The Rise of Fascism

Recent Titles in Crossroads in World History

The Enlightenment: History, Documents, and Key Questions
William E. Burns

The Rise of Christianity: History, Documents, and Key Questions
Kevin W. Kaatz

The Rise of Fascism

HISTORY, DOCUMENTS, AND KEY QUESTIONS

Patrick G. Zander

Crossroads in World History

BLOOMSBURY ACADEMIC
NEW YORK • LONDON • OXFORD • NEW DELHI • SYDNEY

BLOOMSBURY ACADEMIC
Bloomsbury Publishing Inc
1385 Broadway, New York, NY 10018, USA
50 Bedford Square, London, WC1B 3DP, UK
29 Earlsfort Terrace, Dublin 2, Ireland

BLOOMSBURY, BLOOMSBURY ACADEMIC and the Diana logo
are trademarks of Bloomsbury Publishing Plc

First published in the United States of America by ABC-CLIO 2016
Paperback edition published by Bloomsbury Academic 2024

Cover design by Silverander Communications
Cover photo: A view of the *Luitpoldarena* during a Nazi assembly, Nuremberg,
Germany, September 11,1938. (Austrian Archives/Corbis)

Bloomsbury Publishing Inc does not have any control over, or responsibility for,
any third-party websites referred to or in this book. All internet addresses given
in this book were correct at the time of going to press. The author and publisher
regret any inconvenience caused if addresses have changed or sites have
ceased to exist, but can accept no responsibility for any such changes.

Library of Congress Cataloging-in-Publication Data
Names: Zander, Patrick G.
Title: The rise of fascism: history, documents, and key questions /
Patrick G. Zander.
Description: Santa Barbara, California: ABC-CLIO, 2016. |
Series: Crossroads in world history
Identifiers: LCCN 2015033421 | ISBN 9781610697996 (hardback) |
ISBN 9781610698009 (ebook)
Subjects: LCSH: Fascism–History. | BISAC: POLITICAL SCIENCE /
Political Ideologies / Fascism & Totalitarianism. | HISTORY / Modern /
21st Century.
Classification: LCC JC481.Z36 2016 | DDC 320.53/309—dc23
LC record available at http://lccn.loc.gov/2015033421

ISBN: HB: 978-1-6106-9799-6
PB: 979-8-7651-1502-2
ePDF: 978-1-6106-9800-9
eBook: 979-8-2161-3998-0

Series: Crossroads in World History

To find out more about our authors and books visit www.bloomsbury.com
and sign up for our newsletters.

Contents

Alphabetical List of Entries

Topical List of Entries

KEY INDIVIDUALS

EVENTS

Night of the Long Knives
Paris Peace Conference
Reichstag Fire
Remilitarization of the Rhineland
Spanish Civil War

ORGANIZATIONS

Blackshirts
British Union of Fascists
Falange Espanola
Gestapo
National Fascist Party (PNF)
National Socialist German Workers' Party (Nazi Party)
Organization for the Vigilance and Repression of Anti-Fascism (OVRA)
Schutzstaffel (SS)
Sturmabteilung (SA)

WRITTEN WORKS (BOOKS, LEGISLATION, TREATIES)

Enabling Act of 1933
Mein Kampf
Nuremburg Laws
Pact of Steel
Treaty of Versailles

PLACES

Fiume (Occupation of)
Guernica (Bombing of)
Vichy, France

IDEAS, CONCEPTS, AND POLICIES

Anti-Semitism
Autarky
Corporatism (Corporative State)
Fasces
Four Year Plan
Racial Hygiene
Rearmament (German)

How to Use This Book

Throughout the course of history various events have forever changed the world. Some—such as the assassination of Julius Caesar—happened centuries ago and took place quickly. Others—such as the rise of Christianity or the Enlightenment—occurred over an extended period and reshaped worldviews. These pivotal events—or crossroads—were departures from the established social order and pointed to new directions and opportunities. The paths leading to these crossroads in world history often were circuitous, and the routes which branched off from them led to developments both anticipated and unexpected. This series helps readers to understand the causes and consequences of these historical turning points.

Each book in this series explores particular crossroads in world history. Some of these events are from the ancient world and continue to reverberate today through our various political, cultural, and social institutions. Others are from the modern era and have markedly changed society through their immediacy and the force of technology. The books help readers to discover what happened, and to understand the causes and effects linked to each event.

Each volume in the series begins with a timeline charting the essential elements of the event in capsule form. An overview essay comes next, providing a narrative history of what occurred. This is followed by approximately 50 alphabetically arranged reference entries describing people, places, themes, movements, and other topics central to an understanding of the historical crossroad. These entries provide essential information about their topics and close with cross references and suggestions for further reading. A selection of 10 to 15 primary source documents follows the reference entries. Each document is accompanied by an introductory paragraph discussing the background and significance of the text.

Due to their critical nature, the events covered in these volumes have generated a wide range of opinions and arguments. A section of original essays presents responses to key questions concerning the events, with each writer offering a different perspective on a particular topic. An annotated bibliography of print and electronic resources concludes the volume. Users can locate specific information in the alphabetical list of entries, the list of entries grouped into topical categories, as well in the detailed index.

The various elements of each book are designed to work together to promote greater understanding of a crossroad in world history. The timeline and introductory essay overview the event, the reference entries offer easy access to essential information about key topics, the primary source documents give firsthand accounts of the historical event, and the original argumentative essays encourage readers to consider different views related to the events and to appreciate the complex nature of world history. Through its combination of background material, primary source documents, and argumentative essays, the series provides insight into historical causation as for those learning about the pivotal events that changed the course of history.

Preface

This book addresses one of the most significant, complicated, and destructive events of modern history—the rise of fascist dictatorship during the first half of the 20th century. This political movement originated and was centered in Europe, though it eventually influenced states across the globe. In Europe, at the end of the First World War in 1918, a variety of conditions came together to shape a new form of ultra-nationalism which eventually found enough mass support in some nations to produce dictatorial regimes during the 1920s and 1930s. In other European states such popular movements developed but never gained the mass support necessary to take power. These regimes and movements together espoused a belief system and a set of political practices that collectively came to be known as "fascism."

Despite its often-violent nature and its tendency to victimize particular groups of people, many thought that fascist dictatorship was a necessary development to stop the spread of communism and to deal with the prolonged economic downturn that nagged Europe from 1918 to 1939. By the late 1930s, fascist or fascist-inspired dictatorships existed in Portugal, Spain, Italy, Austria, and Germany. It was the aggressive expansionist behavior of these dictatorships (particularly those of Italy and Germany) as they moved to conquer neighboring states that eventually took the world into the largest, most destructive conflict in human history—the Second World War. That war cost an estimated 60 million lives, and it left many powerful developed nations in ruins. During that conflict one fascist dictatorship—Nazi Germany—initiated an organized and industrialized project of mass murder against the Jews of Europe. Known as "the Holocaust," by war's end it would see more than six million Jews and millions of non-Jews murdered in specially designed "death camps."

How did the world come to such a disastrous moment? To even begin examining that question first requires gaining an understanding of fascism. Fascism changed nations dramatically during the 1920s and 1930s, suppressing individual freedoms and producing thousands of political victims. The fascist dictatorships also aggressively challenged the world order put in place by the Paris Peace Conference immediately after the First World War. That threatening behavior was the primary factor in drawing the world back into total war from 1939 to 1945. As such, the origins and development of this political phenomenon demand study and understanding. That is what this volume seeks to help provide. This book is intended to be an introduction to the subject for high school and undergraduate college students. It is designed to provide a brief historical narrative, but principally to serve as a study aid and reference resource.

The work is structured to help readers gain an understanding of fascism. It begins with a timeline of events to provide the chronological order of the developments, and to help show the relationships between events. Next is an essay on the origins and development of fascism. It introduces the key individuals, events, and ideas that brought this political movement to prominence. An encyclopedic section follows, and includes the most important individuals, events, ideas, documents, and other items, listed in alphabetical order. The entries provide in-depth definitions and explanations. The subsequent section is a list of some of the important documentary sources for the present understanding of fascism. This section contains brief explanations of the documents and their significance followed by excerpts from the documents themselves. This enables readers to hear for themselves the voices of those who helped bring about the "fascist era." Next is a Key Questions section which investigates some of the scholarly issues surrounding the study of fascism. Because fascism was practiced in so many different nations, various movements and regimes often employed different practices or espoused contradictory principles. This section attempts to investigate such contradictions and to get at the true nature of this phenomenon. Last is an Annotated Bibliography. It includes some of the most helpful sources available on the subject along with brief explanations of those sources. Together, these tools should help readers gain a clearer understanding of the political creed that became so powerful—and brought the world to such anguish and destruction.

Timeline

May 10, 1871   The Franco-Prussian War ends with Prussia having se-
                  verely defeated the French. Napoleon III is driven from
                  France and the country creates the Third Republic. Prussia
                  uses the victory to form the unified German Empire. In
                  the years to come, French far-right intellectuals develop a
                  type of "proto-fascism" in the climate of national humili-
                  ation born of the defeat.

July 29, 1883   Birth of Benito Mussolini in Predappio, Forli, Italy.

April 20, 1889   Birth of Adolf Hitler at Branau am Inn, Austria-
                  Hungary.

December 22,   Captain Alfred Dreyfus is convicted of treason, setting off
1894   the prolonged "Dreyfus Affair" that would see France dra-
                  matically polarized. In the controversy, nationalist anti-
                  Semitism rose to a fever pitch despite the true criminal
                  having been identified.

January 22, 1905 The Russian Revolution of 1905 breaks out, leading to
                  the creation of the Duma (Russian Parliament). These re-
                  forms would make possible the eventual fall of the mon-
                  archy in 1917 and the Bolshevik Revolution.

June 28, 1914   The assassination of Archduke Franz Ferdinand in
                  Sarajevo put into motion the events leading directly to the
                  outbreak of the First World War.

July 28, 1914   Austrian forces move into Serbian territory, commencing
                  World War I.

July 1, 1916	The Battle of the Somme begins, resulting in a massive slaughter and producing serious disillusionment among soldiers and the public of the Allied powers.
February 25, 1917	Popular demonstrations break out in Petrograd in Russia leading to mutinies in the army and eventually the abdication of Czar Nicholas II (by March 15, 1917).
November 7, 1917	Russian Bolsheviks led by Vladimir Lenin capture the key locations in Petrograd and so seize the government. They retain the government through Civil War, and by 1923 they build the world's first communist state, the Soviet Union.
January 18, 1918	President Woodrow Wilson of the United States makes a speech to the U.S. Congress listing "Fourteen Points" concerning reasons for the start of the First World War and including potential remedies for these tensions. The "Fourteen Points" emerge as the guiding principles of the Peace Conference that follows the war.
November 9, 1918	Declaration of Germany's Weimar Republic in Berlin, after the collapse of the German forces on the western front and the abdication of Kaiser Wilhelm II.
November 11, 1918	Representatives of the German Republic sign an armistice at Compiegne, France, effectively ending hostilities in the First World War.
January 10, 1919	Proceedings commence at the Paris Peace Conference.
March 23, 1919	Benito Mussolini forms the *Fasci di Combattimento,* a political protest and paramilitary group that by 1921 evolved into the National Fascist Party.
June 28, 1919	Representatives from Germany's Weimar Republic are compelled to sign the "Treaty of Versailles," in the Versailles palace Hall of Mirrors. The Treaty places all blame on Germany for the war, removes Germany's overseas colonies, severely limits Germany's military, reduces Germany's geographical boundaries, and establishes a schedule of crushing reparations payments. The Treaty is a source of national humiliation through the 1920s and contributes to the rise of Nazism.
September 10, 1919	The Treaty of Saint-Germain is signed at the Paris Peace Conference, which formally dissolves the Austrian Empire and creates the Republic of Austria. Merger of Austria into the German state is prohibited.

September 12, 1919	Italian nationalist and proto-fascist Gabriele D'Annunzio leads 2,600 members of the Italian army and other supporters in the occupation of the city of Fiume on the Yugoslavian coast which would last until Dec. 24, 1920.
September 12, 1919	Adolf Hitler joins the *Deutsche Arbeiterpartei* (DAP) or German Workers' Party as its 55th member. By February 1920, it evolved into the National Socialist German Workers' Party (or Nazi Party).
November 9, 1921	Benito Mussolini formally establishes his *Partito Nazionale Fascista* (PNF) converting his loose organization of fighting squads into a functioning political party that will run candidates in Italy's 1921 elections.
October 27–28, 1922	The "March on Rome" takes place as thousands of Benito Mussolini's "Blackshirts" converge on Rome pressuring King Victor Emmanuel III to name Mussolini prime minister of Italy.
September 13, 1923	The Spanish military, led by General Miguel Primo de Rivera, establishes a dictatorship in Spain that would last until 1930.
November 8, 1923	Adolf Hitler and the Nazi Party fail in their armed attempt to seize the government of Munich, known as the "Beer Hall Putsch."
April 1, 1924	After a very visible trial, Adolf Hitler is sentenced to only five years in prison for the crime of High Treason. He served only nine months in Landsberg Prison.
June 10, 1924	After speeches denouncing Mussolini's Fascists as criminal and violent, Italian Socialist Giacomo Matteotti is bundled into a car and stabbed to death by Fascist operatives in Rome. Whether Benito Mussolini actually ordered this murder remains a controversial topic.
July 18, 1925	The first volume of Adolf Hitler's book *Mein Kampf* (*My Struggle*) is released in Germany; the book was partially autobiographical and served as a manifesto for the Nazi Party.
April 26, 1928	After a military coup in Portugal, Antonio Oleivera de Salazar is named finance minister. He soon consolidated his power establishing a dictatorship in that country, calling his new fascist-style government the *Estado Novo*.

October 29, 1929	After years of disproportionate growth in stock prices, the New York Stock Exchange suffers a massive collapse leading the United States and Europe into the "Great Depression."
October 1, 1932	Sir Oswald Mosley launches the British Union of Fascists, begins advocating fascist dictatorship for Britain, and publishes *The Greater Britain*.
January 30, 1933	After three years of economic and parliamentary crisis, the German president, Paul von Hindenburg, decides to appoint Adolf Hitler, leader of the Nazi Party, as chancellor of the German nation.
February 27, 1933	In Berlin, the German parliament building, known as the *Reichstag*, burns down. Marinus van der Lubbe and a small group of communists were found guilty of setting the blaze, although the question of their involvement remains controversial.
March 23, 1933	As a result of the *Reichstag* fire, the German government banned the German Communist party and then passed a piece of legislation known as the "Enabling Act," which essentially gave Chancellor Adolf Hitler unlimited political authority.
October 23, 1933	In Spain, Jose Primo de Rivera—the son of deposed Spanish dictator Miguel Primo de Rivera—founds the *Falange Espanola*, an explicitly fascist political party.
February 6, 1934	A group of extreme right-wing political groups—including the fascist-inspired *Croix de Feu*—riot in the Place de la Concorde in Paris. The riots were not well organized and did not produce any clear political results, although France's prime minister Eduard Daladier was forced to resign.
June 30 to July 2, 1934	Adolf Hitler orders a series of political murders of leaders challenging his authority within the Nazi Party. The most prominent of these was Ernst Rohm, leader of the SA or "Brownshirts." The event came to be known as the "Night of the Long Knives."
July 25, 1934	The Austrian chancellor, Engelbert Dollfuss, leader of the fascist Fatherland front in that country, is murdered by members of the Austrian Nazi party in their failed coup attempt.

August 2, 1934	German president Paul von Hindenburg dies and, with his death, the German Parliament agrees to eliminate the position of the presidency making the position of Reich-chancellor and Fuhrer, the ultimate authority in the nation.
June 18, 1935	Britain and Germany sign the Anglo-German Naval Agreement which allows Germany to increase its naval fleet size in violation of the Versailles Treaty, but with the agreement of one of the major democracies.
October 5, 1935	Benito Mussolini commences the invasion of Abyssinia (Ethiopia). The Italian victory results in Abyssinia becoming a colony of Italy until its liberation by the British during 1941.
September 15, 1935	Two acts of severely anti-Semitic legislation, "The Law for the Protection of German Blood and Honor" and "The Reich Citizenship Law," are announced in the German Parliament. They become known as the "Nuremburg Laws."
March 7, 1936	Violating the terms of the Treaty of Versailles, Hitler moves the German military into the Rhineland.
July 17, 1936	A group of Spanish generals, disenchanted with the new left-leaning Republican Government, commence a revolt leading to the Spanish Civil War that would last until 1939.
October 4, 1936	A group of Jewish and left-wing labor organizations stop the British Union of Fascists from marching in East London (known as the "Battle of Cable Street"), marking a symbolic victory against fascism in Britain.
October 18, 1936	Hitler makes Hermann Goering head of the "Four Year Plan," the national economic initiative to prepare Germany for a European war.
April 26, 1937	In the Spanish Civil War, the German "Condor Legion" uses massive aerial bombing to destroy the Basque city of Guernica, shocking world opinion.
March 12, 1938	Adolf Hitler formally annexes Austria into the Nazi German state in a move known as the the *Anschluss*.

September 30, 1938	British prime minister Neville Chamberlain announces an agreement whereby Britain would allow Hitler to take the Sudetenland in Czechoslovakia if Hitler committed that this would be his last move of annexation in Europe.
November 9–10, 1938	In a state-sponsored program of violence, German para-military forces launch an attack upon Jews throughout the nation. Because of the volume of broken glass on the streets, the event became known as *Kristallnacht*.
May 22, 1939	The "Pact of Steel," a military alliance between Nazi Germany and Fascist Italy, is signed in Berlin. This provides Hitler with the protection he feels he needs to launch his invasion of Poland.
August 23, 1939	The Nazi Soviet Non-Aggression Pact is signed between Nazi Germany and the Soviet Union, committing each nation to non-belligerence against the other.
September 1, 1939	Hitler launches the invasion of Poland, commencing the Second World War.
July 10, 1940	Germany completes the conquest of France leading to the creation of a Nazi-held district in Northern France and the creation of a quasi-fascist French government in the south (known as the "Vichy Government" after its new capital city).
July 10 to October 31, 1940	The Battle of Britain takes place as German air forces try to force British submission by massive aerial bombing. Germany eventually fails in its attempt.
September 27, 1940	Representatives from Germany, Italy, and Japan sign the "Tripartite Pact," at Berlin, formally binding those powers together against the "Allies."
June 22, 1941	Nazi Germany launches Operation Barbarossa, a massive ground invasion of the Soviet Union, despite the fact that Germany and the Soviets are alliance partners.
December 7, 1941	The Japanese attack the American naval fleet at Pearl Harbor, HI, resulting in the United States joining Britain and the Soviet Union in the war against the "Axis Powers."
January 20, 1942	A conference is held in the Berlin suburb of Wannsee involving key Nazi officials to coordinate plans leading to the program of the mass extermination of Jews—the Holocaust.

June 4–7, 1942	The Battle of Midway turns the tide of the war in the Pacific, giving the United States the initiative against Japan.
October 23 to November 4, 1942	The British defeat a combined German and Italian force at the Battle of El Alamein in North Africa, leading to the first major defeat of the war for Nazi Germany.
July 25, 1943	Italy's Fascist Party removes Benito Mussolini from power, arrests him, and confines him to a mountaintop prison.
June 6, 1944	The "D-Day landings" take place as part of Operation Overlord on the beaches of Normandy giving U.S., British, and Canadian forces a foothold on the north coast of France.
April 28, 1945	Benito Mussolini and his mistress, Clara Petacci, are discovered by Italian partisan troops and shot near Lake Como. Their corpses are transferred to Milan the next day and hung up in the public square to public vilification.
April 30, 1945	As Soviet troops move into Berlin, Adolf Hitler and his wife Eva Braun commit suicide in an underground bunker beneath the Reich Chancellery. German surrender follows in a matter of days.
August 6, 1945	The United States drops an atomic bomb on the city of Hiroshima in Japan hoping to produce an immediate surrender by the Japanese.
August 9, 1945	After the Japanese refuse to surrender, the United States drops a second atomic bomb on the city of Nagasaki.
September 2, 1945	Japanese officials formally sign surrender documents on the USS *Missouri*, effectively terminating all hostilities of the Second World War.
November 20, 1945	Proceedings begin at the "Nuremberg Trials," which seek to find the truth behind Nazi atrocities and to punish those guilty of war crimes and crimes against humanity. The trials last until October 1946.

Historical Overview (1919–1945)

In the years immediately following the First World War, an ultra-nationalist political creed developed in Europe as a response to many of the changes brought about by that conflict. This political movement became known as "fascism." Economic distress, fear of the spread of Communism, radical cultural change, and particularly a sense of national victimhood all contributed to a growing sense of anxiety among many Europeans during the 1920s and '30s. Believing parliamentary democracy to be inadequate to deal with this array of problems, many turned to extreme political solutions—Marxism (Socialism/Communism) on the left, and on the right the system of fascist dictatorship. Fascism—named after the Italian political party in which it first was established—gained enormous followings in nations where such problems were particularly acute.

Fascist or fascist-inspired dictatorial regimes were established in Italy, Germany, Portugal, Austria, and Spain. Later, as a result of German domination during World War II, fascist-style puppet regimes also were established in places such as France, Romania, Hungary, and Norway. There were also sizeable fascist movements in virtually every other European nation, though they never gained enough popular support to take power. By the 1930s the most powerful of the fascist dictatorships (Italy and Germany) began to expand their territorial claims. Their aggressive invasions and annexations of neighboring nations would by 1939 bring the world back into global conflict.

In this Second World War, Germany and Italy would join together with Japan (which developed its own fascist-style system during the war) to form the "Axis Powers." These nations sought to dramatically expand their domination over territories in Europe and Africa and, for Japan, in the Pacific Rim. They would be challenged and eventually defeated by a large coalition of nations, the most significant of which were Great Britain, the United States, China, and the Soviet Union. The Second World War caused enormous destruction around the globe, leaving many nations in ruins and costing an estimated 60 million lives. This was the sacrifice necessary to extinguish the dictatorships of Nazi Germany, Fascist Italy, and Imperial Japan, and to discredit fascism as a mainstream political system.

WHAT IS FASCISM?

What exactly *is* fascism and how is it defined? This question has proven notoriously difficult to answer for scholars. Because fascism was established in so many different nations, many of these created their own particular rhetoric, policy priorities, and political practices. When trying to compare the many regimes and movements that generally are accepted as being "fascist," many inconsistencies arise. There are some common denominators, however, that help provide at least a fundamental and basic definition.

Fascism begins with the premise that the "nation" is the supreme authority to which all other things (even individual freedoms or democratic rights) must be subordinated. The survival and the purity of that national community typically are seen by fascists as the most urgent of political priorities. Fascists of the time were anti-democratic, believing that representative government was outdated and futile. They instead advocated an authoritarian system with a single political party in control and with a single individual—seen to embody the national will—given unlimited dictatorial power. Fascists were rabidly anti-Marxist, believing that the growth of Socialism/Communism was the greatest threat to world civilization. Fascists certainly believed in the private ownership of business and production, rather than state ownership as advocated by Marxist theory. Fascists, however, also believed that to maximize the benefits of industry to the nation as a whole the national state should dictate policy to industrial producers and not the converse. In other words, fascist theory advocated the state direction of the privately owned means of production. In practice, such industrial policies could be very inconsistent and in some fascist countries state-owned industries were not uncommon.

One of the most conspicuous of fascist principles was the glorification of violence and the belief that violence was a legitimate method to accomplish political objectives. From street violence perpetrated against opposing parties, to the use of torture, summary executions, and concentration camps, fascist regimes used extraordinary violence against their own citizens. Fascists also glorified war as the best and most natural way for the powerful to "rise to the top," and as the best means to develop the strongest traits in the national community.

Fascist ideology consistently emphasized what some have called, "exclusive nationalism." This is the idea that there are certain defining characteristics of a nation that must be protected and cultivated for that community to thrive. These might be physical traits (e.g., skin color, hair color, facial features), or cultural traits (e.g., language, religion, food, common history, political affiliations). A collection of such traits is celebrated as the essence of the national community.

Under this ideology, people attempting to enter the nation from the outside and whose traits differ from the nation's defining traits must be kept from penetrating the nation because they pose the risk of "polluting" or "corrupting" it. Slogans such as, "Italy for the Italians!" and "Britain First!" commonly were used among fascist groups in their particular countries to express "anti-alienism." There also (supposedly) was the problem of those citizens *inside* the nation who did not conform to the accepted definition of the national community and instead possessed different physical, political, or cultural attributes. According to fascists, such individuals had to be purged to prevent their corroding of the national community from within. Such purging often was performed using the methods of violence and oppression mentioned above. Fascist dictatorships were inconsistent as to exactly how purging was carried out in practice. In Germany, the biological "race" was seen as all important and racial "others," especially Jews, had their rights taken away, were violently assaulted, and eventually during the Holocaust were murdered *en masse*. In other fascist dictatorships, however, considerations other than race were more important. In Italy it was mostly political "others"—such as Marxists—who were purged. In Spain approximately 200,000 supporters of the left-leaning Republic were executed by the Franco regime to preserve what Franco called "True Spain."

ORIGINS IN ITALY

Fascism began as a political force in Italy immediately following World War I. Benito Mussolini—who had been a violent and difficult youth—created the first explicitly fascist organization. A sometime school teacher, Mussolini eventually joined the Socialist Party of Italy in the early 1900s, where he found great success. Mussolini fell out with the Socialist party, however, over the question of Italy's entry into World War I—the party was against entry and Mussolini became an enthusiastic proponent. He eventually was expelled from the party over this difference. Mussolini then began publishing his own rabidly nationalist newspaper, *Il Popolo D'Italia* (*People of Italy*).

When that war was over Italy was on the winning side, having joined with Britain, France, Russia, and the United States against Germany, Austria, and the Ottoman Turks. The Italians had joined those nations because of a secret treaty (the 1915 Treaty of London) which promised that if the Allies were victorious, Italy would be rewarded with extensive territory in Central Europe. At the Paris Peace Conference, however, Italy was denied those territories as part of a wider effort to eliminate secret diplomacy going forward. Italian governmental officials walked out of the Peace Conference and returned home to Italy having secured only the tiniest of additional territory. In Italy this result added to an existing sense of national victimhood and some Italians began to describe Italy's war experience as their "mutilated victory." As a result, Italy's government fell and new elections were held.

For the next two years, however, Italy's political situation remained highly fluid and unstable. Governments were elected and fell repeatedly due to a lack of unified support. The country foundered politically and faced other major dislocations as well. Italy's economy suffered greatly as war production ended. Wages decreased drastically and laborers were dismissed in significant numbers. Italian workers responded with a wave of thousands of industrial strikes. In this atmosphere the Italian Socialist Party began to expand rapidly and started to play a much more important role in Italian life. Socialists became the leading party in the Italian Parliament and were elected to numerous local government positions as well. Socialist leaders also established "Labor Exchanges" in the countryside that helped peasants attain higher wages for their seasonal agricultural labor. This period—from 1919 to 1920—became known as the *Biennio Rosso* or the "red two years." After the success of Russia's Bolshevik Revolution in 1917, many Italians who were unsympathetic to Socialism began to fear that Italy was headed for a similar Marxist uprising.

Into this mix of political instability, economic turmoil, and social tension stepped Benito Mussolini. In 1919, he formed a small band that grew into a formal political party in only a few years. He initially called this small group his *Fasci di Combattimento* or "combat leagues." Many of those who joined were demobilizing soldiers from Italy's elite forces known as the *arditi*. These veterans of the *arditi* often retained their military uniforms—which included a black shirt. As such, Mussolini began to call them his "Blackshirts," and increasingly formed them into a paramilitary-type private army.

The Blackshirts' chief political activity became known as *squadrismo* ("squadism"), which consisted of organizing into squads and traveling to towns where Socialists were in charge of local government. Once there, the Blackshirts often inflicted terrible violence, demolishing newspaper offices, ransacking city halls, and especially beating and torturing Socialist members of government and staff. Blackshirts celebrated such violence and often bragged about their use of castor oil, which when forced down the throat of a victim could cause that person to vomit themselves into unconsciousness or even death. Mussolini's early Fascist squads found their political identity as the one group in Italy that would fight (violently) against the rise of Socialism. The national government was in such a state of instability that it could do very little to stop the Blackshirts, and local police rarely got involved because they often supported the Fascists' anti-Marxism.

As this situation continued, Mussolini's disparate groups gelled into a formal political party—the National Fascist Party or *Partito Nazionale Fascista* (PNF). Some of its candidates were elected to the parliament—including Mussolini—supported by mostly middle-class voters and landowners with large holdings. By the end of 1922, the king of Italy, Vittorio Emmanuel III, faced a growing political crisis. No existing party leader seemed to have the support necessary to form a new government, and the Fascists increasingly pressured the country to bring Mussolini to power. In late October 1922, the Fascists staged a massive march of citizens from all over Italy, and converged on Rome—which escalated the crisis. Running out of alternatives, key governmental leaders and the king agreed to ask Mussolini to become prime minister and to form a government. Although Mussolini had used illegal violence to force the issue, he in fact took power by constitutional means.

Once he was in power, Mussolini set about making Italy a single-party dictatorship. Over the next three years he changed the electoral laws which, by 1923, gave the Fascists a sizeable majority. Mussolini then used that majority to gradually outlaw all opposition parties, making the Italian Parliament simply a Fascist Party Congress. Leaders of the opposition parties—particularly those of the Marxist left—often were imprisoned. In 1924 one Socialist, Giacomo Matteotti, stood up in Parliament and spoke against these brutal tactics. He was found murdered weeks later. Whether Mussolini directly ordered this murder remains a controversial topic, although it temporarily cast a pall over his regime.

Despite the violence of Fascism in Italy, many people around the world admired Mussolini, accepting his methods as necessary in Italy to eliminate the Marxist threat and to bring political stability. Outside observers, however, gave Mussolini the most credit for changing the economy. By the late 1920s Mussolini reorganized the Italian economy along the lines known as *Corporatismo* ("Corporatism"). Under this new organization, a "corporation" was formed as a board including representatives from senior management, government representatives, specialists in science and technology, and labor. Together these board members regulated an entire industry with the mission of maximizing that industry's benefit to the nation as a whole. Mussolini was applauded for this and some suggested that he solved the seemingly insoluble problem of class conflict. While he was putting such corporations together, however, Mussolini also outlawed trade unions and strikes. As a result of this process—most historians agree—Mussolini destroyed the power and leverage of Italian labor. Corporatism, however, emerged as a leading objective among those other fascist groups that agitated for power in other nations.

ORIGINS IN GERMANY

As in Italy, in Germany fascism was a set of ideas embraced by many, but initially driven by the activities and vision of a single individual—Adolf Hitler. Hitler was born in Austria but became a fanatic Pan-Germanist early in his life, possibly to defy his abusive father. As a young adult, Hitler applied for admission into the Royal Academy of Arts in Vienna to study painting, but was twice rejected. After this, he lived a poor and precarious existence in Vienna until he was able to move to Munich. Soon after his arrival the First World War began and young Hitler was able to join the German army. He served in the trenches as a communications runner, was decorated for bravery, and achieved the rank of corporal. He was recovering in a hospital from exposure to poison gas when he was devastated by the news of Germany's surrender. After the surrender Hitler remained in the army and was assigned as a "political officer," monitoring local political groups around Munich. As he investigated the *Deutsche Arbeiterpartei* (DAP) (German Workers' Party) he was electrified by that party's political message which seemed to echo all his own political convictions. Despite a lengthy list of detailed objectives, the party stood for five essential principles:

1. Re-unifying the German speaking peoples into a single great German nation;
2. Overturning the Treaty of Versailles (signed at the Paris Peace Conference) which took away Germany's overseas colonies, restricted its borders, limited its armed forces, and imposed crushing reparations payments;
3. The futility of representative government and advocacy of an authoritarian system for Germany;
4. Purging Germany of all Marxist (Socialist/Communist) organizations and influences; and
5. A conviction that many of Germany's most serious problems were caused by Jews and advocacy of purging Germany of Jewish populations and influences.

Hitler quit the army and joined the party as its 55th member in 1919. In the days that followed, the party's name was changed to the National Socialist

German Workers' Party (*Nationalsozialistische Deutsche Arbeiterpartei*) (NS-DAP) also called the Nazi Party, and Adolf Hitler emerged as its unquestioned leader. As Mussolini had done, Hitler would form the party's membership into paramilitary squads with military-style uniforms (the *Sturmabteilung* [SA] or "Brownshirts").

Although the NSDAP still was a small party centered in Munich, in 1923 Hitler believed the time had come for his group to attempt to seize the government. He staged an armed coup in Munich (remembered as the "Beer Hall Putsch"), but his forces were overcome and he himself was arrested. Hitler would stand trial for high treason but, amazingly, although he was found guilty he was sentenced to only five years in prison—and he only served about nine months. In prison he wrote a book called *Mein Kampf* or "My Struggle," which served as his autobiography and the manifesto for the Nazi Party. Nazi principles were laid out in detail, but Hitler added one as well, saying that it was Germany's destiny to one day expand into Eastern Europe and to attack and conquer the Soviet Union.

After his release from prison Hitler was allowed to resume his political activity. The Nazi Party, however, made few inroads in the late 1920s. As Germany's economy slowly recovered in this period, few were willing to listen to the ravings of Nazi speakers. In 1929 the American Stock Market crashed and dragged most of Europe into the Great Depression. Germany was especially hard hit—experiencing an approximately 33% unemployment rate, and the collapse of the country's banking system. Germans then were more ready to listen to extreme solutions to deal with such terrible conditions. By 1932 the Nazi Party and the German Communist Party were the two largest parties in the German Parliament (*Reichstag*). Paul von Hindenburg, the president of Germany's government (which from 1918 was known as the "Weimar Republic"), tried to find a new candidate to run the country, deal with its challenges, and reduce the level of violence and tension in its politics. He and his inner circle eventually decided that making Adolf Hitler the chancellor of Germany would accomplish these things. In January of 1933 Adolf Hitler was named chancellor by Hindenburg, thus taking power by constitutional means.

Soon after Hitler formed a government, there was a disaster in Berlin—the German Parliament building burned down. A small group of admitted Communists was arrested and tried for the crime, although to date the group's guilt is still in question. Hitler, however, used this episode to ask Parliament for extraordinary powers to deal with what he said was a war launched by the Communists. Parliament on March 23, 1933, passed the "Enabling Act" which essentially gave Hitler absolute power—from this point on, Hitler could wield dictatorial power.

After using political murders to eliminate any of his challengers within the party in July 1934 (an event remembered as the "Night of the Long Knives"), Hitler soon after was voted chancellor for life by the *Reichstag*. With this level of power he set about eliminating all opposition parties and imprisoning their leadership in "concentration camps." He also used this power to arrest and imprison those he felt were corrosive to the state and to the German race—such as homosexuals, chronic alcoholics, and criminals. Hitler passed laws that removed Jews from positions of influence in government, business, academia, and cultural life. He also launched programs of public works to rebuild slum areas and to build modern highways. This helped reduce the unemployment statistics.

By 1935, Hitler had begun to launch a nationwide effort to rearm Germany. Since 1920, Germany had endured limitations of its armed forces as a condition of the Treaty of Versailles. Hitler refused to honor these conditions and began a massive rearmament program which mobilized most of Germany's industrial base. By 1937, Germany enjoyed virtual full employment. This helps explain the remarkable levels of popular support that the Nazi regime enjoyed despite its violence and intense racial discrimination.

THE EXPANSION OF THE DICTATORSHIPS

Fascist or fascist-inspired regimes also developed in Portugal under the Salazar dictatorship, and briefly in Austria with the regime of Engelbert Dollfuss. Salazar remained in power until 1968, but Dollfuss was murdered in 1934 by members of the Austrian Nazi Party. Dollfuss's "Fatherland Front," a political coalition of the far right, was continued by Kurt Schuschnigg until 1938. Fascist mass movements also developed in places such as Britain, France, Belgium, Ireland, and Spain. It was the Italian and German dictatorships, however, that began to expand their boundaries and take the world back into global war.

In 1935, Benito Mussolini launched an invasion of the African nation of Abyssinia (modern Ethiopia). The Italians had been humiliatingly defeated in Abyssinia in 1896 at the Battle of Adowa as they attempted to expand their East African Empire. Now, Mussolini hoped to avenge that defeat and to expand his Fascist Empire. By 1936, Abyssinia had been brutally conquered, with the Italians infamously using poison gas on the Abyssinians to achieve victory. The League of Nations imposed weak economic sanctions, but made no military move to stop Italian aggression. Mussolini, outraged by the sanctions, moved increasingly away from good relations with the democracies and toward a formal alliance with Hitler's Germany.

Hitler made his first serious expansionist move in 1936 by re-occupying the area known as the "Rhineland." That region of westernmost Germany along the Rhine River was restricted by the Treaty of Versailles as a demilitarized zone—Germany was to have no military presence in that region at all. Hitler announced that this was German territory and that the Germans no longer respected the treaty's unreasonable conditions. On March 7, 1936, he moved the German army into the area. Worried about starting a full-scale war, however, neither France nor Britain moved to intervene.

Also in 1936, the Spanish Civil War began. Spain had become deeply politically polarized during the 1930s with political agitation often breaking out into violence. After elections in early 1936, the democratically elected government had some far-left elements which some top officials in the Spanish army found unacceptable. These officers organized a rebellion and attempted to seize the government in July. The military troops were stopped, however, mostly through the action of ordinary people, Marxist political groups, and trade unions. As the situation settled down into stalemate, Spanish General Francisco Franco emerged as the leader of the "Nationalist" cause against the "Republican" government and its defenders. Franco appealed to both Hitler and Mussolini and received a great deal of material and military aid. The Republic appealed to France and Britain, but neither of these democracies was willing to intervene. Only the Soviet Union agreed to help. As a result, in the years to follow, Soviet military troops and equipment often faced German or Italian forces on the battlefield. By 1939, the Soviets had withdrawn and Franco's Nationalist forces were victorious. Francisco Franco went on to establish his own quasi-fascist dictatorship which lasted until his death in 1975.

In 1938, Hitler moved again, this time absorbing Austria into the Nazi state. A movement had been growing in Austria since the Great War to see the country combined with Germany. Earlier in the decade, however, Italy had declared its support of an independent Austria and effectively had guaranteed its sovereignty. After Italy's invasion of Abyssinia, however, Italy found itself isolated diplomatically and, as a result, grew increasingly friendly with Hitler's Germany. By 1938 that relationship had become quite close, and Italy was no longer willing to stand in the way of German annexation of Austria. On March 12, 1938, German troops marched into Austria and by the middle of that month German law reflected Austria as being part of Germany.

Hitler justified his actions by insisting that he was merely correcting the wrongs made by the various decisions of the Paris Peace Conference in 1919. In reconfiguring Europe's nations in Central Europe, Hitler said, the German-speaking people had been divided up amongst several nations. He would bring them all back together under the German Reich. As part of this mission Hitler in 1938 announced his intention to bring the German-speaking majority in the far-western area of Czechoslovakia (known as the Sudetenland) back into the German nation. This caused extreme concern because both France and Britain had treaty agreements with Czechoslovakia to come to its aid in the case of that country being invaded by another. If Hitler moved to annex the Sudetenland the result could be another European war. To prevent this, at the very last moment British prime minister Neville Chamberlain flew to Munich for emergency meetings. After multiple conversations, Chamberlain returned to Britain and announced to the world that he and Hitler had reached an agreement to prevent war. The agreement stipulated that Hitler would be allowed to seize the Sudetenland without the intervention of France or Britain. In exchange, Hitler had assured Chamberlain that this would be his last expansionist move. In the weeks and months to follow Hitler did seize the Sudetenland—but he did not stop there. Hitler moved his troops into the rest of Czechoslovakia and seized its capital, Prague. It was clear by this point that Hitler's word meant nothing, and worries escalated that any further move would drive the world back into war.

Hitler moved again in the following year; but first the Germans concluded a rather astonishing agreement with Joseph Stalin's Soviet Union in August of 1939. This was nearly unthinkable because of the extreme ideological differences between fascism and Communism. For years proponents of each system had accused the other of being the greatest threat to western civilization. Now Nazi Germany, the most powerful of the fascist dictatorships, and the Soviet Union, the only Communist state in the world, had agreed to a "non-aggression" pact. This meant that neither would intervene against the other in the case of expansionist aggression. In only a week's time it became clear why this pact had been concluded. On September 1, 1939, Hitler launched a massive invasion of Poland. Both Britain and France had alliance treaties with Poland—and Hitler was convinced they would back down and not honor them. But, two days later both France and Britain declared war on Germany. The Second World War had begun.

As mentioned, World War II caused the greatest mass destruction in human history. It cost approximately 60 million lives and left numerous modern industrialized nations in ruins. Along the way, Adolf Hitler launched a plan intended to exterminate all the Jews (and some other "undesirables") in Europe. Known as the "Holocaust," this plan used industrialized death camps to systematically execute and then incinerate nearly six million Jews from 1942 to 1945. The camps of the Holocaust killed almost as many non-Jewish victims, including Communists, homosexuals, Roma Gypsies, and Jehovah's Witnesses, among others. After the destruction of the war and then the exposure of the horrors of the Holocaust, fascism became an almost entirely discredited political philosophy. As the world began to piece itself back together after the war, the cry of "Never Again!" became the phrase most associated with fascism. But, in the postwar world some regimes have had startling similarities. The Afrikaner Republic in South Africa and its apartheid policies, the Peron Regime in Argentina, the Milosovic Regime in Serbia, and the government of Sadam Hussein in Iraq, have all borne frightening resemblance.

Fascism: A to Z

ABYSSINIAN WAR (SECOND ITALO-ABYSSINIAN WAR)   The Abyssinian War was a war of imperial conquest fought from October 1935 to May 1936. It was initiated with the invasion of Abyssinia (modern Ethiopia) by the forces of the Kingdom of Italy, governed by Benito Mussolini and his Fascist Party (*Partito Nazionale Fascista*) (PNF). The war resulted in the exile of the Abyssinian Emperor, Haile Selassie, and Abyssinia being incorporated into the Italian Empire where it remained until its liberation in 1941. The invasion of Abyssinia marked the first in a series of aggressive acts by the fascist dictatorships that eventually led to the outbreak of the Second World War.

Benito Mussolini, dictator of Fascist Italy from 1922–43, seems to have planned the conquest of Abyssinia as early as 1932. Earlier in its history, Italy had suffered a humiliating defeat to the Ethiopians at the Battle of Adowa in 1896, attempting to enlarge its territory in East Africa. Avenging that defeat was part of the motivation for Mussolini's venture. Economic motivations included finding supplies of natural resources and larger markets for Italian industry as well as increasing the living space for Italy's supposedly virile and expanding population. Historians also point to Mussolini's using the Abyssinian conquest as a case of "social imperialism," distracting the Italian people from poor economic and social conditions in Italy by appealing to their national pride through foreign conquest.

Italy possessed territory in East Africa in the coastal lands of Eritrea and Italian Somaliland. This region's inland territory, however, shared a disputed border region with Abyssinia. On December 5, 1934, in that disputed frontier land at a small town called Wal Wal, there was a skirmish between Italian and Abyssinian soldiers leaving more than 100 Ethiopians and 2 Italians dead. This led to a controversy known as the "Abyssinian Crisis" in the League of Nations, with Emperor Haile Selassie appealing for protection from the League. In the end, however, the League did not condemn or take action against either nation.

By October 1935, Mussolini was fully prepared for a military invasion. Although no declaration of war was announced, the invasion began on October 3, 1935, involving nearly one million Italian and Eritrean troops led by General Emilio De Bono. De Bono's forces made significant progress in the first two weeks of the campaign against Abyssinia's rather primitive armies. The Abyssinians were commanded by local nobles known as a "Ras," but were using inferior firearms, possessed only very few pieces of artillery, and had no combat aircraft. The Italians seized Adowa as well as the ancient city of Axum and eventually made their way to Makale. This, however, was as far as De Bono was willing to advance given his supply and transport problems and his caution with the lives of his troops. Mussolini was impatient for further advances. Frustrated by slow progress, Mussolini removed De Bono from command and replaced him with Marshal Pietro Badoglio in December 1935. The Abyssinians launched their own major offensive at the end of December, known as the "Christmas Offensive." They were able to turn back Italian gains to a small degree and to kill several thousand Italian troops. The offensive bogged down, however, and Badoglio—receiving authorization from Mussolini—began the use of massive aerial bombing and, infamously, poison gas. Badoglio's forces dropped mustard gas in bomb form (and later by spraying) not only on Abyssinia's military, but also on civilian populations—despite this being a violation of the Geneva Convention. Italian forces committed other war crimes as well, including the bombing of Red Cross medical facilities.

In November, the League of Nations passed limited economic sanctions on Italy, supported by Britain and France, though neither nation wanted to alienate Italy. Hoping to preserve good relations with Mussolini, Britain's foreign secretary Sir Samuel Hoare and France's foreign minister Pierre Laval met to draft a proposal for a peace agreement. They granted about two-thirds of Abyssinia to Italy, but provided Abyssinia a corridor of territory to the coast giving it access to the Red Sea. Their draft was leaked to the public by the press. Public opinion was scandalized by the rewarding of Italian aggression with territory and was so vehement that both Hoare and Laval were forced to resign. Nothing came of their agreement.

In January 1936, Badoglio won a major victory at Tembien. Soon after, in February, the Italians assaulted the mountain stronghold at Amba Aradam—held by Abyssinia's most legendary commander Ras Mulugueta and his army—using massive aerial bombing. With his forces nearly exhausted now, Haile Selassie launched one last offensive in March at Mai Ceu. The Italians had intercepted Abyssinian communications and repelled them easily. After this defeat Haile Selassie fled the country and eventually went into exile in Great Britain. On June 30, 1936, the emperor spoke again at the League of Nations condemning Italy's aggression and indicting the League for its failure to provide collective security against Mussolini's naked aggression. In that speech he issued the famously prophetic warning that "It is us today. It will be you tomorrow."

Italy would take formal possession of Abyssinia by May 1936 and eventually settled some 3,600 colonists. Abyssinians, however, continued to assault the Italian administration with guerilla-style attacks right into the Second World War. Italian forces were thrown out of Abyssinia in 1941 by the British Army and the emperor was returned to power.

See also: Ciano, Count Gian Galeazzo; Mussolini, Benito.

Further Reading

Gooch, John, *Mussolini and His Generals* (New York: Cambridge University Press, 2007).
Hardie, Frank, *The Abyssinian Crisis* (Hamden: Archons Books, 1974).
Mack Smith, Denis, *Mussolini's Roman Empire* (New York: Viking Press, 1976).

ANSCHLUSS *Anschluss* is the German word literally meaning "annexation" or "union," and is used to describe the military occupation and formal absorption of the Republic of Austria into the German Reich during March of 1938. Austria was not maintained as a foreign imperial territory, but was incorporated as contiguous German territory and governed accordingly. The *Anschluss* represented the first formal conquest by Adolf Hitler of a foreign nation in the series of annexations by Germany that would lead to the Second World War.

Until the First World War, the Austrian Empire (later the Austro-Hungarian Empire) had grown to constitute most of Eastern Europe. It was composed of dozens of ethnic groups including Germans, Italians, Hungarians, Czechs, Slovaks, Slovenians, Serbs, Croats, Bosnians, and many others. For centuries its emperors had been the descendants of the Habsburg dynasty. The Austrian Empire had been the initiator of the First World War after the assassination of its Crown Prince Franz Ferdinand and its subsequent conflict with Serbia. Austria went to war with its principal allies—the German Empire and the Ottoman Turkish Empire—to fight against Serbia, France, Russia, and Britain (later Italy and the United States joined that coalition). Austria thus was on the losing side in the war and was forced to submit to terms at the Paris Peace Conference of 1919. Per the Treaty of St. Germain, Austria was stripped of its imperial territories (most of which would see new nations created based on ethnic majorities) and relegated to the borders of the traditional German-speaking region of Austria, with Vienna as its capital. The Habsburg Monarchy was dissolved and replaced with a Republican system. Some Austrian diplomats at the conference had pushed for unification with Germany at this time, but Article 88 of the Treaty of St. Germain strictly prohibited this.

As the new Republic of Austria progressed through the 1920s, the Austrian population grew divided as to the most desirable future for its nation. Citizens' visions of the future mostly were guided by their concern that Austria was now too small and lacked the resources to ever be a strong and viable nation in the new world of European politics. Some advocated the return of the Habsburg Monarchy and imperial status. Others defended Austria's independence and its Republic, but thought that a "partnership" with Germany would be the best way to gain strength and viability. Still others—particularly the growing Austrian branch of the Nazi Party—aggressively promoted the liquidation of the nation through a full integration of Austria into the German nation. This school of thought gained significant popularity after Hitler's appointment as chancellor of Germany in January 1933.

As a native of Austria, Hitler had a complicated relationship with the land of his birth. This certainly impacted his own private motivations for erasing that nation and absorbing it into his German Reich. Hitler's publicly announced motivation was his mission to undo the catastrophe of the Paris Peace Conference which had divided the German race into several small nations. Equating race with state, Hitler insisted he would bring all the German-speaking people together into one geographic nation and under one leader.

Hitler's designs were undermined, however, by the relationship between Mussolini's Italy and Austria. In March 1934, Mussolini had signed an agreement known as the "Rome Protocols"; in essence, it made Italy the protector and guarantor of Austrian sovereignty. Mussolini would demonstrate his seriousness in this matter later in 1934 when the Austrian dictator Engelbert Dollfuss was murdered in a coup attempt sponsored by the Austrian Nazi Party (and directed by German Nazi officials). The coup attempt failed, but during the chaos Mussolini massed Italian troops on the Austrian border. Later, in April 1935 at Stresa, Italy, Mussolini signed an agreement with France and Britain pledging the three nations to work together in the case of any threat to Austrian independence.

In late 1935, however, Mussolini invaded Abyssinia with great consequences for the Austrian situation. The invasion caused tension between the Stresa partners and undermined any collective action. The war in Abyssinia also absorbed Mussolini's energy and resources, making Austria less of a priority. Finally, with Germany's war machine growing so powerful and most of Mussolini's own military on a different continent, Italy could no longer act as a protector of Austrian independence.

Recognizing this, Adolf Hitler increasingly pressured the Austrian government to include members of the Austrian Nazi Party as part of its government and pressed for some kind of fusion of the two German lands, although what exact form that fusion would take was not made clear. By February 1938, these demands became more threatening with discussion of armed force. Hitler routinely alluded to the need for the ethnic Germans of Austria to enjoy "racial self-determination" by being allowed to join with the German Reich. The Austrian government—now led by Chancellor Kurt Schuschnigg—continued to agree to small concessions to Hitler's demands. Conspicuously, Schuschnigg never issued a strong rejection to Hitler nor did he begin preparations for Austrian military defense. In February, Schuschnigg went to Hitler's retreat at Berchtesgaden for talks. Hitler issued further demands and threats including the insistence that members of the Austrian Nazi Party be made ministers in Schuschnigg's government. Again Schuschnigg complied, unwilling to provoke military confrontation.

In early March, Schuschnigg seized on the idea of holding a referendum on the issue of retaining Austria's complete independence. If Austria's people voted for complete independence, any attempt by Hitler to seize Austria based on his claim that the Austrians deserved the right to choose German citizenship, would be totally discredited. Hitler was outraged at the idea of a referendum. He began to give orders for the Nazi Party in Austria to prepare for a Nazi takeover (this was discovered by Austrian police). Additionally, Hitler then demanded that Schuschnigg be removed as chancellor and the Austrian Nazi Artur Seyss-Inquart be installed in his place. For several days, Austrian president Wilhelm Miklas refused to comply.

As the day of the referendum (March 13) approached, Hitler decided to take preemptive action. On the morning of March 12 he sent his military troops across the Austrian border. With the troops on the move, Schuschnigg finally was removed and Nazi Seyss-Inquart became chancellor. Nazi troops, however, met no resistance; rather, great numbers of Austrians cheered for them as they arrived. In the days that followed, the German SS led by Heinrich Himmler rounded up most of the anti-Nazi leadership in Austria, including known Marxist leaders, members of the former government, and trade union leaders. Intimidation by Nazi troops influenced anyone else who objected to the Nazis to remain silent. As such, Hitler was able to enter Vienna on March 14 to mass adulation. Soon after, his government passed the "Re-unification Law," which dismantled Austria's status as an independent nation and dissolved its national government. Austria was made a "*Gau*" or regional province of the German nation and became geographically part of the German Reich. The Austrians would be given their referendum by Hitler on April 10, 1938, and this time the question put to the nation was "Do you acknowledge Adolf Hitler as our Fuhrer and the reunion of Austria with the German Reich which was effected on March 13, 1938?" Austrians overwhelmingly voted yes, though this remains controversial as so many of the anti-Nazi leadership had been forced underground, were arrested, or had left the country. In the days to come, Hitler used the Austrian nation for its natural resources, drafted its men into his growing army, and began subjecting Austria's Jews to the same repressive laws that persecuted them in Germany.

See also: Dollfuss, Engelbert.

Further Reading

Brook-Shepherd, Gordon, *Anschluss: The Rape of Austria* (London: Macmillan, 1963).
Evans, Richard J., *The Third Reich in Power* (New York: Penguin, 2005).
Shirer, William L., *The Rise and Fall of the Third Reich* (New York: Fawcett Crest, 1960).

ANTI-SEMITISM "Anti-Semitism" is a term which describes the prejudice against and hatred of Jews, and discriminatory actions against them associated with that hatred. Feelings against the ethno-religious community of Jews dates back to the Middle Ages in Europe. In the modern age, however, anti-Semitic feeling grew and changed during the 19th century, modified by the new conceptions of the Darwinian theories of natural selection and the competition between species. Those who applied such scientific theories to human populations became obsessed with the idea of race and racial struggle. This led to a growing view that Jews were a biologically separate racial group rather than just a religious community. Anti-Semites typically considered Jews to be unable to assimilate into their national communities and a corrosive element undermining their national identity from the inside.

In the 20th century, anti-Semitism became one of the prominent features of fascist ideology and particularly of Nazism in Germany. As Adolf Hitler and his Nazi Party gained popularity and eventually took power in 1933, Hitler's regime began to translate anti-Semitic rhetoric into policy and action. Jews were removed from prominent positions in business, academics, and culture. They also often were arrested and deported to detention camps. During the Second World War, the Nazi regime intensified such persecution and organized special killing squads to murder Jewish populations in Nazi-occupied territories, and then constructed the death camps of the Holocaust.

In the most glaring crime against humanity in the modern age, these camps exterminated nearly six million Jews and almost as many non-Jews.

Much of the early intellectual tradition of fascist thought originated in France in the decades following the French loss of the Franco-Prussian War of 1870–71. The humiliation of that defeat led conservative right-wing intellectuals to construct an ultra-nationalist and exclusionist belief system that emphasized the sacred nature of the French national community and the dangers of foreign influences. In 1894, in the midst of this climate, an officer in the French military named Alfred Dreyfus was accused of spying for the Germans. Though a respected officer, Dreyfus was Jewish, and this set off a wave of anti-Semitic feeling in France. This popular anti-Semitism emphasized the conception of Jews as a "nation within a nation" and hence inherently an enemy of the French nation. Dreyfus was found guilty and sent to the prison camp at Devil's Island. Over several years his family fought to clear his name and gathered evidence that undermined the guilty verdict. This set off a renewed conflict between ultra-nationalists who refused to listen to any evidence vindicating Dreyfus and those who condemned the prejudiced mind-set of the political right. In the end the real spy was identified but Dreyfus still was not acquitted, although he was pardoned and set free. The Dreyfus Affair deeply divided France and contributed to the shaping of anti-Semitic thought in Europe, setting up Jews as a perceived threat to national identity, national purity, and national security.

The National Socialist German Workers' Party or Nazi Party (*Nationalsozialistische Deutsche Arbeiterpartei*) (NSDAP) in Germany made anti-Semitism a key feature of its political program in the early 1920s. Nazi ideology considered Jews to be biologically inferior and thus a threat to the Germanic or "Aryan" racial stock. The Nazis also believed Jews to be in charge of capitalist "international finance" which invested in foreign enterprise to the detriment of the German national economy. Additionally, Nazis and other anti-Semites of the period viewed Jews as controlling Marxist movements and Soviet Communism—which Nazis considered the greatest threat to world civilization. Espousing this rather contradictory view, Nazis and other anti-Semites believed that Jews were in control of a world conspiracy to economically destabilize and morally undermine the societies of non-Jewish nations to further their own financial enrichment.

This ideology supposedly was proven with the publication of a treatise written in Russia entitled, "The Protocols of the Elders of Zion." This pamphlet supposedly exposed the Jewish project to achieve world domination. It was shown to be a forgery and a hoax by 1921, but the Nazis and other anti-Semitic movements continued to insist on its validity. The Nazis even required its study in the German school system after Hitler came to power.

Only months after becoming chancellor, Hitler in January 1933 was able to push through legislation that made legal the removal of Jews from their jobs and positions. Jews lost their jobs in business, at universities, and in key positions of Germany's cultural life. In this early process of forcibly removing Jews from their livelihoods there often arose confusion and questions. Specifically, there was confusion as to who was really considered to be a Jew. To deal with such questions, the Nazis in 1935 passed a set of laws known as the "Nuremburg Laws." These laws established the regulations stipulating that a person who had three or four Jewish grandparents was "officially" Jewish. These Nuremburg Laws also announced that Jews no longer were considered German citizens and thus enjoyed none of the legal rights of German citizens.

In 1938, after the assassination in Paris of a German diplomat named Ernst vom Rath by a Jew named Herschel Grynszpan, Nazi Party leaders—particularly Joseph Goebbels—began to organize a state-sponsored act of vengeance against Germany's Jews. This developed into the mass rioting and violence remembered as *Kristallnacht* ("Crystal Night," or "Night of Broken Glass") that erupted during the night of November 9–10, 1938. The Nazi SA (or "Storm troopers") played the leading role in smashing the shops of Jewish-owned businesses and throwing the merchandise out into the streets, burning synagogues in every major city, and generally assaulting Jews. Harassment included beating Jews randomly, smashing in apartment doors and assaulting them, humiliating them in public, and there were also mass arrests. Some 30,000 Jews were arrested and deported to concentrations camps.

When the Second World War broke out, the Hitler regime made a calculated effort to cleanse any occupied territories of people considered biologically inferior. These included Poles, Czechs, Russians, and many others. In every territory, however, Jews were the primary target. By 1941, the *Schutzstaffel* (SS) ("Protective Squadron") had organized special killing squads known as the *Einsatzgruppen* ("Deployment Groups"), to round up Jews and herd them into segregated areas. They systematically then shot the Jewish victims and buried them in mass graves. By 1942, this method of execution was proving too slow and problematic for Hitler's ambitions and so the enormous apparatus of the Holocaust was planned. This was intended to bring about what Hitler called the "Final Solution"—the extermination of all Jews in Europe.

The Germans used the railroad system to link major cities with the existing network of detention camps. Many of those camps then were converted into industrialized killing factories where inmates were murdered in gas chambers and their corpses incinerated in ovens. In some of the camps, Jews were used as slave labor and worked to death on starvation rations. Exactly how many died in the Holocaust remains unclear, but estimates range from 8 million to 14 million human beings, most of them Jews (Gilbert, 245).

Anti-Semitism was a central feature in a few other fascist movements as well, but German Nazism was by far the most fanatical. Racial and anti-Semitic beliefs were not at all central to the early policies or rhetoric of Mussolini's Italian Fascism. Famously, Mussolini even had a Jewish mistress. But by the late 1930s, as Mussolini's government became increasingly close to Hitler's and increasingly dependent upon Nazi Germany for security, Mussolini began to lean toward anti-Semitism. In 1938, Mussolini passed laws in Italy that discriminated against Africans (a result of the conquest of Ethiopia in 1936) and against Jews. During the Holocaust the Italian government deported nearly 60,000 Jews and sent them to Nazi camps. The British Union of Fascists (BUF), established in 1932, in the first two years of its existence was quite adamant about its rejection of anti-Semitism. After 1934, however, the BUF increasingly turned to anti-Semitism to attract members and its press became stridently anti-Jewish and racist. Spanish and Portuguese regimes were only marginally anti-Semitic and neither made racial struggle or anti-Semitism a central feature of their programs. The Vichy French regime was not stridently anti-Jewish in its rhetoric or policies, but during the Holocaust the regime sent nearly 76,000 Jews to the Nazi death camps in the East.

See also: Hitler, Adolf; Holocaust; *Kristallnacht*; *Mein Kampf*; National Socialist German Workers' Party (Nazi Party); Racial Hygiene; *Schutzstaffel* (SS).

Further Reading

Brustein, William, *Roots of Hate: Anti-Semitism in Europe Before the Holocaust* (New York: Cambridge University Press, 2004).

Gilbert, Martin, *The Routledge Atlas of the Holocaust* (London: Routledge, 2002).

Goldhagen, Daniel Jonah, *Hitler's Willing Executioners: Ordinary Germans and the Holocaust* (New York: Vintage, 1996).

Hitler, Adolf, *Mein Kampf*, translated by Ralph Manheim (Boston: Houghton Mifflin, 1971 [1925]).

Johnson, Eric A., and Karl-Heinz Reuband, *What We Knew: Terror, Mass Murder, and Everyday Life in Nazi Germany* (Cambridge, MA: Basic Books, 2005).

AUTARKY "Autarky" is the term that describes the condition of an entity being entirely self-contained and self-sufficient. Generally, this concept is applied to a nation or empire, and most often is applied to its economic practices. An entirely autarkic economy would neither lend money to nor borrow money from other nations, nor would it import or export raw materials or manufactured goods. Examples of truly autarkic economies are extremely rare, but "autarkic" policies are more common, seeking to at least limit exchange with outside nations, and to protect home industries. In the "fascist era" autarky became a central economic objective of most of the fascist movements and regimes.

The vision of economic autarky grew to be a central tenet of fascism as it became clear that such an economically independent status was necessary to accomplish other fascist objectives. The fascist dictatorships of Italy and Germany each celebrated the growth of armed strength and glorified violence and warfare as purifying and invigorating experiences for a national community. Consistent with such beliefs, Italy launched aggressive military conquests of Abyssinia and Albania. Hitler's Germany likewise sent military troops into Austria, annexing that nation, and soon after invaded the nation of Czechoslovakia. Both Italy and Germany gave significant military aid to the Nationalist cause in Spain's Civil War. Finally, Hitler's massive military invasion of Poland resulted in the commencement of the Second World War.

Both Hitler and Mussolini were fascist dictators determined to assert the power of their respective nations through military strength. After the First World War, however, the Paris Peace Conference had established a League of Nations, and most of the world's great powers were attempting to work together diplomatically to *prevent* armed conflict. To preserve international stability, heal the economic downturn, and prevent another mass slaughter like that of the First World War, the democracies of Britain and France especially attempted to use their economic leverage to undermine the aggressive militarist adventures of the fascist powers.

The fascist dictatorships discovered that the democracies (often working through the League of Nations, but sometimes independently) could inflict serious hardship through the use of economic sanctions. Finding this to be the case, fascist powers increasingly turned to strategies of economic autarky. If their nations could find a way to become economically independent, then the democracies would not have the power to control or block their foreign policy objectives of bullying, manipulation, or outright military conquest. Economic independence would enable political independence.

In Italy there had long been a program, as part of the Mussolini government, to reduce the nation's economic dependencies, particularly for strategic raw materials. But it was Mussolini's invasion of Abyssinia in October 1935 that eventually produced limited economic sanctions. These sanctions mostly involved agricultural produce and did not include key strategic industrial items vital to Mussolini's war effort. Nor did Britain and France agree to close the Suez Canal to Italian shipping. Still, Mussolini reacted to these mild economic sanctions as an all-out assault on the Italian nation. He would announce a new economic program making economic autarky Italy's primary economic objective. He declared to the Fascist Confederation of Industrialists that, "The dominating problem . . . will be securing in the shortest possible time, the maximum degree of economic independence for the Nation . . . the possibility of an independent foreign policy cannot be conceived without the corresponding possibility of economic self-sufficiency." The invasion of Abyssinia, according to Mussolini, would help facilitate this economic self-sufficiency providing myriad new supplies of cheap raw materials and new markets for manufactures. Thus, his invasion of Abyssinia had been pursued partly for reasons of increased autarky, and then produced the sanctions that spurred Mussolini to make autarky an essential prerogative.

In Germany, Hitler also made economic autarky his number one economic objective. Recognizing the power that democracies wielded over Germany through economic restrictions, Hitler faced a dilemma given his deeply held objectives for an eventual mass conquest of Eastern Europe (including the Soviet Union). As such, in 1936 Hitler announced at the Party Rally in Nuremburg his new "Four Year Plan." This was a plan to make Germany an autarkic industrial and agricultural economy by 1940. Hitler created a Four Year Plan Office and made Hermann Goering its chief. Goering thus began a furious program of finding substitute materials (including synthetics) for the raw materials Germany lacked, and bringing most of Germany's industrial production under his own office's supervision.

In November 1937 Hitler held a secret meeting with mostly military staff during which he explained that Germany could not achieve total autarky on its own. He also explained that an integrated economy with the rest of the world's great powers was undesirable. This, he asserted, was the chief reason that the conquest of "the East" had to begin soon. Germany needed the natural resources, capital, and "living space" of Eastern Europe for it to achieve total self-sufficiency. At the same time, the Four Year Plan continued to make Germany as autarkic as realistically possible so that, when the time came for war, Germany would suffer as little as possible from any economic measures taken by the democracies. Like Mussolini, Hitler was mired in a strange contradiction—desiring to withdraw from a world economy into total self-containment and security, but needing to attack and conquer other lands to provide the economic resources to reach that point.

Autarky was emphasized the most by Britain's largest fascist organization, Oswald Mosley's British Union of Fascists (BUF), founded in 1932. Unlike Italy or Germany, Britain already possessed an enormous empire that contained plentiful resources of all types. The BUF did not advocate any expansion or conquest. Rather, its party program emphasized withdrawal from an unstable political climate, and a chaotic world economy. To ensure national security, the BUF advocated a massive armaments program for Britain, and for economic security, the conversion to an autarkic economy. Britain, Mosley said, had to institute policies of outright exclusion of foreign goods to protect the home market for its home industries. Those things that Britain did not possess—such as key raw materials—could be found in the empire. Thus, Mosley's economic vision emerged as an imperial autarky, with raw materials, goods, and services circulated within the British Empire without restrictions or tariffs, but with the legal exclusion of foreign (non-empire) goods and capital. The British Union of Fascists, though, never came close to taking power in Britain.

In Spain, after the Civil War was won by the Nationalists, Francisco Franco established his own fascist dictatorship and economic autarky was a central policy. Franco instituted stringent restrictions on all economic resources, raw materials as well as foodstuffs and manufactures. This was done to preserve his own political independence, but also, strangely, to punish the Spanish people for having been corrupted by outside influences. By restricting Spanish economic exchange he hoped to limit the exchange of foreigners and foreign ideas as well.

See also: British Union of Fascists; Four Year Plan; Goering, Hermann; Mosley, Sir Oswald.

Further Reading

Carr, William, *Arms, Autarky, and Aggression: A Study in German Foreign Policy, 1933–1939* (New York: Norton, 1973).

Overy, Richard, *Goering* (London: Phoenix, 1984).

Richards, Michael, *A Time of Silence: Civil War and the Culture of Repression in Franco's Spain* (New York: Cambridge University Press, 1998).

Skidelsky, Robert, *Oswald Mosley* (New York: Holt, Rinehart, & Winston, 1975).

BALBO, ITALO (1896–1940)   Italo Balbo was an important official within the Italian Fascist movement, and later within the Fascist government of Benito Mussolini. Balbo's career lasted from his involvement as a "Blackshirt" squad leader in the early 1920s to his post as Italy's minister for air, his time as the colonial governor of Libya, and finally to his term as commander and chief of Italian North Africa during the Second World War. A visible and popular member of the Fascist leadership, he was seen by many as the eventual successor to Benito Mussolini.

Balbo was born in Ferrara in Northern Italy on June 6, 1896, to middle-class parents. His father, Camillo, was a local schoolmaster. Camillo always had dreamed of a career in the military and regaled his sons with stories of military glory and filled them with his passionate nationalism. As a young adult, Italo Balbo attended university in Florence and studied law. Before he was able to complete his studies, however, Italy faced the question of entering the First World War. Balbo was an adamant supporter of Italy entering the war and joined the Royal Army. He took part in major military operations on the Austrian front and was decorated for bravery. After the war, he returned to Florence to complete his studies including a research thesis on Mazzini, the famed Italian nationalist intellectual.

In the days immediately after the war, Balbo was among those who were worried about the expansion of socialism and "internationalism," and so he joined Mussolini's Fascist Party in 1921. He emerged as a capable squad leader of the Ferrara branch of the "Blackshirts" as they conducted violent operations against local socialist groups. Balbo's talents as a Blackshirt leader helped him become one of the four chief organizers of Mussolini's "March on Rome," the nationwide convergence on the capital by Mussolini's supporters that helped him to take power in October 1922.

Balbo's contributions helped him to be named one of the founding members of the Fascist Grand Council, the leadership board of the Fascist Party which regulated party affairs. In what became a one-party state, this council wielded tremendous power. In 1924, however, Balbo was accused of having been involved in the murder of an anti-Fascist priest, Don Minzoni, near his hometown of Ferrara. The actual assailants who cracked Minzoni's skull were known to the police, but they were members of Balbo's branch of the Blackshirts. Accused of having orchestrated the murder, Balbo sued a newspaper for libel over the matter and was acquitted—but his reputation was deeply marred by the incident. He moved to Rome and in 1925 Mussolini made him an undersecretary in the Ministry of Economics. In November 1926, however, Balbo received the appointment that changed his life. Though he'd had little in the way of training (just a short stint in the Royal Air Corps during the war) Mussolini named Balbo secretary of state for air. This was a project that Mussolini took very seriously, hoping to use Balbo's appeal to help make Italy truly "air-minded." Balbo responded by quickly learning to fly and becoming a first-class aviator. He worked to sponsor Italy's entries in international air races, and to sponsor Italy's daring airmen in their pioneering flights, such as Umberto Nobile's flight in an airship to the polar regions. Balbo also worked with the military to help build the powerful *Regia Aeronautica*, the Italian national air force.

Balbo probably is best remembered, however, for twice leading great fleets of Italian-built airplanes across the Atlantic Ocean to publicize Italy's progress in aviation. These propaganda expeditions became known as the "Air Armadas." The first took place in 1930 with the fleet of planes flying from Italy to Rio de Janeiro. The much more famous second of these expeditions in 1933 took the Italian "Armada" to Chicago for that city's Century of Progress Exhibition celebrations. There the Italian planes landed spectacularly on Lake Michigan and the pilots later flew to New York where they were honored by a parade and enjoyed dining with the president. Back home in Italy, Balbo was promoted to marshal of the air forces.

In November 1933, Balbo received another appointment. It appears that Balbo was becoming disillusioned with some of the policy directions of Fascism, and never supported Mussolini's economic policies of creating a "corporative" state. Due to these tensions and to get him out of Rome, Balbo was assigned to be the colonial governor of Italy's Libyan territories. Mussolini wanted no rivals. In Libya, Balbo at first pursued policies that he hoped would expand the boundaries of the colony at the expense of British and French territory. But the outbreak of the Abyssinian crisis during 1935–36 created serious tensions with those nations, and Balbo began to create secret plans for invading British Egypt. Mussolini never put those plans into action. During 1938, Balbo began to have serious doubts about Italy's forming a close alliance with Nazi Germany and made these clear to Mussolini, to no avail. He was the only Fascist official of note to oppose that alliance.

As the Second World War broke out in 1939, Balbo was named commander and chief of Italian Forces in North Africa. Again he put together extensive plans for an Italian invasion of British Egypt, which was to take place in July of 1940. Before these plans could be ratified or acted upon, however, Balbo died in an air accident. Mistaking the identity of the plane, Balbo's own forces shot down his plane as he attempted to land at Tobruk on June 28, 1940.

See also: March on Rome; National Fascist Party (PNF).

Further Reading

Segre, Claudio G., *Italo Balbo: A Fascist Life* (Berkeley: University of California Press, 1987).

Stone, Marla, *The Fascist Revolution in Italy: A Brief History with Documents* (Boston: Bedford/St. Martin's, 2013).

BEER HALL PUTSCH   The Beer Hall Putsch (or Munich Putsch) was a failed attempt by Adolf Hitler and his young Nazi Party to seize control of the local government of Munich during November 8–9, 1923. After a brief political meeting in a large beer hall where Hitler and his inner circle forced local officials to support them at gunpoint, legions of Nazi storm troopers marched into the city center toward the government buildings. They were met by armed police, however, and a brief gunfight ensued, killing 4 police officers and 16 Nazis. Adolf Hitler was arrested and stood trial for treason. He eventually was found guilty, but only served 9 months in prison.

By 1923, the National Socialist German Workers' Party (*Nationalsozialistische Deutsche Arbeiterpartei*) (NSDAP) still was a small, local political party based in Munich. Its leader, Adolf Hitler, had made himself the unquestioned leader of the party and he undoubtedly was the most charismatic speaker of the group. With his recent consolidation of power within the group he made the decision during that year that his party, small as it was, needed to seize the moment and take control of the Munich city government. From here, he believed, the Nazis could use Munich as a base for a further effort to seize control of the national government and dislodge the Weimar Republic. Hitler was convinced of the potential success of such a move for two principal reasons. First, he greatly admired the March on Rome carried out by Mussolini and his "Blackshirts" in Italy during October 1922. Mussolini had used a mass movement of his supporters to pressure the king of Italy to appoint him prime minister. Hitler believed such a mass demonstration of force might produce similar results for him and his Nazis. Additionally, the popular political mood was ripe for a radical change.

In 1923 Germany was mired in the midst of a "hyper-inflation," which was wiping out the savings of middle-class Germans and wrecking the German economy. That same year, French troops had occupied the Ruhr Valley industrial district, which served as a further source of anger and humiliation to Germans. Squeezed by hyper-inflation, economic distress, and the Allied Powers as they enforced the Treaty of Versailles, the German public was becoming more willing to listen to radicals like Hitler who swore to overturn the treaty.

Hitler and his Nazi storm troopers had been engaging in almost constant political agitation and street violence during 1923. The chaotic and violent political climate had forced the Bavarian prime minister to create a special ruling council in Munich made up of three conservative politicians with notable military reputations. This council of three banned Hitler's plans for a series of mass meetings in Munich that autumn, and with this Hitler felt he was in a difficult position. If his party was not active in such a politically volatile time, he feared mass defections from its membership. Under this pressure he organized the coup attempt. He was able to secure the support of some notable extreme right-wing political figures, including the legendary General Erich Ludendorff who would in fact take part in the eventual action.

On the evening of November 8, one of Munich's ruling council, Gustav von Kahr, was giving his own political speech at one of Munich's largest beer houses, where it was typical for hundreds to gather for beer, song, and political debates. This particular hall was known as the *Burgerbraukellar* and it was here that Hitler and his inner circle intended to launch their coup attempt. They interrupted the meeting, seized the microphone, and used firearms to force the council members off stage and into a back room. There, holding the men at gunpoint, they insisted that they publicly support the Nazi seizure of power. Hitler even promised Kahr an important position in any government he created. There was a long period of silence outside as the men holed up in the small room resisted Nazi demands. Meanwhile, Hitler spoke to the stunned crowd. Using his power as an orator he explained the group's intent and insisted that this was not aimed at the people of Munich, nor the police, but at the Jewish-led government in Berlin, which had betrayed Germany by surrendering in the First World War five years before. The crowd gradually warmed to Hitler's fanatical speech and eventually the crowd transformed into a frenzied mass of support and applause.

By the next morning, Hitler and his Nazi Storm Troopers headed into the center of town to seize the municipal government. On their way to the buildings of the Bavarian Defense Ministry the crowd of uniformed and armed Storm Troopers was intercepted by the Bavarian State Police force. In the great *Odeonsplatz*, the largest square in central Munich, the police gave orders for the Nazis to cease their march. They ignored these pleas and marched forward, with Hitler and Ludendorff among those in the front lines, and the police fired into their ranks. A brief gun battle followed which killed four members of the police. The Nazis fired back, but eventually scattered. The Nazis lost 16 members and saw a number of their group wounded, including both Hermann Goering and Adolf Hitler. The coup attempt ended as an abject failure.

As a result, Adolf Hitler stood trial for treason. His trial, however, was managed by two judges that were sympathetic to his cause and who despised the Weimar Republic. They allowed Hitler to make long, rambling speeches denouncing the Weimar Republic, ranting about Germany's Jews and about Marxists of all shades. It was the press coverage of this trial and the reprints of his long-winded tirades that really made Hitler a national figure. He was found guilty but, incredibly, was sentenced to only five years in prison—of which he would serve only nine months. It was during his internment in Landsberg Prison that Hitler wrote his autobiographical political manifesto, *Mein Kampf.*

In later years, as the Nazi Party gained strength and eventually rose to power, the 16 who died in the gunfight became almost legendary figures, celebrated for their bravery and ultimate sacrifice—their supposed valor standing as an example for all Nazis. Known as the "blood martyrs," that group was celebrated with almost religious veneration and symbolism including a "blood flag" that routinely was displayed for Nazi ceremonies and still carried bloodstains of the Nazis who died at the Beer Hall Putsch.

See also: Hitler, Adolf; National Socialist German Workers' Party (Nazi Party); *Sturmabteilung* (SA).

Further Reading
Evans, Richard J., *The Coming of the Third Reich* (New York: Penguin, 2003).
Gordon, Harold J., *Hitler and the Beer Hall Putsch* (Princeton: Princeton University Press, 1972).
Pridham, Geoffrey, *Hitler's Rise to Power: The Nazi Movement in Bavaria 1923–1933* (New York: Harper & Row, 1973).

***BIENNIO ROSSO* (RED TWO YEARS)**   The *Biennio Rosso* (or "Red Two Years") is the term used in Italian historiography to describe the expansion of the Marxist and Socialist causes in that country during the period from the end of World War I in 1918 through 1920. The strengthening of the Socialist movement inspired extreme fear on the part of the commercial and landowning classes in Italy, which worried that Italy might experience the same type of worker and peasant revolution that had taken place in Russia during 1917. It was this growth in the Socialist movement that gave Benito Mussolini's earliest Fascist groups their political identity as his paramilitary squads, known as "Blackshirts," began to fight against leftist activities and institutions with savage violence. This situation ultimately created the chaotic political environment that enabled Mussolini to take power later in 1922.

The *Biennio Rosso* saw the Socialist movement grow in several ways, but three areas in particular dislocated the Italian economy and worried the right-wing political faction—party politics, industrial relations, and involvement in the peasant workforces in the countryside. In party politics, the Italian industrial workers traditionally had supported the Italian Socialist Party (*Partito Socialista Italiano*) (PSI). After the First World War, the peasantry of Italy also began to vote for Socialists in overwhelming numbers. The *Partito Populare Italiano* (PPI) also emerged as a second party representing workers' and peasants' interests. Together the PSI and PPI represented a majority in the Italian parliament by 1919. After the 1919 elections the parliamentary representatives of the two parties entered their first parliamentary session singing "The Red Flag," the universal anthem of revolutionary Marxists.

Italy also saw extraordinary turmoil in its industrial relations during the *Biennio Rosso*. During the First World War, in Italy—as in so many other nations—industrial production was increased to meet the extreme needs of a war economy. Several industries had been taken over by the government to ensure coordination with objectives of national defense. When the war was over these industries were returned to private management, and most of Italy's factories had to significantly reduce production because wartime production had ended. This caused wage decreases and widespread layoffs. Italy's workers—knowing full well that industrial capitalists had made astronomical profits during the war—insisted on higher wages, better conditions, and job security. The result was an unprecedented wave of strike actions led by trade union leaders that often coordinated with Socialist organizations. In 1919, nearly half a million workers in Italy went on strike; by 1920, that number was more than a million (Finaldi, 37). As part of these industrial actions there emerged a new kind of workers' action—the "factory occupation." Organized workers went into the factories—often armed—threw out the ownership and the managers, and took control of the functions of production for themselves. As a result of so many workers' disputes, Italy's economy was in near chaos by 1921.

Socialist organizations also established a collection of "peasant leagues" or workers' exchanges in the countryside, concentrated in the south of Italy. In the southern regions, landholders tended to own enormous amounts of land and farmed in plantation style. Peasant agricultural workers sometimes lived permanently on these great estates, but many were seasonal workers. The landowners employed workers during the planting and harvest seasons and generally paid quite low wages. The "peasant leagues" sought to organize the peasant workers and to negotiate with landowners and force them to pay higher wages.

Italy's industrial leaders were exasperated with the chaos of strikes and factory occupations, and they were losing money. Big landowners were furious at having to pay increased wages to part-time workers. Even worse for the owners, there appeared to be no hope for changing the situation through government legislation, as the government was becoming dominated by the workers' and peasants' parties. Landowners' anxieties grew as they contemplated the possibility of a Communist revolution—which quite possibly might threaten their lives and which would surely mean that their property would be taken by the state.

Into this situation stepped Benito Mussolini's *Fasci di Combattimento* ("Fascist Combat Leagues"). Where socialist politicians had been elected in municipal governments, these black-shirted Fascist "squads" would arrive in groups nearing a hundred and assault the town's governing institutions. Socialist newspaper offices were smashed or set on fire; Socialist politicians were tortured, roughed up, and sometimes beaten to death. It was in this earliest phase of nationalist-inspired violence against the Socialists that Mussolini's Fascists defined themselves. Fascism, as a broader political phenomenon, would become far more complex; but in its earliest days, this was how Italian Fascism found its political role and identity.

See also: March on Rome; Mussolini, Benito; National Fascist Party (PNF).

Further Reading

Di Scala, Spencer M., *Italian Socialism: Between Politics and History* (Amherst: University of Massachusetts Press, 1996).

Finaldi, Giuseppe, *Mussolini and Italian Fascism* (Harlow: Pearson, 2008).

Kennett, Wayland, *The Italian Left: A Short History of Italian Socialism in Italy* (London: Longmans, 1949).

BLACKSHIRTS   Originating in Italy, the "Blackshirts" were the paramilitary groups organized by Benito Mussolini which acted as the violent political force for his early Fascist organizations. From 1919 to 1921 Mussolini called his Fascist "squads" the *Fasci di Combattimento* or "Fascist Combat Groups." After 1921, his organization emerged as a formal political party, with candidates running for the Italian government. The "Blackshirts" remained a vital part of Mussolini's organization, however, even after it became a political party.

Sir Oswald Mosley's British Union of Fascists also created a paramilitary organization of young men who lived in barracks, trained in boxing and street fighting, and physically fought against any political opposition. Mosley also called his paramilitaries "Blackshirts" and created a uniform similar to that used by the Italian Fascists. The use of such uniforms became an almost universal trapping of fascist movements everywhere.

In its earliest days, Mussolini's organization was able to recruit a great number of members from Italy's demobilizing soldiers immediately after World War I. Italy's elite forces in that war were known as the *arditi* and their uniform included a black shirt and tie. Many of these demobilizing soldiers joined Mussolini's Fascists and kept their military uniforms. This earned them the nickname "Blackshirts." A full black uniform eventually became the official uniform of this paramilitary group.

The group first found its political identity in engaging in brutal attacks upon the institutions of Socialist government from 1919 to 1922. Italy's political system had been racked with significant change in the years immediately after the First World War, and the period from late-1918 through 1920 became known as the *Biennio Rosso* or the "Red Two Years." This nickname was applied because of the great expansion of the Socialist movement in Italy during those years. The Italian Socialist Party gained the majority in Parliament and a wide movement of strikes and factory occupations nearly paralyzed the Italian economy. As a result, Mussolini's political organization decided it must fight back and defend the rights of the "nation"—really the commercial and landowning classes. To do this he used his "Blackshirts."

They were divided into "squads" and deployed for action, hence the Italian term used at the time to describe their activity—*squadrismo*. They typically would choose towns that had elected Socialists to power in local government, or towns where there was a significant Socialist Party organization. The Blackshirts would smash the offices of socialist newspapers, often setting them on fire. They also broke into town halls, kidnapping, or—more often—torturing and beating Socialist officials. They used blackjacks, brass knuckles, and clubs, but the Blackshirts seemed most proud of their use of castor oil, a violent purgative. Forcing bottles of castor oil down the throats of their political enemies could cause those victims serious permanent health problems, or at times force them to vomit uncontrollably. The Blackshirts were so proud of such activities that they celebrated their use of castor oil in party songs.

In October 1922, as a political crisis brewed in Rome, the various branches of Mussolini's Blackshirts staged a nationwide choreographed "March on Rome." From all over the country armies of black-shirted men rode in cars, trucks, trains, and came on foot to occupy the center of Rome, putting increasing pressure on the Italian king to appoint Benito Mussolini prime minister. The king's decision was a highly complex one, but certainly the mass demonstrations by the Blackshirts as they filled the streets and squares of Rome, chanting for Mussolini, was an influential factor in his making the decision to ask Mussolini to form a government.

Mussolini would retain the Blackshirts as a paramilitary force and as part of his official government apparatus after becoming prime minister and then dictator of Italy. Separate from Italy's established armed forces, they often were used to create crowd scenes for public speeches and to violently oppress those in opposition. Some Blackshirt squads formed armed regiments that fought next to the army in conflicts such as the Spanish Civil War and in the conquests of Abyssinia (1935–36) and Albania (1939).

As Mussolini's Fascist movement was the first in Europe to come to prominence and then to political power, the Italian example often was used by other fascist organizations. The use of a violent paramilitary force, in uniform (like Mussolini's Blackshirts), became one of the most commonly used trappings of fascist movements. These included the creation of the "Brownshirts" in Germany, the "Blueshirts" in Spain and in Ireland, and the "Greyshirts" in South Africa.

In Britain, Sir Oswald Mosley launched his British Union of Fascists (BUF) in late 1932. In an imitation of Mussolini's techniques, Mosley would create his own paramilitary army and dress them in a black-shirted uniform. They were used to keep order at rallies, for marches, and for fistfights against those in political opposition on the streets. In London, Mosley's Blackshirts lived in barracks-style housing at his party headquarters in Chelsea, known as

"Black House." In 1936, the British Government passed laws outlawing the use of uniforms in political demonstrations. These measures were aimed directly at the BUF and eliminated the public use of the black shirt as a symbol of violence and intimidation.

See also: British Union of Fascists; March on Rome; Mussolini, Benito.

Further Reading
Parenti, Michael, *Blackshirts and Reds: Rational Fascism and the Overthrow of Communism* (San Francisco: City Light Books, 1997).
Pugh, Martin, *Hurrah for the Blackshirts! Fascists and Fascism in Britain Between the Wars* (London: Jonathan Cape, 2005).

BRITISH UNION OF FASCISTS The British Union of Fascists (BUF) was the largest and most visible of the explicitly Fascist political organizations in Great Britain, operating from 1932 to 1940. Founded by Sir Oswald Mosley, a famous and glamorous politician, the organization was able to attract most of the membership away from the other much smaller existing fascist parties in Britain. In addition to being a party of agitation and political pressure it also was a formal political party, running candidates in several by-elections during the 1930s. The group experienced a peak of popularity in 1933, when it received public support from Lord Rothermere and his newspaper the *Daily Mail.* After a group of setbacks, however, including Rothermere's withdrawal of support, the party went into decline. It experienced a brief rebound in its popularity during 1939 as it fervently rejected war with Nazi Germany and campaigned for peace. After the Second World War broke out, the party continued to function but in 1940 finally officially was banned by the government and most of its key membership imprisoned.

Sir Oswald Mosley was elected to the British Parliament in 1918 as a Conservative, but soon grew impatient with that party's ultra-conservative approach to the slumping economy and its oppressive measures in Ireland. He switched to the Labour Party by 1924. After Labour's victory in 1929, Mosley was given a minor position in the government (chancellor of the Duchy of Lancaster), but was assigned to work under Jimmy Thomas (an old Trade Union leader) to solve the unemployment problem, which by now was acute. Mosley embraced the new economic ideas being propagated by John Maynard Keynes that urged state-stimulation of consumer buying power to revive the economy and employment. As such, Mosley recommended a full program of state-sponsored public works and a program of deficit borrowing to finance it. The program was rejected by the more conservative-minded of the Labour cabinet, and Mosley was furious. He resigned from the government, and eventually presented the same ideas to the Trade Union Congress, where they again were rejected. Mosley subsequently made a stunning speech in the House of Commons promoting his ideas and condemning the government for its lack of vision. He then resigned from the Labour Party and founded his own party—the New Party. This party emphasized the needs for the modernization of industry, the use of public works and deficit financing, and streamlining the government's cabinet to a small committee of five key officials to run the country. His party ran candidates in the 1931 election, but none was elected, and Mosley himself lost his seat in parliament. Over the next several months he toured Asia and Europe examining economic and political questions. During his travels he visited Fascist Italy, where he was significantly impressed with Mussolini's approach to government and the Duce's ability to get things done with dictatorial powers. When Mosley returned he began to convert his moribund New Party into a new kind of party. By October 1932 he would launch his British Union of Fascists, advocating a fascist dictatorship for Britain, for Mosely himself to be its "leader" with dictatorial powers.

As part of launching the party in 1932, Mosely published his manifesto entitled, *The Greater Britain*. In that book Mosley explained his views on the nature of the new political world of the 20th century, changed so dramatically by the Great War. He particularly emphasized that the progress of science and technology had created a new set of economic realities that made the old economic theories and practices obsolete. He advocated a dictatorship where a dictator—elected by the people in a plebiscite—would have absolute power. Mosely proposed eliminating the party system in politics and re-creating the parliament based on Mussolini's "Corporative" system. The parliament was to be organized by "Corporations" which would contain boards of representatives that were elected by members of their own industries and professions. These elected representatives were to have backgrounds as senior management, technical experts, and workers. Once elected, they would make decisions in parliament to be applied within the industries they represented.

Another of Mosley's core policies was the conversion to an "autarkic" imperial economy. Mosley believed Britain and its imperial possessions could create an economy that was completely self-sufficient and self-contained. The empire held sources for any raw materials needed for industry, and Britain would redevelop agriculture and manufacturing devoted to its home market and its empire markets. There would be legal restrictions against international borrowing or lending, and foreign goods would be kept out of Britain not by tariffs (which Mosley found too weak a barrier), but by outright legal exclusion. The ability then for Britain to provide its own food, procure any raw materials from the empire, employ its people at increased wage levels (controlled by the state), would create an economy no longer dependent upon exports of capital or manufactures. Being completely economically independent, Mosley argued, meant that Britain would have no need of involvement in any overseas conflicts that did not threaten Britain or its empire directly. To further insure this, Mosley was adamant about the need for Britain to rearm with the most modern weaponry available. These were then the most fundamental policies that composed the program of the BUF: a single-party dictatorship, parliament organized on the corporative model, an autarkic imperial economy, and massive rearmament.

With these policies in place Mosley's BUF began to take shape. Mosley began using the "fasces" as the party's principal symbol and insignia, borrowing from Mussolini's Italian Fascist Party. He soon created a unique symbol for the BUF, however. It was a circle (representing the unity of the state) with a lightning bolt moving diagonally through the center of the circle (representing swift, decisive action). The party also assembled a paramilitary corps of young men—dressed in an official uniform—to provide the muscle and violence, if necessary, to make the party's presence known and to intimidate any of its enemies. Their uniform was made up of black trousers and a black turtleneck shirt. The corps became known as the "Blackshirts," just as Mussolini's private army had come to be known. They earned a reputation for violence and thuggery as they "kept order" at BUF speaking engagements, silencing any hecklers or protestors with brutality.

In 1933 the party launched its weekly newspaper, called *The Blackshirt*, which ruthlessly attacked the "Old Gang" democratic politicians and advocated BUF policies. The name of the publication was changed a year later to *Action*, which lasted until the demise of the party in 1940. As the Depression intensified during 1932 and 1933 the BUF had a surge of membership and popularity. This reached its peak during 1933 as Lord Rotheremere, the second richest man in Britain, publicly endorsed the BUF in the pages of his newspaper, the *Daily Mail*. Rothermere was an advocate of most of Mosley's policies, and was also a supporter of fascist dictatorships on the continent as the best barrier against the threat of Bolshevism from the Soviet Union.

In 1934, however, the popularity of the BUF began to fade quickly because of a combination of factors. First, the facts emerged about Hitler's series of political murders in June, which came to be collectively known as the "Night of the Long Knives." The naked brutality and illegality of this began to generate questions about fascism even among those who had initially supported it. Next, a BUF Party rally at the Olympia arena in London saw a number of hecklers removed and savagely beaten on the sidewalks outside the coliseum. These beatings were photographed and publicized in Britain's press, again turning public opinion. Finally, Rotheremere himself stopped his official support for Mosley in the *Daily Mail*. There remains a great deal of speculation as to why he withdrew his support. Mosley would claim later in his autobiography that Rotheremere had been forced to do this by powerful Jewish advertisers in his press.

The BUF from its founding had pledged to reject the racism and anti-Semitism characteristic of Nazism and of some of the other British fascist organizations. Mosley continually emphasized that a nation which governed an empire composed of numerous races and cultures had no place for racism. It even was said that the BUF had a few Jewish members. This also would change during 1934. As Jewish organizations publicly protested against the BUF and attacked Mosley as a potential "British Hitler," Mosley began to change the party line, increasingly including anti-Semitic rhetoric. During 1935, some of the more rabid anti-Semitic members of the party were put in charge of the party's newspaper and the character of that publication became even more conspicuously racist and anti-Semitic.

After Mosley reorganized the party during 1935 because of financial strains, two of those highly anti-Semitic members left the party to form their own fascist organization. William Joyce and John Beckett would form the National Socialist League, an organization much more closely modeled after the Nazi Party and its anti-Semitic and racially based ideology. On October 4, 1936, the BUF planned a march through the East End of London, an area of strength for the BUF due to the high number of Jews who lived in the area and the resulting anti-Semitic attitudes of other residents. Jewish groups and several Socialist and workers' groups organized a protest, sealed off the streets, and refused to let the BUF march. After much tension the march was cancelled. The event was remembered as the "Battle of Cable Street," and marks an important symbolic victory in the British stand against the rise of fascism in that country.

As 1937 and 1938 progressed with the Spanish Civil War raging and Hitler's annexations of Austria and Czechoslovakia, the BUF launched the "Mind Britain's Business," campaign which advocated non-intervention by Britain in European affairs. As these events in Europe brought the world closer to war, in 1939 the party again experienced a boom in popularity, as Mosley and other members campaigned relentlessly for Britain to remain neutral in any European conflict.

When war did come, the BUF continued to function, though public opinion turned overwhelmingly against it. As Britons awaited possible invasion from Germany there were questions about the BUF secretly aiding the Germans and hoping to be put in power as a puppet government in the event of a successful German occupation. Due to such concerns, in 1940, under the famous law Defense Regulation 18B (which allowed the government to imprison citizens without trial), the British government moved to officially ban

the BUF (and the other Fascist groups) and arrest the majority of its prominent members. This included Oswald Mosley and his wife, Diana, but included numerous others. After 1943, as the threat of Nazi invasion passed,
the BUF members gradually were released from prison. Although other "neo-
fascist" groups emerged in Britain in the postwar years, the British Union of
Fascists was never revived.

Although the BUF had a well-known leader, a thorough political program,
and moments of high visibility, the party never came close to winning any
election. It was an utter failure in terms of electoral politics, and never put a
single candidate into a parliamentary seat. Its agenda, however, often could be
promoted by far-right Conservative MP's, fascist pressure organizations, and
powerful members of the press.

See also: Blackshirts; Mosley, Sir Oswald.

Further Reading
Linehan, Thomas P., *British Fascism, 1918–39: Parties, Ideology and Culture* (Man-
    chester: Manchester University Press, 2000).
Pugh, Martin, *Hurrah for the Blackshirts! Fascists and Fascism in Britain Between the
    Wars* (London: Jonathan Cape, 2005).
Skidelsky, Robert, *Oswald Mosley* (New York: Holt, Rinehart & Winston, 1975).

CIANO, COUNT GIAN GALEAZZO (1903–1944)   Count Gian Galeazzo Ciano was a prominent member of the Fascist government in Italy from
the mid-1920s through the Second World War. He served as Italy's foreign
minister from June 1936 to February 1943, and played a significant role
in Italy's involvement with Nazi Germany and other nations in the chain of
events leading to the outbreak of the Second World War. Having married
Edda Mussolini, the daughter of the Italian dictator Benito Mussolini, he
was among the closest of the dictator's associates. In the latter stages of World
War II, however, as Italy came under military threat from the Allies, Ciano
supported making peace and lost the support of his father-in-law. In the
days to come, Ciano would be among those in the Fascist Party that deposed
Mussolini and imprisoned him. Mussolini's subsequent rescue by the Nazis
(and Ciano's subsequent capture) resulted in Ciano's trial and conviction for
treason. He was executed in 1944. His diaries from 1937 to 1943 are an
essential source for understanding the diplomatic environment leading up
to the Second World War and for understanding the inner workings of the
Italian government during the war.

Gian Galeazzo Ciano was born in Livorno, Italy, on March 18, 1903. His
father, Costanzo Ciano, was a well-to-do businessman and diplomat who had

distinguished himself in Italy's navy during the First World War. As a reward for his performance in the navy, Costanzo was given the title of "Count" by Italy's king Victor Emmanuel III, a title that would later pass to his son. Costanzo was an enthusiastic member of the Fascist Party (PNF) in Italy from its earliest days and became a close member of Benito Mussolini's inner circle. This was reinforced by his continued support of Mussolini after the notorious Matteotti murder in 1924. In 1926, in an unpublished document, Mussolini even designated Costanzo Ciano as his replacement should he die in office.

Young Galeazzo proved himself a distinguished student and was able to attend Rome University where he studied philosophy and law. While still at the university he spent a short period attempting to make his living as a writer, both in journalism and as a writer of short stories and plays. He achieved very little success with this endeavor. After graduating from Rome University in 1925, Galeazzo's father encouraged him to apply for a position in Italy's diplomatic corps. His father's connections enabled Galeazzo to secure a position as a vice-consul in Brazil. In 1927, he was given a new assignment as a secretary of legation in Beijing, China. After two years he was recalled to Rome. During his period back in Rome, Galeazzo met and courted Edda Mussolini and the two were married on April 24, 1930. After their brief honeymoon, he resumed his assignment in China.

As Mussolini's plans for a war of conquest in Abyssinia moved forward, Galeazzo returned to Italy and signed on for service in the *Regia Aeronautica* (Italy's military air service) as a bomber pilot. He was made commander of the 15th Bomber Squadron and became famous for a rather foolhardy attempted landing at enemy-held Addis Ababa in 1936, where his plane was shot to bits in the attempt. Enjoying a new level of popularity and respect from Mussolini, however, he was made Italy's foreign minister on June 9, 1936.

As foreign minister, Ciano was a key player in Italy's work with Nazi Germany during the buildup to the Second World War. He was involved with Italy's military aid to Spain during the Spanish Civil War, and was present at the Munich conferences of late 1938 that saw Czechoslovakia deserted by Britain and France. Despite his participation and involvement with Italy's increasing closeness with the Third Reich, Ciano had serious reservations about such close relations with the Nazis. His chief worry was the seeming inevitability of Hitler causing a general war in Europe, and Italy's lack of preparedness. For this reason he was only reluctantly willing to endorse the signing of the "Pact of Steel" in 1939.

As the Second World War progressed into 1943, the Italian forces in France, Greece, and North Africa had performed poorly. Success in each case had only been assured by German aid. In 1942, Italian forces had been routed in North Africa, paving the way for an Allied invasion of continental Europe that would proceed through southern Italy. As the Allies made their way through Sicily and up the "boot" of the Italian peninsula, Ciano consistently called for a withdrawal from the conflict and for separate terms with the Allies. Because of this, Mussolini removed him from his post as foreign secretary and made him ambassador to the Holy See in the Vatican. This way, Ciano was still in Rome to be monitored by Mussolini's secret police, the Organization for the Vigilance and Repression of Anti-Fascism (*Organizzazione per la Vigilanza e la Repressione dell'Antifascismo*) (OVRA). As the Allies continued to progress and came closer to Rome, however, the Fascist Grand Council met on July 24, 1943. With the realities of Italy's situation openly discussed, the council made the extraordinary move of removing Mussolini from his position and granting full powers to the king of Italy. Mussolini was arrested hours later and imprisoned in a mountaintop jail, to ensure his isolation. Ciano had been among those who voted for his deposition.

Ciano received an unpleasant surprise when he was dismissed from his post by the new government convened after Mussolini's ouster. The new government already was moving to change sides in the war and join the Allies. Ciano almost certainly would be arrested and executed in such an event. Because he was in such a vulnerable position, he traveled north hoping to find sanctuary with the Nazi forces. Hitler, meanwhile, had conceived and planned a rescue operation, using German commandos, to break Mussolini out of jail and bring him to safety in Germany. With this accomplished, Hitler set up Mussolini as dictator of the region in the far north of Italy that became known as the Italian Social Republic. When Ciano made contact with Nazi forces he was taken into custody. His vote to oust Mussolini then came back to haunt him. Mussolini and Hitler both insisted that he be put on trial for treason. He was found guilty, and on January 11, 1944, he was executed by a gunshot to the back of the head while he was tied to a chair.

His wife Edda, who had escaped Italy to Switzerland with her lover, retained Ciano's papers. These eventually would be compiled into two volumes of a published diary. This diary of his days as foreign minister from 1937 to 1943 is an invaluable source for historians in tracking the progress of events and particularly the workings and positions of the Italian government during the interwar period and during the World War II itself.

See also: Abyssinian War; Mussolini, Benito, National Fascist Party (PNF).

Further Reading

Ciano, Count Galeazzo, *Ciano's Hidden Diaries 1937–39,* translated by Andreas Mayor (New York: Dutton, 1953).

Ciano, Count Galeazzo, *The Ciano Diaries 1939–43*, edited by Hugh Gibson (New York: Doubleday, 1946).
Moseley, Ray, *Mussolini's Shadow: The Double Life of Count Galeazzo Ciano* (New Haven: Yale University Press, 1999).

CORPORATISM (CORPORATIVE STATE)   "Corporatism" (*Corporatismo* in Italian) is the term applied to describe an approach to industrial organization as developed by Benito Mussolini and his Fascist Party in Italy from 1922 to 1943. It involved assigning a board of specially appointed (or in some cases elected) officials to monitor, control, and manage entire sectors of industry. Although Fascist leaders and theorists always adamantly maintained the priority of private ownership of business, they also believed that business should be conducted to maximize the benefits of industry to the whole national community. The Corporative system was developed to ensure that industry was managed not for the optimal benefit of a select few companies, but for the entire nation. Mussolini eventually fully implemented this philosophy, creating his Chamber of Fasces and Corporations in 1939. Other fascist regimes and movements celebrated this system as an ingenious way to eliminate the war between classes, and virtually all fascist movements of the era included Corporatism as a feature of their political program.

The first instance of such an organization for industry being proposed actually occurred during the occupation of the city of Fiume by Gabriele D'Annunzio in 1920. D'Annunzio worked with the Syndicalist intellectual Alceste De Ambris in designing the system in their "Charter of Carnaro," which was to act as a constitution for D'Annunzio's state. That state collapsed almost immediately, but Benito Mussolini and his Fascist Party in Italy were deeply influenced by it. During the 1920s and 1930s Mussolini worked to reorganize labor relations and issued the Charter of Labor in 1927, which clearly outlined the rights and duties of laborers in the new Fascist state. The Corporate model was the basis of the regulations and Mussolini worked to create the Chamber of Corporations through the 1930s. In 1939, Mussolini actually replaced the Chamber of Deputies (representatives elected by regional vote) in the Italian Parliament with the Chamber of Corporations (representatives elected by industry).

The way that the system worked was through the creation of a board of qualified representatives associated with a particular sector of industry. There was an Iron and Steel Corporation, for instance, and a Transportation Corporation. These representatives were selected from four specific areas of expertise: (1) top management from the top companies; (2) government representatives from the Fascist Party; (3) those with special expertise in that industry's science and technology; and (importantly) (4) representatives selected from labor.

This Corporation's board then would oversee and manage an entire industry composed of privately owned companies. The Corporations had the authority to mandate policies, such as wage levels, production levels, and the methods for introducing new technological innovations. Mussolini received tremendous admiration around the world for having solved what seemed to be an unsolvable problem—the class war between workers and employers.

Theoretically, in Corporatism, labor officials would help form the very policies under which their workers would labor. In practice, however, Corporatism had a limited impact and did not really create a truly cooperative environment in industrial relations. In the process of creating this system, Mussolini outlawed all non-Fascist trade unions, and made all strike activity illegal. In essence, although labor was represented in these Corporations it had no leverage of any kind. Employers, managers, and government officials had no real reason to listen to the priorities and demands of labor because labor had no legal recourse. Thus, many scholars believe that the chief result of the Corporative system in Mussolini's regime was the crushing of the Italian labor movement.

The Corporative system became a very visible and even essential feature of fascist theory and practice outside Italy. A similar system of boards and labor relations was created in Nazi Germany and called the "Labor Front." Franco's Spain and Salazar's Portugal also attempted to create similar organizations for their industrial communities. The "Fatherland Front" under Engelbert Dollfuss's brief dictatorship put plans in place for a Corporative organization for Austria's economy. In Britain, the British Union of Fascists made the Corporative system one of the principal features of its program. Its leader, Sir Oswald Mosley, in fact intended to replace the existing British parliamentary system (elected by geographical regions) with a Corporative system under which members of parliament were elected by members of their own industries. It would be an industrially based parliamentary system (as Mussolini did in fact implement in 1939). This was discussed at length in his book *The Greater Britain* (1932) and in the party's book *The Coming Corporate State* (1934). In the United States, Franklin D. Roosevelt also experimented with a form of Corporatism when he passed the Nation Industrial Recovery Act in 1933, creating the National Recovery Administration (NRA). This program created boards empowered to regulate and pass policies for entire industries to help stabilize the economy and improve working conditions. These codes of policies and regulations were found to be unconstitutional by the Supreme Court in 1935, however, in the case of *Schechter Poultry Corp. vs. United States*. Thus the program was dismantled.

See also: British Union of Fascists; Fiume (Occupation of); Mussolini, Benito.

Further Reading

Mosley, Sir Oswald, *The Greater Britain* (London: BUF, 1932).

Sarti, Roland, *Fascism and the Industrial Leadership in Italy 1919–1940—A Study in the Expansion of Private Power Under Fascism* (Berkeley: University of California Press, 1971).

CZECH CRISIS OF 1938   The Czech crisis was a chain of events during the period from April 1938 through September 1938 during which Hitler's Germany threatened war unless it was granted territorial claims on the borderlands of Czechoslovakia. The crisis involved several other European nations as well—particularly Britain and France, as each of those nations maintained a treaty of military alliance with Czechoslovakia. After multiple talks, Germany, France, Britain, and Italy signed an agreement on September 29 to settle the crisis. This agreement allowed Germany to annex the border-land areas of Czechoslovakia (known as the Sudetenland) into the German Reich, and left an international commission to settle other disputed border areas. The Czechs, who were not invited to the conference, had no choice but to capitulate because their treaty allies—Britain and France—refused to honor their treaty obligations. After annexing the Sudetenland areas, how-ever, Hitler would move to take most of the rest of Czechoslovakia as well, proving that his word meant nothing. The Czech Crisis and the failure of the "Munich Agreement" it produced, stand as the most prominent failures of the policy of "appeasement," by which the British and French governments had hoped to reach peace with the fascist dictatorships.

The nation of Czechoslovakia had been established as a result of negotia-tions at the Paris Peace Conference immediately following the First World War. On its westernmost boundaries, Czechoslovakia bordered Austria to the south and Germany to the west and north. Along those borderlands there was a population that included a German-speaking majority. Those lands became known collectively as the "Sudetenland," and it was the "national question" surrounding this territory that was the essence of the Czech crisis of 1938. By the early 1930s a large branch of the Nazi Party within the Sudetenland had developed—known as the "Sudeten German Party" (SDP). The SDP worked closely with the Nazi government to provoke discord in the region, giving Hitler the public justification he wanted for a full military annexation of the area.

Germany bullied and intimidated Austria into a surrender of its sovereignty in March 1938. After Germany's formal annexation of the entire nation of Austria—an act which became known as the *Anschluss*—Germany surrounded Czechoslovakia's entire western region. It was at this point in April 1938 that Hitler personally met with Konrad Henlein, the leader of the SDP, and directed the group to begin demonstrations and provocations against the Czech government. On April 24 the SDP submitted a list of demands to the Czech government demanding full equal rights as Czech citizens and, significantly, an autonomous government for the Sudetenland. Czech president Edward Benes readily agreed to the majority of the demands, including full citizenship, but would not agree to make the Sudetenland an autonomously governed region. After this, the SDP continued its work of creating riots and disturbances throughout the region, and demanding full autonomy.

While this was happening, Adolf Hitler—who had been planning to take Czech territory for some time—moved into the final stages of preparing for a military invasion. His top generals had produced a plan, known as Operation Green, and insisted that it should take place on or before October 1. The Czechs were busy preparing military defenses along the border, and this would allow the Germans to move in before those defenses were complete and effective. As the situation moved into the summer it became increasingly clear that Germany would intervene in the Czech situation. This caused real alarm, as both Britain and France had alliance treaties with Czechoslovakia committing them to military action if Czech security were threatened. To most in the western democracies, the thought of entering another continental war with Germany was horrifying and unacceptable. The British and French governments both made this clear to the Czech government, strongly urging it to accept any demands the Sudetens made. French foreign minister Georges Bonnet even went as far as to tell the Czechs that France would publicly endorse Czech independence but was not prepared to go to war over it.

On September 12 Hitler made a speech in Nuremburg accusing the Czech government of atrocities against the Sudeten Germans, including forcing them from their homes and attempting to exterminate them. He went on to make clear that Germany would act as the protector of the Sudetens and assure their national and racial "self-determination." This produced a long chain of negotiations between Germany and the western democracies. Hitler's demands changed during these negotiations; sometimes he only demanded the Sudetenland for Germany, and other times he demanded the wholesale elimination of Czechoslovakia. Eventually, the British and French agreed in principal for the Germans to take the Sudetenland and pledged they would not intervene. As these negotiations carried on, Hitler made another provocative speech in Berlin. He demanded that the Czechs cede the Sudetenland by midday on September 28 or Germany would invade.

No cession had occurred on September 28 and as the hours neared for a German invasion, the Italian dictator, Benito Mussolini, announced he had arranged a 24-hour delay. He also announced that he had arranged last-minute talks with British prime minister Neville Chamberlain. Chamberlain hurriedly flew to Munich for talks. In the early hours of September 30, an agreement was reached. The agreement allowed Germany to absorb the Sudeten region into the German Reich, and left other disputed territorial questions to be resolved by an international commission. Britain and France would not honor their existing treaties with Czechoslovakia by intervening militarily. Hitler suggested—though it was not made clear in the agreement—that this would be his last expansionist move in Eastern Europe. The Czechs—who were not part of the conference—were appalled, and had little choice but to accept, as they otherwise would have to face the German military alone, with no help from their allies. The Czechs bowed to the conditions of the new agreement soon after.

Hitler's forces moved into the Sudetenland during October. By early 1939, however, the Germans moved farther into Czechoslovakia, taking the regions of Bohemia and Moravia, and installing a puppet fascist regime in Slovakia. Some other small borderlands were annexed by Hungary and Poland. This violation of the agreement and naked aggression essentially ended the attempts by the western democracies to "appease" the dictators. After the Czech crisis it became clear that no commitment made by Nazi Germany could be trusted.

See also: Hitler, Adolf.

Further Reading

Crowhurst, Patrick, *Hitler and Czechoslovakia in World War II: Domination and Retaliation* (London: Tauris Academic, 2013).
Evans, Richard J., *The Third Reich in Power 1933–1939* (New York: Allen Lane, 2005).
Faber, David, *Munich, 1938: Appeasement and World War II* (New York: Simon & Schuster, 2008).

DOLLFUSS, ENGELBERT (1892–1934)   Engelbert Dollfuss was an Austrian politician who by May 1932 became chancellor of that nation and emerged as a fascist-style dictator until his murder by Austrian Nazi Party members in July 1934. Due to crises in the Austrian parliament during March 1933, Dollfuss was able to shut it down and rule by emergency decree, thus making himself a dictator. As dictator he suppressed opposition parties and finally created a one-party state under a conservative coalition group known as the "Fatherland Front." Although a dictator in fascist style, Dollfuss banned the Austrian Nazi Party and modeled his dictatorship more closely on Mussolini's Italian state. On July 25, 1934, in the midst of an attempted seizure of the government by the Austrian Nazi Party (directed by German Nazis) Dollfuss was shot to death. The coup attempt, however, eventually failed.

Dollfuss was born on October 4, 1892, in Texing in Lower Austria. He was the illegitimate son of peasant parents, although his mother would later marry a village notable. His peasant roots and his firm Roman Catholic faith deeply influenced his life as a politician. He briefly attended seminary, but switched to studying law and economics. His education was interrupted by the First World War. He served as an officer in the Austrian army in the Alpine campaign and won eight medals for bravery. It was during his tenure in the military that he seems to have become interested in a career in politics.

When the war was over, Dollfuss applied for work in government service and obtained a bureaucratic position in the Ministry of Agriculture in his home region in the south. In 1927, he was promoted to the position of director of the Austrian Chamber of Agriculture. During the 1920s he had joined the Christian Social Party, Austria's majority party of the conservative right. The remarkable reforms he managed to push through (including a system of social insurance for Austria's farmers) earned him the promotion to head of Austria's nationally owned railway system. Dollfuss again distinguished himself through effective management. His mounting accomplishments came to the attention of the leaders of the party, and in 1931 Dollfuss was made a member of the cabinet and named minister of agriculture and forests. These were particularly difficult years for Austria as the nation was hit hard by the Great Depression, and the nation's banking industry was on the verge of collapse. As a result, government support and stability was difficult to achieve. Because of this, the president of the Austrian Republic, Dr. Wilhelm Miklas, in May 1932 asked young Dollfuss (then only 39 years old) to form a government. Dollfuss accepted and became chancellor of Austria, having only one year of federal government experience to his credit. One of his first crucial moves was to secure a large loan from the League of Nations in July of 1932. In the following months, Dollfuss found increasing troubles with Austria's Socialist leaders, though he did initially attempt to create a coalition with them.

By the spring of 1933 the Austrian parliament was in deadlock over many crucial issues, not the least of which was the question of Austria's continuing independence. On the far left, Austria's Communists and Socialists wanted to form a union with the German Communists or with the Soviet Union. On the extreme right, the "Pan-Germanists" and the Austrian Nazis advocated merging Austria into Hitler's Third Reich, after Hitler came to power. Dollfuss—attempting to maintain a political center—rigidly opposed any loss of Austrian independence. In May 1933, a parliamentary crisis emerged over an issue of whether to punish striking railway workers. To win the vote on the issue, the Socialist president of the parliament (Karl Renner) had to resign his position to cast a vote. With this done, the conservative vice presidents resigned their positions to vote on the other side. The result was that parliament found itself in chaos with no one occupying the leadership positions to manage it. Dollfuss stepped in and closed the parliament session. Then—using the emergency sections of the existing constitution—Dollfuss began to rule by decree without a functioning parliament. By May, he had outlawed most of Austria's political parties including the Nazi Party, and created a single right-wing coalition party that he named the "Fatherland Front." Its insignia was a black cross on a white background with red borders on either side—a statement reinforcing Austrian independence (flag colors) and Austria's commitment to the Catholic Church. The Socialists were furious over having lost their party organizations and the parliamentary forum for debate and government. As such, they used their own paramilitary force, the *Schutzbund,* to agitate and to prepare for some kind of armed protest. To fight the *Schutzbund,* Dollfuss increasingly was forced to use a far-right paramilitary group called the *Heimwehr.* The *Heimwehr* were not supporters of the Nazis generally, but did support a union with Germany. Dollfuss' dependence upon them to keep the Socialists in line meant that he was allowing those with deeply opposing political views to greatly influence his government. Use of the army was not adequate for the challenge as Austria's forces were limited to only 30,000 men by the Treaty of Saint Germain (1919), signed immediately after World War I.

On February 12, 1934, the Socialists finally let loose an armed attack on the state. The *Schutzbund* used weapons it had been secretly storing to attempt to seize the government and return to a democratic system. Dollfuss used the army and the paramilitary fighters of the *Heimwehr* to confront the *Schutzbund* in a conflict known as the Austrian Civil War of 1934. The war lasted only about four days, and Dollfuss infamously is remembered for having had his troops fire artillery into the workers' housing projects in Vienna to bring a speedy end to the war. With the Civil War over and the Socialists crushed, Dollfuss moved to create a new constitution for Austria that would construct a fascist-style state-governing apparatus. The system would retain the office of president but the chancellor would continue to run the country. Parliament no longer would be a functioning part of the state, but a set of groups would be established that represented various industries and professions. These would have the function of advisory councils to the chancellor, but would have no power to initiate laws or to veto any decision the chancellor made. The Church would retain its prominent role particularly in the area of education.

With a new constitution in place that formally eliminated any opposition parties and any future institution for them, the Austrian branch of the Nazi Party began to plan an uprising of its own. Aided and directed by key Nazi officials in Germany, the uprising began on July 25, 1934. As armed

Nazi paramilitaries poured into the Austrian Chancellery building, Dollfuss and some key ministers attempted to flee but instead ran straight into a group of Nazis. One Nazi, Otto Planetta, fired two shots into Dollfuss, who then was laid out on the couch in his own office. As medical care became available, however, the Nazis refused to allow Dollfuss to be treated, and as a result he bled to death. The coup eventually failed as several key members of the government were able to escape and made it to the army barracks and alerted the troops. The Austrian military remained loyal to the state and was able to put down the rebellion. There seems no question that Adolf Hitler knew about and supported the Austrian Nazi coup. Whether he had ordered the murder of Dollfuss is less clear and remains controversial. Dollfuss was replaced by a member of his cabinet, Kurt Schuschnigg, who served as Austria's chancellor until the country was forcibly annexed by Germany in March 1938.

See also: *Anschluss.*

Further Reading

Bischof, Gunter, Anton Pelinka, and Alexander Leffner (eds.), *The Dollfuss-Schuschnigg Era in Austria: A Re-Assessment* (New Brunswick: Transaction Publishers, 2003).

Brook-Shepherd, Gordon, *Dollfuss* (London: Macmillan & Co., 1961).

ENABLING ACT OF 1933   The "Enabling Act" is the term given to a piece of legislation passed by the German Parliament (the *Reichstag*) on March 23, 1933, which gave the power to initiate and enact laws to the German Cabinet, led by Chancellor Adolf Hitler. The official title of the legislative act was the "Law to Remedy the Distress of the People and Reich." Its precise stipulations allowed for the German chancellor to enact law without any involvement of or approval by the *Reichstag*. Additionally, the law made it permissible for such laws to deviate from the existing constitution. The resulting effect of the law was to place virtually absolute power in the hands of the chancellor, Adolf Hitler, making him a de facto dictator of the German state.

The background to the passage of the law begins with the political platform of the Nazi Party from its beginnings. The Nazis always had rejected the system of liberal democracy and particularly had railed against the complex set of political parties operating in Germany. As such, the elimination of party politics and the establishment of an authoritarian system was a fundamental objective of the Nazis.

After a long period of economic and political crisis, the president of Germany's Weimar Republic, Paul von Hindenburg, reluctantly appointed Adolf Hitler as chancellor in January 1933. The laws of the constitution, however, constrained Hitler in his efforts to bring the full Nazi program into effect, as the constitution gave the *Reichstag* the power to initiate and enact legislation, and granted the president the executive authority to provide the final signature making a resolution a formal law of the land. Several political parties had representatives in the *Reichstag* that adamantly opposed the Nazi Party's aims. These included the German Communist Party and the Social Democrats, as the most deeply opposed. On February 27, 1933 (not even a month after Hitler's appointment as chancellor), the old German Parliament building, the *Reichstag*, was set on fire. Nazi police arrested a small group of men—including a Dutchman named Marinus van der Lubbe—who claimed to be Communists. Whether these men set the fire, or if it was the Nazis that actually perpetrated the crime and then arrested scapegoats, remains unknown and controversial. Hitler, however, used the fire to skillfully lever himself into absolute power. He announced to the *Reichstag*, now meeting in the Berlin Opera House, that the fire had been the first act of a coming assault on the German state by the Communists—essentially the start of a civil war. With such a threat looming, Hitler issued the "*Reichstag* Fire Decree," which suspended certain civil liberties guaranteed by the constitution and gave the serving government temporary authority to rule by decree. Hitler used this to suppress the German Communist Party, to search and ransack the party's headquarters, and to arrest its leaders. With the suspension of habeas corpus, as outlined by the decree, Hitler could imprison people at will and without trial.

With this accomplished, Hitler hoped to go further by placing such absolute power in his hands permanently. He always was quite concerned that at least the appearance of legality be maintained, and so he sought to have an act of legislation passed by the *Reichstag* which would do this. It essentially amounted to the *Reichstag* voting away its own power and its own place in the functioning of the state. For such a law to pass, the existing constitution required a two-thirds majority. Hitler knew that he could count on the Nazis in parliament and some other allied parties. Hitler also knew that his most vigorous opponents, the Communist Party deputies, no longer could vote against it, as they all were banned or jailed. The Social Democrats would surely vote against it, and there was a question about the Catholic Centre Party. Hitler then was going to have to rely on the Catholic Centre deputies all voting for the law in order to see it passed. To this end, Hitler began negotiating with the head of the party, Ludwig Kaas, and eventually obtained Kaas' assurance for his party's vote. Hitler offered in return a commitment that he would never move to suppress the Catholic Centre Party and that he would protect many Catholic traditional rights and roles, including the Church's place in the system of education. In a speech to the *Reichstag* on the day the law was to be voted upon, Hitler introduced the resolution and emphasized throughout his address the important place of the Church in German life and the need to keep its rites protected. It seems a strange, almost irrelevant subject, given the substance of the bill, but this was a reiteration of his commitments to the Catholic Centre Party to assure its votes. The ploy worked as the vast majority of deputies voted for it, with only the Social Democrats voting against. The Opera House, where the *Reichstag* was now forced to meet, was filled with Nazi SA members or "Storm Troopers," as an intimidating influence.

With its passage, Adolf Hitler emerged as the sole leader of the German Reich with dictatorial power, and the *Reichstag* passed into irrelevancy. Hitler used this power to eliminate all other political parties, making Germany a single-party dictatorship. The *Reichstag* then became a kind of "Party Congress" where Hitler made speeches and the members roared their approval, but under the Nazis the *Reichstag* no longer functioned as a true legislative branch of government.

See also: Hitler, Adolf; *Reichstag* Fire.

Further Reading

Evans, Richard J., *The Third Reich in Power, 1933–1939* (New York: Allen Lane, 2005).

Kershaw, Ian, *Hitler 1889–1936: Hubris* (New York: W.W. Norton, 1998).

Tobias, Fritz, *The Reichstag Fire,* translated by Arnold J. Pomeranz (New York: Putnam, 1964).

FALANGE ESPANOLA   The *Falange Espanola* is the name of the most important of the explicitly fascist parties established in Spain during the 1930s. Founded by Jose Antonio Primo de Rivera in 1933, the party actively engaged in street violence during the days of the Spanish Republic, attempting to subdue the forces of the political left. During the Spanish Civil War, the *Falange* actively supported Franco's "Nationalists" and, at war's end, it was folded into the larger coalition of the far right known as the *Falange de Tradicionalista y de las JONS (FET de las JONS)*. The Falangist program was modeled after the Italian and German models, though it also emphasized traditional Spanish elements for the state such as the Catholic Church and Spain's imperial past.

The *Falange* was founded by Jose Antonio Primo de Rivera, the son of Spain's military dictator, General Miguel Primo de Rivera, who had ruled Spain from 1923 until 1930. General Primo de Rivera's dictatorship had been somewhat fascist in character, as the general greatly admired Benito Mussolini's Italian Fascist state. That regime, however, mostly was concerned with preserving traditional Spanish Institutions rather than advocating the more modernist revolutionary objectives of fascism. The Primo de Rivera dictatorship fell apart by the end of the 1920s, and after a brief period, Spain finally exiled Primo de Rivera, eliminated the monarchy, and established its Second Republic during 1931.

The first governments elected by the Spanish people were somewhat left-leaning and immediately began pursuing modern reforms such as granting women the vote, allowing divorce, and reforming education—at the cost of the Catholic Church's influence. This enraged the traditional right-wing citizenry as well as those on the extreme right—including Jose Antonio Primo de Rivera, who had seen his father exiled in disgrace. Jose Antonio began to work with other political intellectuals to put together a program that was more modernist than his father's, accepting that the world had changed in the new era. On October 29, 1933, Jose Antonio formally launched his new political party, the *Falange Espanola*, as a political pressure group, but also as a formal political party that would run candidates in future elections.

In the first two years of its existence, the *Falange* mostly was involved in demonstrations, publications, and street battles, particularly against Socialists and Anarchists of the far left. The party's program began to take firmer shape with the publication of its "Twenty-Seven Points," the party's brief manifesto. The party advocated a fascist-style dictatorship, but no return to the monarchy. The *Falange* was fiercely anti-Marxist and also advocated maintaining or expanding Spain's imperial holdings. While the left had emerged as stridently anti-religious, the *Falange* advocated retaining a role for the Catholic Church and respecting its place in Spain's history, although what part it genuinely wanted the Church to play in a fascist state was not entirely clear.

In the years after the 1933 election—which had brought a more moderate government to power—a right-wing coalition known as the CEDA gradually had become more powerful by getting ministers appointed to key positions. By 1936, the left had unified enough to challenge that government and elections were called for February 1936. In the 1936 election the *Falange* ran many candidates, but none were elected. Out of the approximately 10 million votes cast, the *Falange* only polled 46,000. This was an indication that the Spanish did not see the *Falange* as a viable or necessary political alternative. The results of that 1936 election, however, placed a much more left-wing government in power, which became known as the "Popular Front" government. Responding to the call of Joseph Stalin, premier of the Soviet Union, all the parties of the Spanish left had coordinated their efforts to ensure the election of a left-wing leaning government. The strategy worked and the "Popular Front" government was in place by the spring of 1936. This, however, caused an extreme reaction on the part of some of Spain's leading military generals—they led a military invasion of Spain to try to seize the government. This resulted in the prolonged Spanish Civil War. Just before the war broke out, the "Popular Front" government moved to suppress the *Falange* and arrested and imprisoned Jose Antonio for illegal possession of firearms. In October, when it was clear he was conspiring with the "Nationalist" leaders, Republican leaders tried Jose Antonio for treason and sentenced him to execution. He was killed by firing squad on November 20, 1936.

During the Spanish Civil War (July 1936 to April 1939), the *Falange* threw itself into military service for the leading general of the "Nationalist" forces, Francisco Franco. The war also stimulated membership in the *Falange* to an unprecedented degree. From only a few thousand official members, the *Falange* membership grew to approximately 200,000. The *Falange* principally was used as internal security and police in cities rather than on the battlefields. The *Falange* also had a prominent women's section known as the *Seccion Feminina* which was led by Jose Antonio's sister, Pilar. The *Seccion Feminina* provided key services for the "Nationalist" forces, including transport, food distribution, and especially nursing care.

Having won the war, General Francisco Franco consolidated his power and folded the organization of the *Falange* into his larger far-right coalition group, which he named the *Falange Traditionalista y de las JONS*. This became his ruling party in a single-party state going forward. As such, the *Falange's* explicitly fascist program was diluted, but the larger traditional right was made increasingly fascist by this blending of forces. Francisco Franco maintained his own extreme-right dictatorship from 1939 to 1975, and debate continues as to the degree to which his regime was truly "fascist" in character.

See also: Franco, Francisco; Primo de Rivera, Jose Antonio; Spanish Civil War.

Further Reading

Payne, Stanley, *Fascism in Spain, 1923–1977* (Madison: University of Wisconsin Press, 1999).

Preston, Paul, *The Politics of Revenge: Fascism and the Military in Twentieth Century Spain* (Boston: Unwin Hyman, 1990).

Richmond, Kathleen, *Women and Fascism in Spain: The Women's Section of the Falange, 1934–1959* (London: Routledge, 2003).

FASCES "Fasces," which is derived from the Latin word *fascis*, literally means "bundle," and describes a symbolic artifact that was significant in the republic of ancient Rome. It is a bundle of wooden sticks or rods bound together in a cylindrical shape, with the blade of an axe projecting from the side. Although politically meaningful to many modern governments and organizations, it was the principal symbol selected by Benito Mussolini for his political organization which became a formal political party in 1921. Mussolini named his political movement after this symbol, calling it the Fascist Party of Italy and using the symbol on its flags and insignia.

The fasces emerged as an important political symbol during the Republican period of ancient Rome. It was carried by officials known as *lictors* who accompanied particularly important government administrators. The higher the station of the government official the greater the number of *lictors* who accompanied the official for ceremonial processions or parades. The highest-ranking legal official in the republican system was the dictator, who was given extraordinary powers and absolute authority in especially challenging situations. As such, the fasces came to be symbolically associated both with judicial powers and with dictatorial powers.

Benito Mussolini used this artifact for its symbolic meaning. The wooden rods on their own could be snapped easily, but bound together in such a tight formation they were unbreakable. This symbolized the unbreakable power of a totally unified nation. The axe blade symbolized the power and authority of the state and also represented violent action. The fasces would remain the principal symbol of the Italian Fascist Party up until the party's suppression after the Second World War. The British Union of Fascists (BUF) also adopted the fasces as its principal symbol during the first two years of its existence, though the BUF later replaced the fasces with its own symbol.

See also: British Union of Fascists; National Facist Party (PNF).

Further Reading

Lazzaro, Claudia, and Roger J. Crum, "Italy's Past and Mussolini's Present: Forging a Visible Fascist Nation: Strategies for Fusing Past and Present," in *Donatello Among the Blackshirts: History and Modernity in the Visual Culture of Fascist Italy,* edited by Claudia Lazzaro and Roger J. Crum (Ithaca: Cornell University Press, 2005).

FIRST WORLD WAR (1914–1918)   The First World War (also commonly referred to as "World War I" or the "Great War") was a global conflict lasting from July 28, 1914, to November 11, 1918. Although it involved conflict in multiple continents and on the seas, the war's central areas of combat were in Eastern and Western Europe. The scale of the war and the casualty rates were unprecedented to that point in human history. Many scholars refer to this scale of warfare as "total war," as the war involved the engagement of entire national economies, armies of millions of men, and the sense that to lose the war meant the loss of national existence. After four years of horrifying casualties, which included more than 10 million dead (Grayzel, 129), the Central Powers (principally Germany, Austria-Hungary, and the Ottoman Turks) were forced to surrender to the Allied Powers (principally Britain, France, and the United States). The psychology of total war and militarization, along with the conditions established as a result of the peace settlement helped establish the mentalities and the political programs of fascist movements. Particularly in nations that had lost the war there was a sense of national diminishment and humiliation. The ultra-nationalist belief system of fascism emerged and promised to bring national renewal after the horrors and strains of the Great War.

The war's origins are complex but chiefly relate to imperial and economic competition between the great powers of Europe in the late 19th century and early 20th century. Germany was particularly antagonistic in its relations with France (which it had utterly defeated and humiliated in 1871 in the Franco-Prussian War), and Great Britain. The German state embarked upon a great military shipbuilding program in the late 19th century with the rather open objective of competing with Britain's power on the high seas. This resulted in a naval arms race that escalated tensions. Further exacerbating these tensions, the powers of Europe had configured themselves into defensive treaty alliances—Germany, Austria-Hungary, and Italy in the Triple Alliance, and France, Russia, and Britain in the Triple Entente.

The immediate trigger of the war was caused by the operations of Pan-Slavist terrorists within the Austrian Empire. Some of these terrorist organizations (hoping to intimidate the Austrians into giving the Slavic peoples a free state) operated from the nation of Serbia. On June 28, 1914, a group of Slavic terrorists carried out the assassination of the Austrian Archduke Franz-Ferdinand on his visit to the city of Sarajevo. With this, the Austrian government intended to eliminate the terrorist threat from Serbia by invading. After a harsh ultimatum was sent to the Serbs, and confirmation that their German allies supported the Austrian invasion was received, Austria declared war on Serbia on July 28. Russia was a close ally of Serbia and mobilized for war to come to Serbia's aid. Due to the array of treaty alliances, Russian involvement triggered a domino-like progression of the various treaty powers entering the war. By August the basic configuration of the war had taken shape, with Germany, Austria-Hungary, and the Ottoman Turks forming the "Central" Powers, and the Russians, French, Serbs, and British forming the Entente or "Allied" Powers.

At the very early stages of the war, in early August, the Germans launched a massive invasion of France. The operation was known as the "Schlieffen Plan" and was intended to knock France out of the war in only two months so that Germany could avoid fighting a war on two fronts—against France in the west and Russia in the East. The invasion, however, was sent through Belgium which was internationally recognized as a neutral nation. Belgium refused to allow the Germans to pass through its territory and gathered its army to fight. The result was a prolonged and bloody fight eventually won by the Germans. After penetrating deep into France and almost reaching Paris, the Germans were halted and the conflict in northern France turned into a stalemate. All along the border of northern France and Belgium opposing armies dug into the earth in a network of trenches. The Schlieffen Plan had failed. This line became known as the "Western Front," and was the principal killing field of the Great War. The casualties in battle were astonishing and unprecedented. This mostly stemmed from the fact that modern weaponry had advanced dramatically, although military thinking and tactics had not. The First World War would see the use of the machine gun, the weaponized airplane, poison gas, the submarine, and the tank. Many commanders, however, still were using tactics leftover from the Napoleonic era, such as the use of cavalry and bayonet charges.

In Eastern Europe the Russians made initial inroads into German territory, but eventually were pushed back and another long line of trenches, earthen works, and barbed wire made up the Eastern Front. In 1915, the Italians entered the war on the side of the Allied Powers. The secret Treaty of London guaranteed Italy a large section of Austrian territory if Italy fought on the Allied side and achieved victory. As a result, another front developed along the Austrian-Italian border. The conflict spread to the Middle East, East Asia, and the Pacific, and European powers fought within their African imperial territories as well. The Western Front, however, continued to be the focus of attention for the most powerful nations. There, many men were recruited, were sent into the trenches, and were killed by snipers, constant artillery barrages, and periodic skirmishes. There was no meaningful movement of the armies or taking of territory, however.

To break this destructive stalemate the Allied Powers conceived a strategy to open another distant front. The British and French sent large numbers of soldiers on an amphibious landing mission in Turkey on the peninsula known as Gallipoli. Their intention was to take the peninsula and then move toward Constantinople (modern Istanbul). This, the Allied commanders believed, would force German troops to be moved from the Western Front to help and thus the balance would be tipped. The landings were a disaster though, with the Turks quite well armed and prepared in their own trench networks. After nearly two months of battle and tens of thousands of casualties for the Allies the commanders pulled out of the area having achieved nothing.

The next major attempt to break the stalemate was launched on the Western Front itself. The plan called for intense Allied shelling of the German trenches for days on end. At this point, the Allied commanders believed the Germans would have abandoned their front trenches. Then a mass movement of Allied troops would make a fast rush to take the trenches from which the Germans would have retreated. During July 1916 this operation was launched, but failed when German troops found it possible to come back to their front trenches and use machine gun fire to decimate the onrushing Allied foot soldiers—most of whom were marching in formation. The result was that the British and French lost 60,000 wounded and dead on the first day. The stalemate continued.

In 1917, the war changed dramatically. The nation of Russia was thrust into political upheaval by its citizens revolting and eventually deposing the Czarist monarchy that had ruled there for centuries. Although Russia stayed in the war during the summer, its forces fell into chaos and desertion. In October, the Communist Bolsheviks seized power in Russia and eventually negotiated a separate peace with Germany and officially exited the war. Also in 1917, Germany's return to a policy of "unrestricted submarine warfare," began to turn public opinion in the United States. The United States had stayed out of the conflict, but was appalled at the German sinking of the British passenger liner, the R*MS Lusitania* in 1915. More than 100 Americans had died in the sinking. Germany had placated American opinion by changing its policy to "restricted submarine warfare," whereby submarine commanders would appear above the surface and ensure that targets were military. Now, in early1917, the Germans returned to an "unrestricted" policy and this convinced many Americans that the German "menace" had to be stopped. Later that same year, the German foreign minister sent a telegram to the Mexican government urging it to join the war with Germany against the United States. If Mexico did so, the telegram suggested, then Germany would help Mexico recover territories lost in the 1840s in the Mexican War (i.e., Texas, New Mexico, Arizona). The British intercepted the telegram and presented it to the U.S. government, which then released the text of the telegram to the American public. The result was a renewed public call for entry into the war. President Woodrow Wilson received approval from Congress to join the war and positioned the move as an effort to secure a decisive victory which would end large-scale warfare in the future.

After the Russian withdrawal, the Germans launched an all-out offensive on the Western Front during the spring of 1918. It initially was quite successful and the German forces came within miles of Paris. French, British, and (later) American forces eventually stopped the offensive and forced the German forces back to their initial lines. By the fall of 1918, the German and Austrian war leaders recognized that they were exhausted of men and supplies. In late October and early November the German high command stepped down, the Kaiser of Germany, Wilhelm II, abdicated his throne and an armistice agreement was reached.

In the aftermath of the cataclysm, a great conference was called at Paris to sort out the details of peace. The conference was guided by the "14 Points" espoused by U.S. president Woodrow Wilson. Among these 14 points were the creation of an organ of world government (a "League of Nations"), the elimination of secret diplomacy and treaties, the construction of new nations based on the "self-determination of peoples," and the principle of arms reduction by all governments. Using these guiding principles, the leaders of the victorious powers at Paris created the League of Nations which began operating in the early 1920s in Geneva, Switzerland. They also redrew the map of Europe creating new nations including Poland, Czechoslovakia, and Yugoslavia. In so doing, the League took significant territory from the German state. The Austrian Empire was dismantled as was the Ottoman Turkish Empire. The Allied leaders also constructed the Treaty of Versailles, which imposed conditions upon the defeated Germany and was especially harsh. The Treaty assigned all blame for the war to Germany and its allies. It removed all of Germany's overseas colonies. It limited Germany's military to token levels and prohibited the creation of a military air force. It also imposed crushing reparations payments in cash and in industrial products for decades to come.

The conditions imposed upon the defeated powers—particularly Germany—gave their populations a sense of national failure and humiliation. In Germany there was a particular anger that the leaders of its new government, the Weimar Republic, had surrendered with Germany still in enemy territory. This action became known among Germany's far right as the "stab in the back." German anger also persisted over the loss of German territory, the inability to defend itself with a potent military, the crippling schedule of payments, and the simple fact that foreign nations policed the enforcement of these conditions. These would all be central issues for the Nazi Party's program as it emerged and promised to right the wrongs of the Treaty of Versailles, and reunify and rebuild the German nation

Although Italy was on the winning side in the war, it also suffered a national humiliation at the war's end. Having joined the war on the Allied side due to the promises of Austrian territory in the Treaty of London, the Italians expected to be given this territory at the Paris Peace Conference. With the priority of building a world with no more secret diplomacy, however, the victorious leaders were not willing to honor the secret treaty that Italy had signed in 1915. Therefore, Italy was granted only tiny areas of territory and the Italian officials walked out of the conference. In Italy this humiliation became known as the country's "mutilated victory," and reinforced an existing feeling of national inferiority relative to the other great powers. This helped foster the climate that allowed Mussolini's defiant and extreme nationalism to flourish among the political far right as his Fascist movement developed.

The war also did something else, particularly to the veterans who returned from duty in the trenches. It created a militarized mentality among ex-soldiers. Many of those who returned found it difficult to reenter normal life and kept their uniforms and even continued to fraternize with their army mates in new paramilitary battalions. In Italy these types were among the most fervent followers of Mussolini's Fascists, and found that they could continue living and fighting as soldiers in his paramilitary fighting squads. In Germany such veterans organized themselves into the *Freikorps* (or Free Corps) who continued to drill and to march, and then helped the new Weimar Republic savagely put down the Communist revolt of 1918–1919. Members of the *Freikorps* were among the earliest and most fervent adherents of Nazism and typically joined the SA which allowed them to continue as a uniformed, fighting force. Such uniformed paramilitary bands became a signature feature of fascist movements.

Two other key conditions produced by the Great War contributed directly to the shaping of fascist ideology. The first of these was the economic "slump" that engulfed most of Europe after the war. War production involved entire industrial economies during the conflict, thus unemployment disappeared and, if anything, there was a labor shortage. Wages rose, working conditions improved, and trade unions flourished. When the war ended, production levels plummeted; therefore wages were reduced and workers were dismissed in great numbers. This economic distress was another of the conditions that helped bring about fascist movements and regimes. The other key factor was that World War I had created conditions so harsh in Russia that the people had risen up and deposed their czar. By late 1917, the Communist Bolsheviks had taken charge of the government and, after a bloody civil war of their own, by 1921 began constructing the Soviet Union—the world's first Communist state. With the success of the Russian Communist revolution, Marxism expanded across Europe. Socialists, Anarchists, and Communists began to believe that the time for revolution had arrived. The determination to turn back Marxism at all costs was yet another central feature of fascist ideology.

See also: Paris Peace Conference; Treaty of Versailles.

Further Reading

Ferro, Marc, *The Great War 1914–1918* (New York: Ark, 1973).

Fussell, Paul, *The Great War and Modern Memory* (Oxford: Oxford University Press, 1975).

Grayzel, Susan R., *The First World War: A Brief History with Documents* (Boston: Bedford/St. Martin's, 2012).

Toland, John, *No Man's Land: 1918—The Last Year of the Great War* (New York: Konecky & Konecky, 1980).

FIUME (OCCUPATION OF)   The occupation of the city of Fiume was an illegal seizure led by the Italian poet and political activist, Gabriele D'Annunzio, during 1919 and 1920. The episode reflected the disgust that many Italians felt about their treatment at the Paris Peace Conference and Italy's sense of national victimhood. D'Annunzio eventually declared a new state in the city (which he called the "Regency of Carnaro"), with himself as dictator. He created a constitution that anticipated many of the features of Mussolini's Fascist regime. After declaring war on the nation of Italy, D'Annunzio and his followers were forced from Fiume by the Italian military in December 1920. Fiume then was made a free and independent state until it was annexed by Mussolini's Fascist government in 1924.

The background to the occupation of Fiume mostly concerned the dissatisfaction of Italian nationalists about the small gains achieved at the Paris Peace Conference. Italy had been part of the Triple Alliance with Germany and Austria in the years leading up to the First World War. When that war broke out in 1914, however, Italy did not join the fighting. Eventually the Italian government concluded a secret agreement with the British, documented in the Treaty of London, signed in 1915. This treaty said that if the Italians joined the British, French, and Russians against Germany and Austria, that, in the event of an Allied victory, Italy would be entitled to large tracts of Austrian territory. At the Paris Peace Conference, however, leaders of the other Allied governments were not willing to honor this treaty. One of President Woodrow Wilson's famous "14 Points"—which were treated as the guiding principles of the Conference—demanded that there should be no further secret diplomacy among nations. Thus, the Conference leaders did not believe that they could honor the provisions of a secret treaty and maintain any credibility. As such, Italy was granted some small bits of territory on the coast of the Adriatic Sea, but certainly not nearly the large tracts of territory it had expected. One of the areas the Italian government did not even claim was the important seaport city of Fiume. Fiume was discussed at the Conference as being part of the territory that eventually became Yugoslavia.

One of the most passionate of Italy's nationalists was the poet and soldier, Gabriele D'Annunzio. He had been an important literary figure in Italy, but during the First World War he emerged as daring war hero. He had been an enthusiastic advocate of Italy's joining the war, and tended to glorify war as the route to pride, glory, and Italy's assertion of its national power. D'Annunzio became a fighter pilot and gained fame for his daring "Flight over Vienna," to drop propaganda pamphlets on the enemy capital. The war intensified his fervent nationalism, and his belief that Italy had proven itself able to stand alongside the Great Powers of Europe. The denial of significant territories at the Peace Conference, however, caused D'Annunzio (like most nationalists) to be furious with the other Allied leaders. Italian nationalists, however, also felt a great deal of anger with their own government officials for not having the forcefulness to claim what supposedly belonged to Italy.

In response to this sense of outrage, D'Annunzio began to make public speeches denouncing the timidity of the Italian government and asserting the need for decisive action on the part of the Italian people. He led a growing troop of returning Italian soldiers and other disgruntled citizens on a march to the city of Fiume. He and his troops were able to take the undefended city and force themselves into the leadership of the city government. D'Annunzio eventually declared the city to be an independent and sovereign state—calling his regime the "Regency of Carnaro," after the Gulf of Carnaro. He used the technique of mass rallies in the city center as well as using flags and other symbols to stir a fanatical national enthusiasm amongst his followers. This was a technique that would be further developed by Benito Mussolini and used in other fascist movements in the future.

D'Annunzio declared himself to be the individual dictator of the city and gave himself the title, "Duce." He also created a political constitution that designed a government system for the future. This "Charter of Carnaro" included a legislative branch of government divided into two houses. The upper house would be a "Council of the Best"—a group of elected officials that represented the community's elite. The lower house would be a group of officials elected and organized by occupation. There would be nine "Corporations" in this chamber, representing nine branches of employment (e.g., industrial, commercial, agricultural, teaching, legal/medical, shipping). This was the embryo of the "Corporative" system later developed by Mussolini's government in Italy and by virtually every other fascist movement.

D'Annunzio would never have the chance to see his vision in full development. In late 1920 he declared war on Italy, hoping to force the Italian government to take the city by force and annex it to the Italian state. The move backfired, however, as Italy sent a group of battleships to fire on the city, and soldiers forced D'Annunzio to evacuate. He handed over the city on December 24, 1920. Afterward, Fiume was made an independent city state, and D'Annunzio retired to his estate in Italy. He would be a great supporter of Mussolini and Fascism, although he remained independent from the regime. In 1924, Mussolini negotiated with the Kingdom of Serbs, Croats, and Slovenes and was able to annex Fiume into the Italian state.

D'Annunzio's political style, his use of rhetoric and symbolism, and the political organization he developed were all deeply influential to Benito Mussolini's Fascist state in Italy and to fascism as a general political movement.

See also: Corporatism (Corporative State); Paris Peace Conference.

Further Reading

Ledeen, Michael A., *D'Annunzio: The First Duce* (New Brunswick: Transaction Publishers, 2000).
Woodhouse, John Robert, *Gabriele D'Annunzio: Defiant Archangel* (New York: Clarendon, 1998).

FOUR YEAR PLAN   The Four Year Plan was a collection of economic policies set in place by Adolf Hitler to support his plans for the rearmament of Germany and an eventual large-scale war. The plan included the acceleration of existing state-sponsored public works programs—such as the building of the Autobahn highway system—and a series of public building projects. The central feature of the plan, however, was forcing Germany's industrial producers into a system of economic self-sufficiency or "autarky." Hitler was convinced that Germany needed complete economic independence to have full freedom to wage war against other nations. If Germany continued to be dependent upon other nations for foodstuffs and key industrial raw materials, then opposing nations could cut off those supplies in the event of war, crippling Hitler's ability to conquer the lands he desired. The plan was launched in 1936 with the intention of making Germany fully self-sufficient by 1940.

The need for such a plan, in Hitler's mind, stemmed from the Treaty of Versailles, signed at the Paris Peace Conference, which imposed penalties on Germany for its role in the First World War. In the Treaty, Germany was named as bearing all blame for the outbreak and continuance of the War. As stipulations of that Treaty, the victorious powers removed Germany's overseas colonies, removed and restricted certain German geographical territories, and imposed a significant program of reparations payments, in cash and in industrial produce.

The Treaty of Versailles also made clear restrictions on Germany's military. Germany's navy was restricted to a smaller number of ships and sailors, and submarines were prohibited. Germany's army was limited to a total force of 100,000 men. The Treaty also prohibited Germany from forming a military air force. Under these conditions, Germany had suffered terrible economic hardship during the 1920s and early 1930s. But the German people also were humiliated and felt a sense of "national" victimization. These sources of anger and humiliation were among those factors that enabled the radical Nazi movement to grow and to come to power in 1933.

Once in power, Adolf Hitler acted upon his political promises by removing Germany from the League of Nations and beginning a steady program of defying the stipulations of the Versailles Treaty. He re-occupied the Rhineland region with German military forces in 1936, against the Treaty's condition that this German territory must remain a "demilitarized zone." Hitler also began a massive program of rearmament. This program's intentions were kept secret through 1933 and 1934, but in 1935 Hitler announced the existence of a German military air force. There was no effort by the League of Nations or the European democracies to stop Hitler's expansion of his military by force. Therefore, by 1936 his rearmament plan was expanding rapidly in industrial terms and in terms of the expansion of Germany's military power.

Hitler was preparing for a war of aggressive conquest, which he had described as his aim in his book *Mein Kampf*, published in 1925. In that book he had made clear two principal objectives for German conquest—to re-unite the people of the German race into a single German Reich, and to attack and conquer the Soviet Union. In conquering the Soviet Union, Hitler hoped to enjoy its almost limitless natural resources, and to create an enormous "living space" or *lebensraum* into which the German race could expand. These were the military and ideological objectives behind the development of the Four Year Plan.

Hitler announced the Four Year Plan at the 1936 Nazi Party Rally. Soon after, he named Hermann Goering, longtime Nazi and head of the German Air Force, as the chief of the Office of the Four Year Plan. Goering spent years working with—or forcing—German industrial leaders to convert their business to be independent of foreign supplies, credit, and export markets. Credit and export markets were of less importance, but Goering insisted upon restricting them to the use of domestic supplies of raw materials. In many cases, of course, Germany did not have supplies of key raw materials for these industries. In such cases, Goering's office encouraged other companies to use scientific innovation to create synthetic or artificial substitutes for such raw materials. Examples of these raw materials that German companies developed included synthetic rubber, synthetic fuels, and synthetic lubricants, among many others.

In his capacity as head of the Four Year Plan, Goering soon emerged as the most powerful figure in the German economy. Economics minister Hjalmar Schacht had been the most eminent figure in Germany's economic recovery to that point. He had been successful in securing a number of foreign loans to finance Hitler's massive rearmament costs to the state. But Schacht resisted the Four Year Plan, saying it was unfeasible and might well be economically harmful. As a result of his disagreement about Hitler's cherished project, Schacht declined in importance in the government and eventually was dismissed in 1937. The rise of Goering and the decline of Schacht are regarded as a further example of the radicalization of Hitler and Nazism as war approached.

In the end Hitler went to war in 1939, much earlier than anticipated. Germany was not yet close to the autarkic objectives of the Four Year Plan; however, due to Germany's success in conquering its neighbors from 1939 to 1942 this presented few visible problems. Germany was able to steal raw materials and industrial facilities, and could force human victims into slave labor as its conquests continued. After 1941, however, as the Soviet Union and the United States each joined the war against Germany, the industrial needs for a conflict of such global scale were beyond the limits of German productive capacity.

See also: Autarky; Goering, Hermann.

Further Reading

Carr, William, *Arms, Autarky, and Aggression: A Study in German Foreign Policy, 1933–1939* (New York: Norton, 1973).

Overy, Richard, *Goering* (London: Phoenix, 1984).

Tooze, Adam, *The Wages of Destruction: The Making and Breaking of the Nazi Economy* (New York: Viking, 2007).

FRANCO, FRANCISCO (1892–1975)   General Francisco Franco Bahamonde was a prominent general in the Spanish army who emerged as the leader of the military revolt against Spain's Republican government in the 1930s. That revolt developed into the Spanish Civil War from 1936 to 1939. With the help of Nazi Germany and Fascist Italy, Franco was able to lead the military forces to victory and establish himself as dictator of Spain. He instituted harsh measures including a strict economic autarky which kept Spain relatively isolated and impoverished during the 1940s. Although Spain was officially neutral during the Second World War, Franco consistently lent assistance to the Axis Powers. In the 1950s Franco worked with the United States, allowing that nation to build military bases in Spain as part of a collective security effort during the Cold War. Franco maintained his personal dictatorship until his death in 1975.

Francisco Franco was born on December 4, 1892, in Ferrol, Spain, near the north coast. His father was a naval officer and it generally was agreed that Franco would follow in his father's footsteps. After the Spanish American

War, however, the Spanish navy was reduced and its officer's academy was closed. Thus, Franco entered the Spanish army. As a young officer Franco was stationed in North Africa and was engaged in the Rif War between Spanish occupying troops and the native Moroccan forces. He acquitted himself well on the battlefield, suffering a serious wound at age 23. He later emerged as a prominent officer in the Spanish Foreign Legion, again stationed in North Africa. There Franco was involved in the humiliating Spanish defeat at Annual in July 1921. That defeat eventually led a Spanish general, Miguel Primo de Rivera, to seize the government and establish a military dictatorship that lasted from 1923 to 1930. During the days of the Primo de Rivera dictatorship, Franco thrived and eventually became the chief of the newly established General Military Academy at Zaragoza.

By 1931, the Spanish people had dissolved the Primo de Rivera dictatorship and voted to eliminate the Spanish monarchy; in its place they established the Second Spanish Republic. The new Republic, however, had a short and uneven life span. Its first government, established through popular elections in 1931, brought an agenda of serious reforms including granting women the right to vote, legalizing divorce, and creating a major plan to redesign the education system to be more secular. Such measures appalled far-right conservatives such as Franco. The new government personally devastated Franco when the decision was made to close the Military Academy, even though Spain's military had far too many officers for its level of troops. In 1933, new elections led to a right-wing backlash and the election of a right-leaning government bent on stopping the rash of liberal reforms begun by its predecessor. This, in turn, incited an uprising by groups associated with the far left, including Communists and Anarchists. The uprising included a serious revolt among the coal miner's unions in the region of Asturias. Franco was assigned to lead troops to crush the uprising using extremely violent measures. There was special contempt for Franco among leftists because he used African troops to smash the will of Spanish citizens. His detractors nicknamed him "the butcher of Asturias."

In 1936, new elections brought another left-leaning government to power. Joseph Stalin in the Soviet Union had called for a "Popular Front" of the left so that all left-wing groups (i.e., Socialists, Anarchists, Communists) would cooperate and participate in elections to help fight the growth of fascism in Europe. This resulted in bringing a Socialist government to power in France, and a left-wing government to power in Spain. Spain's new government included some Socialists in key positions and insisted it would continue its agenda of liberal reforms for Spain, including land reform. For the conservative right this seemed too much, and the nation started to become dangerously polarized.

Politics was spilling onto the streets of Spain, as extreme-right fascists of the *Falange Espanola* fought openly with left-wing groups. In the military, a group of high-level generals believed that the new left-wing government could not be tolerated. The Spanish army in the past had stepped in and seized the government in times of supposed emergency, and had developed a type of traditional military coup d'état known as a *Pronunciamiento* ("Pronouncement"). This action is what the generals then planned, and it led to a bloody and prolonged civil war that tore the nation apart.

The action of the generals began in mid-July 1936 with Franco transporting approximately 30,000 soldiers from North Africa up the south coast, intending to eventually capture Madrid. Other generals moved with their troops as well. In the days that followed, however, the ordinary people of Spain rose up with whatever weapons could be mustered and stopped the advance of the Spanish army forces. The popular troops were led mostly by the series of political trade unions which included the Socialist *Union General de Trabajadores* ("General Union of Workers") (UGT) and the Anarchist *Confederación Nacional del Trabajo* ("National Confederation of Labor") (CNT). But, together they were able to stop the advance of Spanish troops all over Spain and a prolonged military stalemate ensued. To deal with this humiliating development, Franco eventually made contact with Mussolini's Italy and Hitler's Germany. Each of those dictatorships pledged significant assistance and in the subsequent years delivered tanks, planes, munitions, soldiers, and supplies. Despite the use of African, German, and Italian armies, Franco's forces became known as the "Nationalists."

The Republican government, under such a dire threat, requested assistance from the western democracies, but both France and Britain refused to get involved in the situation. France and Britain, in fact, created an international committee to guarantee non-involvement in the Spanish Civil War. Italy and Germany had representation on that committee, but ignored its stipulations completely and continued to help Franco's forces. As a result, the only nation that gave the Republic any assistance was the Soviet Union. The Soviets sent significant assistance, and a bizarre situation developed which often involved Soviet military forces fighting German and Italian military forces in Spain—neither side fighting for the maintenance of a democratic republic. Over time, the fragmentation of the Republican forces, now under Soviet domination, and the fading will of the Soviets to continue assistance meant the dissolving of the popular defense. By 1939, Franco was able to finish off the Republican forces. In late February of that year the British and French governments officially recognized Franco's government and on March 28, 1939, Madrid fell. From that point on, the rest of the war was merely a "mopping up" operation.

Franco took power as a dictator. He consolidated all the right-wing parties into a single political party known as the *Falange Espanola Tradicionalista y de las JONS*, with himself as chief. He also made the decision not to restore the Spanish monarchy. Spain's king Alfonso XIII remained in exile. Franco immediately began to take retribution on those parties that, in his mind, had been responsible for the war—the forces of the left. From 1939 to 1943, he arrested and executed approximately 200,000 people, and thousands more escaped over the border to France (Beevor, 405). Franco also used prison labor from the political arrests to build a great monument to the Nationalist forces with an enormous cross overlooking a monastery at the bottom of a deep ravine. The monument was christened the *Santa Cruz del Valle de los Caidos* (the "Valley of the Fallen").

Franco's regime officially was neutral during the Second World War, but in reality Spain consistently lent aid to the Axis Powers. Spain allowed the Axis forces access to Spanish islands for use as submarine bases. It also sent a great deal of raw materials to Germany to aid in war production, and in fact supposedly sent a volunteer force to fight for the Germans in the Soviet Union.

At home, Franco passed a number of laws that isolated Spain economically and culturally, and he used political repression to eliminate all opposition. Opposing political parties were outlawed and their leaders rounded up and executed. The Basque Nationalist Party was outlawed and went into exile. Other languages including Basque or Catalan were suppressed. The Catholic Church had its official position and status restored. As such, the Church continued to have a prominent role in education and laws regarding moral behavior reflected the Church view. As an example, homosexuality was made a criminal offense.

The Franco dictatorship began to loosen its repressive grip in the 1950s as the United States courted his government for cooperation in defense initiatives. Spain's strategic position was attractive to the U.S. military for establishing bases in the collective security effort of the Cold War. After 1957, Franco began to allow a group known as the "technocrats," to open up the Spanish economy somewhat. Toward the end of his life he also began to make arrangements for the return of the Spanish monarchy. In 1969 he designated Prince Juan Carlos as his successor. Franco had seen to Juan Carlos' education and was confident that Juan Carlos would not bring about liberalization after his death. Franco died on November 20, 1975, after a long illness.

There is much debate as to whether Franco's dictatorship was truly "fascist," or whether his was merely a conservative military dictatorship. Those that argue against his "fascism" contend that his was not a Populist movement nor was it revolutionary or Modernist. Those that do consider his dictatorship to be fascist point to his deep involvement with Hitler and Mussolini, his use of violence to "purify" his national community, and his regime's relationship to big business. Whatever the level of true fascism in his dictatorship, his estimation of Juan Carlos proved incorrect. The new king moved to bring a democratic system to Spain in the mid-1970s. After his death, Franco was entombed at the *Valle de los Caidos,* which perhaps is the only monument to fascist dictatorship that still stands.

See also: *Falange Espanola*; Spanish Civil War.

Further Reading

Beevor, Anthony, *The Battle for Spain: The Spanish Civil War, 1936–1939* (London: Wiedefield and Nicolson, 2006).

Payne, Stanley, *Franco: A Personal and Political Biography* (Madison: University of Wisconsin Press, 2014).

Preston, Paul, *The Politics of Revenge: Fascism and the Military in Twentieth Century Spain* (Boston: Unwin Hyman, 1990).

Richards, Michael, *A Time of Silence: Civil War and the Culture of Repression in Franco's Spain, 1936–1945* (New York: Cambridge University Press, 1998).

GESTAPO   The "Gestapo" is the name used for the secret state police force which operated in Nazi Germany from its inception in 1933 to the last days of the Second World War. The full name of the organization, in German, is the *Geheime Staatspolizei.* The Gestapo was given responsibility for identifying all threats to the national state or to the Nazi Party. These included all cases of treason, espionage, or physical attack. The Gestapo used its own internal espionage, phone tapping, and torture to achieve its objectives. Recent scholarship, however, is increasingly demonstrating that the Gestapo also used a wide network of informants to arrest and remove those people who were not necessarily threats to the state, but who simply did not conform to societal norms. The Gestapo operated as a separate entity until 1934 when its leadership was taken over by Heinrich Himmler, who also was the head of the *Schutzstaffel* (SS). By 1936, the Gestapo was made a formal unit of the SS and remained such until the collapse of the Nazi government in 1945.

The Gestapo was established on April 26, 1933, with Rudolf Diels appointed as its first director. A kind of power struggle ensued—reflective of how the Nazi state worked—between Hermann Goering and Heinrich Himmler for control of the agency. Although Goering was the chief of police for Prussia, the largest region in the Reich, Himmler was busy consolidating power over most of the other provincial police forces. Himmler also was in control of Hitler's elite guard forces, the SS. On April 20, 1934, the Gestapo officially was transferred to Himmler's organization. On June 17, 1936, Hitler announced the consolidation of all police in the state under Himmler. This organizational move formally made the Gestapo a branch of Himmler's growing SS organization. The Gestapo offices were established in Berlin at number 8 Prince Albrechtstrasse, a large building with a nondescript, gray exterior and a labyrinth of sound-proofed cells in its basement for detentions, interrogations, and torture.

The work of the Gestapo was distinguished from the processes of the ordinary criminal justice system by a series of laws that allowed it to operate outside the limits of the existing German judicial system. These new laws and judicial precedents stated that the Gestapo was not subject to judicial review, and that the organization had no accountability (or relationship with) the administrative courts of the land. The Gestapo often used this independence to arrest and remove individuals—without any due process of law—into "protective custody" for an indefinite period. In essence, the Gestapo had been given a license to act as the regime's tool of repression without any check on its power, other than Adolf Hitler or its own administrative leaders. In 1939, this power was strengthened further. The organization was elevated to the level of a ministry called the Reich Security Main Office (RSHA). During the Second World War, one of the RSHA's first actions was to create a written policy allowing the agency to arrest and execute any individual suspected of undermining the war effort. No trial was necessary in the German court system; rather the Gestapo compiled a briefly worded statement passing judgment, and then the sentence of death was carried out.

The Gestapo compiled a huge mass of files on suspects and victims, but it did not do much work in compiling statistics that measured the extent of its work. As a result, historians have difficulty assessing the true scale of political repression during the Third Reich. Many Gestapo offices destroyed their records at the end of the war. Where those records do still exist historians have been surprised to find that the Gestapo operated less on the directives and suspicions of top politicians (although it certainly did this). Extant records, however, suggest that legions of ordinary people consistently denounced their coworkers, neighbors, and even family members to the Gestapo. Their crimes often only were private indications of dissatisfaction with the regime or—just as commonly—a person simply did not fit in with German societal norms. Strange behavior (including alcoholism and homosexuality) often was reported to the Gestapo by such ordinary informants, and those people so denounced often were arrested and sentenced to terms in concentration camps where the majority of them died during the Second World War.

See also: Hitler, Adolf; *Schutzstaffel* (SS).

Further Reading

Browder, George C., *Hitler's Enforcers: The Gestapo and the SS Security Service in the Nazi Revolution* (New York: Oxford University Press, 1996).

Gellately, Robert, *The Gestapo and German Society: Enforcing Racial Policy 1933–1945* (New York: Clarendon, 1990).

Johnson, Eric A., *The Nazi Terror: The Gestapo, Jews, and Ordinary Germans* (New York: Basic Books, 1999).

GOERING, HERMANN (1893–1946)   Hermann Wilhelm Goering was a German fighter pilot in the First World War and became a prominent member of the Nazi Party during the early 1920s. He rose to become one of Adolf Hitler's most trusted henchmen and would be entrusted with numerous positions and responsibilities during the period of Nazi rule. He was made the minister of the interior in Prussia—Germany's largest province—and was made the commander in chief of the German military air force, the *Luftwaffe* in 1935. He remained commander of the *Luftwaffe* until the end of the Second World War. In 1936 Goering was made head of the Four Year Plan, the economic initiative launched by Hitler to prepare Germany for war by making the nation as economically self-sufficient as possible. Though Goering lost much of his influence with Adolf Hitler after the failures of the *Luftwaffe* during World War II, he remained in his positions and spent increasing time in the looting of art treasures from the Nazi-occupied territories. At the end of the Second World War Goering was tried and convicted for war crimes and crimes against humanity at the hearings at Nuremburg.

Goering was born in Rosenheim, Bavaria, on January 12, 1893. His father was a diplomat and governor of German imperial territories in Africa and was on assignment in Haiti at the time of Hermann's arrival. His mother had returned to Germany to give birth. After giving birth to Hermann his mother left for Haiti; the parents would not see their son again until he was three years old.

When the First World War began in 1914, Goering joined an infantry regiment and fought in the trenches along the Western Front. He was hospitalized for rheumatism and it was while he was recovering that he became interested in the flying corps. After some rejections he finally was able to transfer to the Air Combat Force during 1916, and was flying reconnaissance missions by 1917. He eventually became a fighter pilot and amassed a total of 22 victories by war's end.

After the war, Goering worked for a small Swedish airline and as a private pilot from 1919 to 1921. He returned to Germany after marrying his wife to begin studies at the University of Munich, and it was here that Goering came into contact with Adolf Hitler and his Nazi Party. Goering was disgusted with the disintegration of the old German power structure and the new influence of Liberal Democrats, Socialists, and Jews. He hoped for a revolutionary movement to sweep away these elements and found such a movement in Nazism. He joined the Nazi Party in 1922 and had become a *Sturmabteilung* (SA) group leader by 1923. Gradually Goering moved up the ranks, having been alongside Hitler during the Beer Hall Putsch in November 1923, even being shot in the leg during the brief gun battle. By the time Hitler took power in January 1933 Goering was a key member of Hitler's inner circle.

Goering played an important role in the aftermath of the *Reichstag* Fire in February of 1933, when the German Parliament building was burnt to the ground by arsonists. As one of the first Nazis on the scene, Goering's henchmen found and arrested a small group of culprits—including the Communist Marinus van der Lubbe—who were tried and executed for the crime. Goering was among those who clamored for action against the Communists and for giving Hitler dictatorial power to deal with the supposed Communist threat. Goering also was part of the coordinating group in the series of political murders known as the "Night of the Long Knives" during June 1934.

Still in the early days of Hitler's regime, Goering was named minister of the interior for Prussia and then air minister. As minister for air, Goering was instrumental in building the infrastructures for a military air force (in violation of the Treaty of Versailles) under the cover of civilian aircraft and facilities. In 1935 the Nazi regime publicly announced the formation of their military air force with Goering continuing under the new title of Reich aviation minister.

It was in 1936 that Goering began to reach the full summit of his powers. In that year Hitler announced the Four Year Plan at the Nazi Party rally in Nuremburg. This was the initiative to make Germany as economically and agriculturally self-sufficient as possible in preparation for war, and it emerged as Germany's highest economic priority. Goering was put in charge of the Office of the Four Year Plan.

Over the years to come, Goering used his power to bully, intimidate, and cajole businesses into cooperation. In the process Goering also took on personal control of massive engineering works and factories. Under his leadership, the Office of the Four Year Plan became the de facto controlling institution of Germany's economy. The finance minister, Hjalmar Schacht, who had done so much to secure overseas loans and was a brilliant economic mind, gradually was moved aside, and was forced out of the government by 1937. The demise of Schacht and the rise of Goering are often cited as one example of the radicalization of the Nazi regime after 1936.

When the Second World War began Goering initially was decorated for the achievements of his *Luftwaffe*, having decimated the Polish air force and gained immediate air superiority in France. He was promoted to the rank of field marshal, but his position as "Reich Marshal of the Greater German Reich" made him superior in rank to all other field marshals. With his military responsibilities continuing, he also continued his economic work in seizing and converting industry in the occupied territories. Beginning in mid-1940, however, Goering's star began to fade. The prolonged air campaign to bomb Britain into submission failed during the summer and autumn of 1940 with the *Luftwaffe* losing numerous aircraft and pilots. The problems continued as Allied bombers and fighters routinely destroyed German aircraft and carpet bombed German cities during 1941 and 1942. With his forces dwindling, the *Luftwaffe* also struggled in Russia, and by late 1943 Germany had all but lost air superiority in any theater of battle. Allied bombing of Germany increased and it became clear that the *Luftwaffe* was virtually helpless to stop it. Hitler began to distance himself from Goering after this point, though he did not relieve Goering of any of his leadership positions.

At war's end Goering was among the top echelon of Nazi officials put on trial for war crimes and crimes against humanity at the Nuremburg Trials in 1945–46. He was the highest ranking of the surviving Nazi leaders. He refused to believe in or acknowledge the horrors of the Holocaust, saying that the films used for evidence must have been Allied fakes. Goering was found guilty, but asked that he be allowed to be shot—a death more befitting a soldier. His request was refused by the court and he was sentenced to be hanged. While awaiting his execution in prison, however, Goering was able to secure poison—probably by bribing guards—and he committed suicide on October 15, 1946.

See also: Beer Hall Putsch; Four Year Plan.

Further Reading
Asher, Lee, *Goering: Air Leader* (New York: Hippocrene Books, 197?).
Mosley, Leonard, *The Reich Marshall: A Biography of Hermann Goering* (Garden City, NY: Doubleday, 1974).
Overy, Richard, *Goering* (London: Phoenix, 1984).

GUERNICA (BOMBING OF)   The city of Guernica is a culturally important city in the Basque region of Spain. During the Spanish Civil War, on April 26, 1937, Guernica was the target of an aerial bombing assault so massive in scale that it was unprecedented at the time. Although the city was of some strategic value, it virtually was an entirely civilian target. The German military used the Guernica operation as a testing case for future plans of aerial terror in subsequent wars. The Spanish painter Pablo Picasso produced an enormous anti-war painting for display at the Paris Exhibition in 1937. Now considered an important masterpiece, *Guernica* depicted the horror of modern warfare. Since the incident, the bombing of Guernica stands as a historical threshold in the development of mass bombing and modern "total war," and as a powerful symbol of the fate of the innocent in such wars.

The Spanish Civil War was fought from July 1936 to April 1939. It began with an attempted seizure of the government by a collection of dissatisfied Spanish military generals, among them the man who would emerge as the leader of the revolt, General Francisco Franco. These generals were unwilling to accept the radical reforming policies of a recently elected government, which included some hardline Socialists. The perceived threat to Spain's traditional order was so great that these generals marshalled their troops—many from Spain's colonies—and returned to Spain in the form of a military invasion. To defend the government, legions of ordinary people—led mostly by far left political leaders and trade union leaders—took up arms against their own military and held back the initial surge. The war thus was bogged down into a prolonged conflict.

On Franco's "Nationalist," side (the military rebels), help was secured from both Fascist Italy and Nazi Germany. This aid came in the form of money, supplies, and food, but also in the form of military materials, ground troops, and aerial forces. The Republican side, defending its right to exist as a democratically elected government, appealed to Britain and France for help. Neither nation was willing to give assistance. As a result, large numbers of ordinary people from around Europe and the Americas went to Spain to fight in the "International Brigades." Desperate, the Republic accepted military aid from the Soviet Union. By 1937, the Soviets were mostly in control of the anti-Nationalist war effort.

By 1937, the war was taking place on many fronts around the country. One of those was in the north, in the lands of the Basque peoples. The Basques were fighting the Nationalists because of their belief that they could better secure regional autonomy from a left-leaning Republican government—a Nationalist, military dictatorship would never allow any increased level of independence. On that Northern Front there was a high level of participation by both Italian and German troops, and by late April they stood the chance of breaking the Basque defenses. The Nationalist objective at this point was to push the Republicans ever northward to the sea, and capture the vital seaport city of Bilbao. One city that lay along this line of advance was Guernica. This city was not particularly large, having only about 7,000 inhabitants, but it was a vital historical center for the Basques and for Basque culture.

On April 25, Colonel Wolfram von Richtofen, Commander of the Nazi "Condor Legion," a bombing squadron of the German *Luftwaffe*, was frustrated with the slowness of the Nationalists' advance. Both the Spanish and Italian forces on the ground had produced weak spots in the Republican line, but were slow to follow them up, and were wasting opportunities for a swift offensive to the sea. Many of the Republican troops that had been scattered from various points of the line had fallen back to the city of Guernica. It was here that Richtofen resolved to break the Republican forces and open a wide path for Nationalist forces. As such, he believed that overwhelming force was needed to bring this about. Early on the morning of April 26, his bombers (mostly Junker 52s), began dropping bombs in dense patterns on the city and in repeated runs. This has since been termed "carpet bombing," and it was the "Condor Legion" that had pioneered this aerial strategy earlier, when bombing the Spanish city of Oviedo.

The result was destruction on a scale that had never been witnessed before. The city was turned into a smoldering skeleton in a single afternoon, and entire families were buried in the rubble. Bomb shelters proved of little or no assistance. To make matters worse, Monday was "market day," when thousands of residents of the outlying lands came into town to sell their produce. This increased the level of human casualties. The actual number of dead and wounded has been hotly debated. At the time, the local Basque government reported 1,654 dead and 889 wounded. Later statistics suggest a number closer to 300 dead (Beevor, 234).

Regardless of the statistics, the scale of the physical destruction immediately struck world opinion as constituting a barbaric war crime, and the press quickly condemned Nazi brutality. Franco's government issued their own press release replying that the "Reds," had set their own city on fire with gasoline to deny resources to the advancing Nationalist army. This has since been proven to be a ridiculous lie, particularly by the war diary of Colonel Richtofen himself and by eyewitnesses (Beevor, 233).

Moved by the horror, the Spanish painter Pablo Picasso would paint one of his most enduring masterpieces, *Guernica*, later that year and displayed it at the Paris Exhibition. Its black and white color scheme and its depiction of helpless victims, wide-eyed with terror, made it a powerful symbol of the atrocities of modern "total war."

See also: Franco, Francisco; Spanish Civil War.

Further Reading
Beevor, Antony, *The Battle for Spain: The Spanish Civil War 1936–39* (London: Wiedenfield and Nicolson, 2006).
Patterson, Ian, *Guernica and Total War* (London: Profile, 2007).

HESS, RUDOLF (1894–1987) Rudolf Hess was a prominent member of the German Nazi Party (*Nationalsozialistische Deutsche Arbeiterpartei*) (NSDAP) from its earliest days and a close associate of Adolf Hitler. He acted as Hitler's private secretary starting in 1925 and in 1932 was appointed Nazi Party Commissioner. Upon the establishment of the Hitler regime in 1933, Hess was appointed deputy führer, and held special responsibility for several key areas of the government including foreign policy, finance, health, and education. He served in this position until 1941, during the Second World War, when he flew secretly to Scotland to try to negotiate a peace with Britain. The British authorities apprehended him and he would spend the rest of the war in prison. At war's end he was tried with other prominent Nazi leadership at Nuremburg, found guilty of "crimes against peace," and would spend the rest of his life in Spandau Prison, committing suicide on August 17, 1987.

Rudolf Walter Richard Hess was born on April 26, 1894, to a German family living in Alexandria, Egypt. His father operated a commercial trading firm in Egypt and was quite prosperous. Thus, young Rudolf was able to return to Germany regularly and eventually attended boarding school there to finish his secondary education. Just as he began his university studies the First World War broke out in 1914. Hess enlisted and served in field artillery regiments and in infantry regiments. He proved himself on the Western Front, being twice decorated for bravery, including receiving the Iron Cross. He was severely wounded in 1917, and spent much of the rest of the war recovering. In the final days of the war he had recovered enough to train as a fighter pilot but was never able to go into combat, as the war ended while he was still training.

Immediately after the war Hess enrolled at the University of Munich, studying economics and history. It was here that he came into contact with the ideas of Professor Karl Haushofer about the relationship between demographics and geographical space, and the need for "living space" or *lebensraum* for communities. He would one day pass these ideas on to Adolf Hitler, and the quest for *lebensraum* would become one of the central points of Nazi ideology. Having become an extreme right-wing Nationalist in his politics, Hess joined a *Freikorps* group while he was in Munich and fought against the Communists during the Spartacist Rising. He developed a lifelong and intense hatred of Marxism and of Jews, believing, like many other Germans, that Jews were carriers of corrosive Marxist ideas. It was in 1920 that he first heard Adolf Hitler speak at a meeting of the NSDAP (Nazi Party). Hess instantly was moved by Hitler's charisma and found that Hitler's political radicalism harmonized with his own political ideas. Hess became a devoted follower and joined the Nazi Party that year.

Hess very quickly made himself part of Hitler's inner circle of party leadership. In 1923, after the French occupation of the Ruhr and the devastating effects of hyperinflation, Hitler and his party attempted an armed seizure of the government. Hess was part of this coup attempt, but when the attempt fell apart, he initially was able to escape capture. Hess eventually was arrested, along with Hitler, and sentenced to serve five years in Landsberg Prison (though they both served only nine months). While in prison, Hitler dictated his book, *Mein Kampf* (*My Struggle*), to Rudolf Hess. Working with other Nazis, Hess helped assemble it into to two volumes that were released in 1925 and 1926, respectively. The book was Hitler's autobiography and also laid out the program of the Nazi Party and its vision for Germany's future.

After release in 1925, Hitler made Rudolf Hess his personal secretary, and Hess accompanied Hitler to all meaningful campaign engagements—often making the introductory speeches himself. The party did poorly in elections in the late 1920s, polling only 2.6% of the vote in 1928. After the crash of the U.S. stock market in 1929, however, Germany was dragged into a severe economic depression. As conditions worsened and multiple governments seemed unable to alleviate them, the Nazis gained in popularity and began to put large numbers of deputies into parliament. In 1933, Adolf Hitler was made chancellor of Germany and Rudolf Hess was named deputy führer. In that special position he had cabinet ministers reporting directly to him in several areas such as economics, foreign affairs, health, and education. He was also the man to sign many key pieces of Nazi legislation into law. These included the Nuremburg Laws of 1935—which stripped Jews of their German citizenship, prevented Jews and Aryans from intermarriage, and laid out the criteria for being considered to be a Jew.

Hess was a full supporter of Germany's rearmament and its entry into the Second World War. After the invasion of Poland, Hitler designated Hermann Goering as his immediate successor in case of his death, and made Rudolf Hess the second in line for the position of Führer. As the war progressed into 1941, however, Hess became increasingly worried about Germany's ability to survive. He secured a German military airplane, made a secret flight to the United Kingdom, and parachuted out over Scotland. He hoped to find the Duke of Hamilton (a famous airman who had been the first to fly over Mount Everest in 1933), who he believed to be an opponent of the war and sympathetic to Nazi Germany. Through the duke he hoped to try to negotiate a secret peace with Britain. His plan failed and he was taken into custody by the British government and jailed for the remainder of the war.

At war's end Hess was transported back to Germany to stand trial for war crimes at the Nuremburg Hearings. During the trials he routinely behaved as if he had severe amnesia and feigned insanity. His later behavior proved this to be a deception. He was found guilty of "crimes against peace," and sentenced to life in prison. He would serve out that sentence in Spandau Prison, in East Germany, but on August 17, 1987, at the age of 93, Hess committed suicide by using an electrical cord to hang himself. There was some controversy over his death with some scholars asserting that Hess might have been murdered by British Secret Service agents to prevent him from disclosing secrets about British misconduct during the war, although this never has been proven. Spandau Prison and Hess' tombstone eventually were destroyed to prevent them from becoming shrines for members of neo-Nazi movements.

See also: *Mein Kampf*; National Socialist German Workers' Party (Nazi Party).

Further Reading

Padfield, Peter, *Night Flight to Dungavel: Rudolf Hess, Winston Churchill, and the Real Turning Point of World War II* (Lebanon, NH: ForeEdge, 2013).

Raina, Peter, *A Daring Venture: Rudolf Hess and the Ill-Fated Peace Mission of 1941* (Bern: Peter Lang, 2014).

HITLER, ADOLF (1889–1945)   Adolf Hitler was the supreme leader of the National Socialist German Workers' Party (*Nationalsozialistische Deutsche Arbeiterpartei*) (NSDAP) also called the "Nazi Party." Hitler guided the Nazi Party to political prominence and then into power during the 1920s and 1930s. He was appointed chancellor of Germany in 1933. By 1934, Hitler had consolidated his power to emerge as the dictator of Germany and held virtually absolute power. His ideology and policies made Germany a racially based political state, where only those people considered to be of Aryan biological stock enjoyed the legal status of citizenship. His policies also propelled Germany into a large-scale and state-sponsored rearmament program, which helped renew Germany's economy and eliminated unemployment.

Eventually, Hitler's objective of reuniting the Germanic peoples (after territories had been broken up by the Paris Peace Conference) influenced him to aggressively threaten and annex neighboring European nations including Austria, Czechoslovakia, and Poland. His aggression was the principal reason for the commencing of the Second World War in 1939. Hitler briefly conquered most of Europe during the period from 1939 to 1941. After this point, with both the United States and the Soviet Union as enemies, however, Germany gradually was subdued and Hitler's dreams were crushed. Although Germany struggled militarily from 1942 to 1945, Hitler's fanatic anti-Semitism produced the program of mass murder known as the Holocaust. Hitler's "Final Solution" used specially designed death camps to exterminate the Jews of

Nazi-occupied Europe. Germany fell in late April of 1945, and Hitler committed suicide to elude capture.

Adolf Hitler was born to Alois and Klara Hitler on April 20, 1889, in the small Austrian town of Braunau am Inn near Linz. The family moved to the city of Passau in Germany briefly before moving back into Austria by 1895, again settling near Linz. It is believed that the brief time spent in Germany affected Hitler's speech patterns, giving him a Bavarian German accent rather than an Austrian accent. Once back in Austria, the family moved into a small farmhouse where Adolf's father settled into retirement and Adolf continued his schooling. Hitler's behavior at school, however, was the source of serious conflict.

Alois was a devoted Austrian civil service worker. Having spent his career in the Customs Service, he'd hoped that his son would follow in his footsteps. Young Adolf, however, resisted this and grew to despise Austria and its Habsburg dynasty while idealizing all things German. This obsessive love of Germany and rejection of Austria perhaps was a way for the boy to defy his overbearing and abusive father. Although his father insisted that young Adolf pursue a career in the Austrian civil service, the boy dreamt of becoming an artist. He hoped one day to go to Vienna to study painting.

Hitler's father died in 1903; and soon after, it was clear that young Adolf was not succeeding in secondary school. In 1905, Adolf left school to follow his dream of becoming an artist and went to Vienna to apply at the Academy of Fine Arts. He was heartbroken, however, when he was rejected twice from the Academy—once in 1907 and again in 1908. Hitler remained in Vienna, however, living a tenuous existence selling small postcards and watercolors to scratch out a living. He eventually ended up living in a series of homeless shelters or "doss houses." According to one of his companions from these days, August Kubizek, whenever they could scrape together the money the two would visit Vienna's Opera House for productions of Wagner. Hitler became a passionate devotee of Wagner's work and particularly the legends of Germany's mythic past. It was also in these desperate days in Vienna that Hitler came into contact with extreme political anti-Semitism. In his own autobiography, *Mein Kampf*, Hitler talks about coming into contact with Jews for the first time and being repulsed. Hitler would have also seen how Vienna's mayor, Karl Lueger, exploited Austrian prejudices against Eastern immigrants by emphasizing anti-Semitism in his political campaigns. Whether Hitler fully formed his extreme anti-Semitism as early as his days in Vienna remains a matter of debate.

Hitler's mother had died while he was in Vienna, and a few years later he received the last part of his parents' estate in inheritance. This gave Hitler the resources to move out of Austria and into his beloved Germany. He moved to

Munich in 1913. The following year the First World War broke out and Hitler was anxious to join the German army. Because his birthplace was Austria, Hitler had to make a special appeal to the German government. Upon his acceptance he served in the 16th Bavarian Reserve Infantry Regiment on the Western Front. He served as a communication runner through the trench networks, and was twice decorated for bravery. His time in the German army intensified his already passionate German nationalism.

In October 1918, Hitler was exposed to poison gas on the battlefield and was hospitalized for the recovery of his eyesight. It was while recovering in a German hospital that Hitler received the news in November of the abdication of the Kaiser, the declaration of the new Weimar Republic, and then the surrender of Germany to the Allies. This, Hitler said later, was the most traumatic moment of his life and he was consumed with sadness, bitterness, and feelings of betrayal. He swore to himself to somehow take revenge on the supposedly cowardly politicians who had betrayed the nation with surrender. This was a popular viewpoint among those of the political right in Germany. The idea that Germany would surrender while still occupying enemy territory seemed insane to them (not accepting the reality of Germany's collapsing forces, dwindling supplies, and mutinies occurring in the navy). The idea that the Social Democratic leaders of the Weimar Republic—many of them Jewish—had so betrayed the nation became known to German nationalists as the "stab in the back," and the government leaders were labeled the "November criminals."

When released from the hospital, Hitler, by now a corporal, remained in the army and took assignment as a "political officer." His job was to monitor local political parties and to ensure that soldiers in the German army were not involved in any subversion. He was assigned to infiltrate a new party that had emerged out of the chaos and frustration of Germany's postwar experience (which had included a brief Communist uprising). The particular party that Hitler went to investigate was called the *Deutsche Arbeiterpartei* (DAP) (German Workers' Party), which sounded potentially Communist.

What Hitler found, however, was that the beliefs and program of the DAP matched his own almost identically. This included belief in self-sufficiency for Germany, that the Treaty of Versailles should be nullified, and in the racial superiority of the German nation. The DAP condemned the liberal democratic system and the Weimar Republic and wanted to return to an authoritarian system. The party thought that Germany needed colonies for its growing population. It believed that Communism was an insidious threat to the nation and that Jews were especially to blame for most of Germany's problems. Hitler became so enamored of the party and its program that he left the army and joined the DAP as a full-time member and activist. The groups' name soon was changed to *Nationalsozialistische Deutsche Arbeiter-partei*) (NSDAP) (National Socialist German Workers' Party) or "Nazi Party." In the party he soon found that he had a remarkable talent. He developed into an impressive public speaker with the ability to whip audiences into a frenzy of political fervor. With this gift, Hitler emerged as the most important member of the party.

Hitler used this notoriety to position himself as the unquestioned and absolute leader of the party. He refused to create committees or share power. Once in complete control he began to structure the party and created the *Sturmabteilung* (SA) ("Storm Troopers") ("Brownshirts"), a uniformed, paramilitary force to use as "muscle" for the party. He also took on a hectic speaking schedule. By 1923, Hitler and his inner circle believed the time was right to attempt a forcible seizure of the local government in Munich. They hoped that having achieved this they could use Munich as a base from which to then seize the national government. The attempt, known as the "Beer Hall Putsch," failed, leaving 16 Nazis dead and Hitler arrested. He was tried for treason, but his judges were sympathetic to his cause and allowed him to make long speeches during the trial. This trial, in fact, is what made Hitler a national figure in Germany. He was found guilty, but was sentenced to only five years in prison, and only served nine months.

In Landsberg Prison, Hitler continued to run the operations of his party—most of his closest staff members were jailed with him. He also used this time to dictate his infamous book, *Mein Kampf.* The first section was his own autobiographical story and the second essentially was the political manifesto of the Nazi Party. In this book, Hitler talked about Germany's destiny lying in the East and insisted that the Germans must someday attack and conquer the Soviet Union. When released from prison Hitler continued his work with the Nazi Party, although its influence was waning. Conditions in Germany were improving and the Nazi appeal was fading. In October 1929, however, the U.S. stock market crashed and Germany's economy went into a full depression. As a result of the distress and chaos that followed, the Nazis gained in popularity at elections, and in January 1933 German president Paul von Hindenburg, appointed Adolf Hitler chancellor of Germany.

Only a month after taking office, Hitler used the fire that burned the German Parliament building as a reason to insist that the Communists were launching an all-out attack on the nation. He was able to persuade the parliament to arrest Communists and eventually to ban the Communist Party. Hitler then was able to push through a law, known as the "Enabling Act," that gave him virtually absolute power. The following year, 1934, President Hindenburg died and Hitler was made the supreme leader of the land, taking the newly created office of "Führer and Reich Chancellor." He was now the dictator of

Germany, using his Nazi Party apparatus to govern and impose his will upon the nation. Despite all this, however, there still existed a group of party leaders whose beliefs differed from Hitler's and who threatened his positon. These in- dividuals were murdered by Hitler's security forces in June 1934, on a night remembered as the "Night of the Long Knives." With his power now fully consolidated, Hitler continued to push though his radical Nazi agenda.

Hitler's policies included those that persecuted Jews, removed their citizen- ship, and tried to force them into emigration. Other programs related to the strengthening of the so-called "Aryan race," were those that removed "unde- sirables" from the community and detained them in concentration camps. The mentally unfit were sterilized, and a program eventually emerged for the euthanizing of "mentally retarded" children and adults.

Hitler also was adamant about putting Germany back to work, and to do this he sponsored a massive plan of public works, including the building of bridges, housing projects, and the famous *autobahn* highway system. Most of all, Hitler coordinated Germany's economy to rearm the country (in violation of the Treaty of Versailles) and to create a massive war machine. This growing military then was used to intimidate neighboring nations into bowing to Hitler's territorial demands.

In 1936, Hitler re-occupied the Rhineland area and moved in German troops. In 1938, he forced the Austrian government to allow him to send his troops into that nation as an occupying force. The Austrians did not fight back, and Hitler almost immediately moved to annex Austria into the Ger- man nation. Also in 1938, Hitler announced his intention to annex parts of Czechoslovakia into Germany to bring the German-speaking people of the Sudetenland into the German Reich. After making a controversial agreement with the British and the French to allow this, however, Hitler moved beyond the Sudetenland and occupied virtually all of Czechoslovakia. In September 1939, Hitler launched a massive invasion of Poland. This time, however, both Britain and France declared war on Germany as a result, beginning the Sec- ond World War.

In the first phases of the war, Hitler pushed his reluctant generals into the invasions of Norway, Denmark, Holland, Belgium, Luxemburg, and finally into France. By the summer of 1940 Hitler held almost all of Europe through outright conquest or through dominating relations with puppet govern- ments. Hitler was at the height of his power. Only the British held out against Hitler, fighting off the German attempts to bomb them into surrendering.

In June 1941, Hitler launched an enormous invasion of the Soviet Union. Although the Soviets and the Nazis had been alliance partners, having signed the Nazi-Soviet Non-Aggression Pact in August 1939, Hitler had always insisted that the conquest of Russia was his ultimate goal for the German people. That same year the Japanese bombed Pearl Harbor in Hawaii, forcing the United States into the war. From that point the war was a slow but steady erosion of the power and conquests of the Axis Powers as the industrial might and resources of the United States and the Soviet Union were brought to bear.

After his invasions of the East, Hitler launched projects to displace Poles, Czechs, Russians, Ukrainians, and others for the benefit of German settlers. In this process he also ordered the segregating and extermination of the Jews of Eastern Europe. Death squads began rounding up and shooting Jews. By 1942, the extermination process had not been as quick or as efficient as Hitler wanted. To bring about what he called the "Final Solution," Hitler directed that plans be made for an enhanced process. The result was the creation of the system of industrialized death camps. The transport, slave labor, and execution of victims (through gas chambers disguised as shower facilities), killed nearly six million Jews and nearly as many non-Jews, though estimates continue to vary.

Through 1943 and 1944, and into 1945, Hitler's armies disintegrated. The Soviets pushed toward Germany from the East, and the United States and Great Britain pushed toward Germany from the West. The goal of these armies was to eventually meet at the city of Berlin. As the armies approached, Hitler and his inner circle moved into an underground network of concrete rooms known as "the bunker." Here, Hitler increasingly lost touch with reality—he commanded nonexistent armies, and even ordered the destruction of German cities and property to keep the Allies from capturing them. When the Soviets reached the outskirts of Berlin, Hitler faced the inevitable. He married his long-time mistress, Eva Braun, and together they committed suicide on April 30, 1945, to avoid capture. Hitler's body was burned by Joseph Goebbels, Hitler's loyal propaganda minister. For years after the war, controversy raged regarding what actually happened to Hitler's body. After the collapse of the Soviet Union in 1991, it was revealed that Hitler's few remains had been taken by Soviet troops in 1945 and kept in secret vaults in Russia.

See also: *Anschluss*; Anti-Semitism; Beer Hall Putsch; Czech Crisis of 1938; Enabling Act of 1933; Four Year Plan; Holocaust; *Mein Kampf*; Night of the Long Knives; National Socialist German Workers' Party (Nazi Party); Nuremburg Laws; Racial Hygiene; Rearmament; *Reichstag* Fire; Remilitarization of the Rhineland; *Schutzstaffel* (SS); *Sturmabteilung* (SA).

Further Reading
Hitler, Adolf, *Mein Kampf,* translated by Ralph Manheim (New York: Mariner, 1971 [1925–1926]).

Kershaw, Ian, *Hitler 1889–1936: Hubris* (New York: W. W. Norton, 1998).

Kershaw, Ian, *Hitler 1936–1945: Nemesis* (New York: W. W. Norton 2000).

Petrova, Ada and Peter Watson, *The Death of Adolf Hitler* (New York: W. W. Norton, 1995).

Shirer, William L., *The Rise and Fall of the Third Reich* (New York: Fawcett Crest, 1960).

Toland, John, *Adolf Hitler* (Garden City, NY: Doubleday, 1976).

HOLOCAUST   The term "Holocaust" is used to describe the initiative launched by Adolf Hitler's Nazi regime in Germany to exterminate all people of Jewish extraction by means of systemized mass executions. Although there have been other episodes of genocide in history, because of its scale and calculated, methodical nature, this project is considered perhaps the most horrifying crime ever perpetrated upon one group of people by another. The Nazi regime proclaimed its intense anti-Semitism from its origins, but focused its attention upon removing Jews' citizenship, removing them from prominent positions in society, and forcing them to emigrate. During the Second World War, in 1941, however, the Nazis launched the coordinated effort to exterminate Jews within Nazi-occupied territories. After 1942 that process was expanded through the use of death camps. These death camps were specially designed for execution using gas chambers and the incineration of the corpses. The Nazi regime is estimated to have murdered approximately six million Jews in only four years of this initiative. The camp system was used to exterminate others as well, including Roma Gypsies, Slavs, Poles, homosexuals, and those considered to be of inferior racial stock. Estimates of the number of non-Jews executed range between three and five million, making an estimated total death toll of the Holocaust between eight and eleven million human beings.

Immediately upon taking power in January 1933, Adolf Hitler began to push through measures that translated the Nazi prejudice against Jews into legislative reality. Jews were removed from important positions in business, academia, and cultural life. There also were limited government-coordinated efforts to create boycotts against Jewish businesses. Such actions prompted thousands of Jews to leave Germany, though many remained due to lack of resources or simply a refusal to leave their own homeland. The government's anti-Semitic measures had proven to be problematic and confusing at times, as there was difficulty in determining exactly who qualified as a Jew and there were legal problems related to the rights of citizens. In 1935, such problems were swept away by the passage of a set of laws that came to be known as the "Nuremburg Laws." These identified exactly who qualified as a Jew (related to the number of one's Jewish grandparents) and removed the status of citizenship from all Jews in Germany. Thereafter anti-Semitism intensified, emigrations continued, and the state began to seize enormous quantities of Jewish property from those who fled. In 1938, after a Jewish man shot a German diplomat in Paris, the Nazi government launched a state-sponsored pogrom. It was carried out during November 9 and 10 and included mass rioting, the smashing and looting of Jewish businesses, random assaults against Jews, and mass arrests. Estimates suggest that up to 7,000 Jewish businesses were vandalized, 1,200 Jewish synagogues were burned, and approximately 30,000 Jewish individuals were arrested, taken from their families, and sent to concentration camps. This event is remembered as *Kristallnacht* ("Crystal Night," or Night of Broken Glass), and marked a threshold in the intensification of the Nazi campaign against Jews.

Concentration camps had existed from the beginning of the regime but originally were not intended for the purpose of mass murder. They were intended to be prisons where "undesirables" (e.g., Jews, alcoholics, homosexuals, Communists, and other political opponents) could be segregated and removed from German society. These camps were unsanitary, often required back-breaking labor, and the guards certainly could be violent and deadly. The network of concentration camps, however, was not yet part of a concerted effort to exterminate Jews. The Hitler regime continued to implement policies intended to force Jews to leave the country.

When the Second World War began, however, this approach to the Jews underwent a change. As Nazi forces came to conquer and occupy neighboring territory they found large percentages of peoples deemed "unfit" for the Aryan race. Large areas of Poland, and later Russia and the Baltic were marked out for the settlement of German people. Native populations were forced out of their homes and often into slave labor in agriculture or industry, serving the Nazi war effort. Jews, however, were a different case. Jews were identified and massed together in large segregated districts in cities that came to be known as "Ghettoes." Such cities included Warsaw and Lodz in Poland, and Riga in the Baltic. With only a starvation diet and no opportunity to work, the people in these ghettoes were confined behind fences in a restricted space that resembled a massive concentration camp in the middle of a large city.

During 1941, the approach to what the Nazis called the "Jewish Problem" changed yet again. The existing strategy of Jewish transport and confinement was proving costly and ineffective for the size of the Jewish population. To remedy this, the elite state security force, known as the SS, was given the task of actually exterminating harmful Jewish elements in the occupied territories in the East. This marked a significant turning point, as the strategy had now evolved into an unqualified effort to reduce or eliminate Jewish populations through mass murder. The method chosen for accomplishing this was the establishment of special police squads or "death squads," known in German as the *Einsatzgruppen*. Their job was to assist the regular army and facilitate the process of "Germanization" in the occupied territories in the East. In the process, however, they specifically were assigned to identify Jews, assemble them into segregated groups, and kill them in mass shooting operations. This often was carried out in the middle of town, but could also be carried out by driving loads of Jews into the countryside in trucks and gunning them down there. Such operations were completed by burying the victims in enormous mass graves, often after the victims had been forced to dig the pits themselves. Such behavior by the *Einsatzgruppen* has generated much controversy among scholars. Some maintain that the willingness of men to participate in these murders, the public tortures that often went with it, and the celebration and honoring of those who killed most efficiently, provides evidence that the German population in general was in favor of, and even enthusiastic about the extermination of the Jews. Other research suggests that many of the *Einsatzgruppen* agents were horrified by their work, tried to get out of it, and often turned to coping mechanisms such as alcoholism.

While debate continues regarding this issue, the fact remains that during 1942 Hitler and the SS high command decided that innovations were needed to accelerate and expand the extermination of Jews. The approach of seeking out Jews in specific communities and murdering them piecemeal was proving too slow and too difficult for those carrying out the work. It was at this point, in early 1942, that a plan was conceived to bring about what Hitler called the "Final Solution"—the extermination of all of the Jews from German occupied Europe. The man who put together the logistical plans for this next stage of the process was Reinhard Heydrich, the head of state security forces within the SS. Heydrich conceived the idea of converting existing concentration camps into specially designed death camps, which would murder their populations by gassing them in chambers disguised as shower facilities. He designed the system that linked all the centers of Jewish detention by railroad. He also advocated rounding up Jews in places such as France, Holland, Belgium, Greece, and Italy in special detention centers and then having them transported by rail to the death camps in the East. In January 1942, this plan was approved and initiated by Heydrich at a conference in the Berlin suburb of Wansee and which has been known as the "Wansee Conference" ever since. The SS, under its supreme commander Reichsführer Heinrich Himmler, began the construction of the camps and implementing the strategy during 1942. Heydrich would never see his conception in full operation as he was assassinated by Czech secret agents (working from London) in June of that year.

In this system Jews were transported to concentration or "deportation" camps in places including Austria, Belgium, France, Germany, Greece, Holland,

Hungary, Italy, and Russia. The SS also continued to segregate Jews in the large Polish and Baltic ghettoes. Jews systematically were transported by rail from these ghettos to the death camp network in the East. Most of these camps were in occupied Poland, including Auschwitz, Treblinka, Belzec, Majdanek, Chelmno, and Sobibor. Other camps where executions were carried out included Dachau in Germany and Riga in the Baltic. At some of the camps—particularly Auschwitz—there were large facilities for laborers. Jews and other "undesirables," if they were deemed fit, were put to work as slave labor, working for companies that were providing arms, munitions, and materiel for the war effort. Their diet was at a starvation level, their living conditions were dangerously unsanitary, and most victims died in a matter of months from overwork, malnutrition, and disease. This was a calculated strategy by the Nazis to get necessary labor completed, and still accomplish the goal of extermination. The millions of others who were not deemed fit for labor—the elderly, the sickly, the weak, and most children—most often were sent directly to barracks areas. Here, whatever property the Jews were carrying was taken. Both laborers and non-laborers had their suitcases, clothing, shoes, wallets, and jewelry seized. Laborers were given thin prison clothes. The others were forced to undress and to move naked into mass shower facilities for cleaning and de-lousing. In those showers, however, the nozzles did not release water, but rather a deadly form of poison gas known as "Zyklon-B." This was specially manufactured for the German government by the largest German chemical corporation I.G. Farben. After everyone in the shower facility had died, guards moved the corpses outside, stacking them in massive piles. From here, the deceased eventually were transported by cart, truck, or wagon to the incineration facilities or ovens. The bodies were systematically burned. Memories that most haunt Holocaust survivors and those who eventually liberated the camps are the smell of burning flesh and the constant rain of human ash.

As the Allied forces made their way across Western and Eastern Europe during 1944 and into 1945, the SS staff running the death camps was put under pressure. They were forced to continue their work in destroying the evidence by burning bodies, but now also were asked to destroy documents. They often abandoned the camps at the last minute before being overrun by Allied troops. Rather than leaving the suffering Jewish survivors behind, the SS staff generally forced them to make the long marches into German territory. At gunpoint these often-emaciated people attempted to keep up on miles-long marches. Those who could not keep up were generally shot on the spot. Others managed to escape into wooded areas to await the arrival of Allied troops. These "death marches" are another example of behavior that suggests utter fanaticism. It would have been far quicker and safer to have left the captives behind, but the SS was determined to keep these Jewish victims with them to suffer their eventual fate. Another more prosaic explanation of the death marches is simply that the SS staff was under orders to keep Allied troops from seeing the human results of the Holocaust.

But U.S., British, and Russian troops certainly did discover the horrors of the Holocaust. As they liberated camps during 1944 and 1945, they found railroad cars full of corpses, mass graves, and the full apparatus of the death camps. The Allied Supreme Commander, General Dwight D. Eisenhower, insisted that these camps be meticulously photographed and that every guard and every document be seized as evidence. He feared that if this were not done that there might be those who denied the Holocaust in future decades.

In Central Europe the Holocaust killed between 80% and 90% of the Jewish population. In Western Europe approximately 25% of the Jewish population was exterminated. Overall, approximately 6 million or about 60% of the total Jewish population of Europe was killed. Many of the key SS personnel involved with the Holocaust were arrested and tried for war crimes and crimes against humanity. Several of them were tried during the 1940s but a few high-profile staff members were found later and tried during the 1960s and 1970s. Many others, however, were able to escape and have never been brought to justice.

See also: Anti-Semitism; Hitler, Adolf; *Kristallnacht*; *Schutzstaffel* (SS).

Further Reading
Friedman, Saul, *A History of the Holocaust* (London: Vallentine Mitchell, 2004).
Gilbert, Martin, *The Holocaust: A History of the Jews of Europe During the Second World War* (New York: H. Holt, 1985).
Goldhagen, Daniel Jonah, *Hitler's Willing Executioners: Ordinary Germans and the Holocaust* (New York: Vintage, 1997).
Johnson, Eric A. and Karl-Heinz Reuband, *What We Knew: Terror, Mass Murder, and Everyday Life in Nazi Germany* (Cambridge, MA: Basic Books 2005).

KRISTALLNACHT *Kristallnacht* ("Crystal Night" or Night of Broken Glass) is the German term that emerged for the night of coordinated, state-sponsored rioting and violence that took place during November 9–10, 1938. The violence was organized chiefly by Joseph Goebbels (Adolf Hitler's minister of propaganda) and carried out by the legions of the SA (*Sturmabteilung* or Brownshirts). Despite the program being organized by the government, however, there was a tremendous level of civilian involvement as well. Jews had their businesses smashed, inventories stolen or destroyed, and their vehicles demolished. Synagogues were burned and vandalized and there also were waves of beatings, tortures, and murders. This attack took place throughout Germany and in the newly annexed territories of Austria. The term *Kristall-nacht* refers to the masses of broken glass on the streets which gleamed like crystal.

The Nazi Party had been fanatically anti-Semitic since its beginnings in the immediate aftermath of World War I. Nazi followers believed that Jews were biologically inferior, and were a menace to the German nation. Nazis believed that Jews were carriers of Marxism and were deeply involved in the speculations of "international finance," which threatened productive nations everywhere. As such, when the Nazis came to power in January 1933, almost immediately the government passed legislation persecuting Jews. Such laws included those that removed Jews from prominent positions in business, academia, and cultural life. Later, the Nuremburg Laws identified exactly who was to be considered a Jew, and stripped all Jews of their German citizenship. The Nazi regime routinely arrested and detained Jews, and regularly seized their property.

In early November 1938, a Polish Jew named Herschel Grynszpan was living in Paris and received a postcard from his parents who lived in Germany. The postcard informed him that they had been deported and were being forced out of their home. Young Grynszpan was so outraged that he purchased a revolver and went to the German Embassy in Paris. There, he was able to shoot a German diplomat named Ernst vom Rath, although the man initially survived the shooting. In Germany, the reaction by the Nazi government was one of fury. Immediately schools were closed to Jewish children and Jewish newspapers were shut down. When, on November 9, it was announced that vom Rath had died from his wounds, Nazi government officials, particularly Joseph Goebbels, began to organize a mass reprisal against the Jews in Germany. The internal security service began to coordinate attacks through the various units of the SA.

The result was a mass pandemonium and violent attacks. The windows of Jewish businesses were shattered and their inventories stolen and strewn about the streets. Mobs broke into Jewish homes and beat or kidnapped members of the household. SA groups worked to set fire to major Jewish synagogues. When the night of chaos and violence was over, more than 30,000 Jews had been arrested at random and shipped to concentration camps. More than 1,200 synagogues were destroyed—mostly by fire—and 7,000 Jewish businesses were ruined (Gilbert, 31). Another significant statistic that might never be calculated is the number of outright murders that took place—which possibly numbers in the thousands.

Kristallnacht marked a significant threshold in Nazi policy toward Jews, as the regime moved from legal suppression to active violence, arson, and murder. Some scholars think that the Holocaust, which killed six million Jews, really began with the horrors of that night. The German public did virtually nothing to stop the violence, but evidence exists suggesting that most Germans were appalled by it. In the aftermath of the violence, the Hitler regime seems to have understood that the German public did not support such ugly and overt mayhem and so Hitler downplayed the event in Nazi propaganda. The world outside of Germany was horrified and infuriated. The United States recalled its ambassador and some other nations cut off diplomatic relations entirely. The Nazi regime would not take such public measures against Jews again.

In the years that followed, the regime launched a massive project of displacement, slavery, and mass executions against Jews. Having learned lessons from *Kristallnacht*, however, the regime also worked strenuously to hide the facts of Jewish persecution and the truth of the Holocaust from the German public.

See also: Anti-Semitism; Hitler, Adolf; Holocaust; Nuremburg Laws.

Further Reading

Evans, Richard J., *The Third Reich in Power, 1933–1939* (New York: Penguin, 2005).
Gilbert, Martin, *The Holocaust: the Jewish Tragedy* (London: Collins, 1986).
Read, Anthony, *Kristallnacht: Unleashing the Holocaust* (London: Joseph, 1989).

MARCH ON ROME   The "March on Rome" was the term given to the coordinated mass movement of the members of Benito Mussolini's Fascist Party, converging on the city of Rome during the period from October 27 to October 29, 1922. The mass movement had been organized by the Fascists to force Italy's king to name Mussolini as prime minister. The plan was to begin with squads of Fascist "Blackshirts" seizing vital pieces of the Italian infrastructure such as the railways and telephone exchanges. It was then to proceed with tens of thousands of Blackshirts and other Fascist supporters arriving in Rome to demonstrate an overwhelming mandate from the masses for a Mussolini government. In fact, the king and his ministers stopped the marchers in place on the 27th through police intervention. Political negotiations between the king and his ministers, however, convinced him to ask Mussolini to form a government. Once Mussolini had taken the position, the "March on Rome," was allowed to continue. Mussolini used the "March on Rome," to create the image that he had taken the government through the overwhelming force of his mass of followers. In fact they arrived in Rome a full 24 hours after he had already been appointed prime minister.

Beginning in 1919, Benito Mussolini had worked to create a political movement. He formed groups of political activists who used violence to attack and undermine the advance of Italy's Socialists. His squads, known as "Blackshirts" after their black paramilitary uniforms, went into towns that had elected Socialists to their municipal government and smashed newspaper offices, ransacked city halls, and beat and tortured Socialist politicians. From this initial identity of anti-Socialist violence Mussolini in 1921 created a true political party—the *Partito Nazionale Fascista* (National Fascist Party) (PNF). The Fascist Party was able to get some deputies elected to the Italian Parliament, but nowhere near a majority. Still, however, the Blackshirts continued their open and violent assaults all around Italy. This had the effect of reducing Italy's politics to chaos at the municipal, provincial, and even national level. Unable to solve the economic problems of the day and struggling to maintain order, Italy saw several governments established but then fall due to lack of coalition support in parliament. In this atmosphere of political instability Benito Mussolini hoped to force himself into control, using the raw force of the Fascist Blackshirts. Mussolini named four of his top party leaders *quadrumvirs* to coordinate the march from different geographical areas of the country. They were to take control of the railways and railway stations where they could, and to take control of the telephone exchanges. Having paralyzed the government's ability to control them, the Fascists marched on to Rome and overwhelmed the city, forcing the king to ask Mussolini to form a government. This was the plan.

The march was launched on October 27, 1922, and in some areas the Blackshirts were successful in taking control of transport and communications. At this point, however, the prime minister, Luigi Facta, and Italy's king, Victor Emmanuel III, met with other key ministers to find a way to deal with the crisis. They all agreed to use the military to crush the Blackshirts and to declare martial law. There also was a directive sent to the Police Prefect of Milan to arrest Mussolini. The army was able to arrest several Blackshirts and to stop their march but, in Milan, the mayor failed to move to arrest Mussolini. Local Fascists had assured him that if and when Mussolini took power he would be rewarded with a post in the cabinet. With such a promise in mind, the prefect ignored his order and Mussolini remained free.

Meanwhile the king was preparing to sign the order to institute martial law but, at this crucial time, he decided against it. Some members of the government convinced him that if the military intervened to control the country they would be outnumbered and overwhelmed by the Blackshirts and Italy could descend into civil war. Because the king would not move forward with Facta's initiative for martial law, Facta resigned as prime minister. Another key minister, Antonio Salandra, was asked to form a government. Salandra thought he could only be successful in stopping the chaos if Mussolini were included in the government. He contacted Mussolini and offered him a prominent post in the new government if he stopped the mass movement of his Blackshirts. Mussolini—sensing that he might be able to leverage himself into the top position—refused. He was right. Salandra, believing that he could not maintain order without Mussolini in his government, declined the position of prime minister. At this point the king thought he had no other option to bring order but to ask Mussolini himself to accept the position of prime minister and form a government. Mussolini accepted on October 29, 1922, and thus technically took power by constitutional means.

The "March on Rome" took on a mythic status amongst the Fascists in the years to come. Mussolini had declared that he had 300,000 Blackshirts on the move. In reality this number was somewhere between 25,000 and 30,000 (Mack-Smith, 54). In some areas only a few policemen were needed to stop the march. Mussolini, however, presented the event to the world press as an overwhelming spectacle demonstrating his ability to use the power and violence of the masses to force Italy into the Fascist era.

See also: Blackshirts; Mussolini, Benito; National Fascist Party (PNF).

Further Reading
Finaldi, Giuseppe, *Mussolini and Italian Fascism* (Harlow, UK: Pearson, 2008).
Gentile, Emilio, *The March on Rome: How Anti-Fascists Understood the Origins of Totalitarianism (and Coined the Term)* (Rome: Viella, 2014).
Mack-Smith, Denis, *Mussolini: A Biography* (New York: Vintage, 1982).

MEIN KAMPF *Mein Kampf,* German for "My Struggle," was the book written by Adolf Hitler which served as his autobiography and as a political manifesto for his Nazi Party. Hitler dictated the book to his staff (including his personal secretary, Rudolf Hess) while serving his sentence in Landsberg Prison for his failed attempt to seize the government in 1923. The book was assembled into two volumes released in 1925 and 1926, respectively. It provides insight into Hitler's rather deranged personal beliefs about his own providential destiny, the development of his obsessive belief in racial struggle, and his fanatical anti-Semitism. Although the book reiterates the policies that the Nazi Party had been espousing for some time, Hitler added a new feature to his vision of German destiny—that of Germany's inevitable conquest of the Soviet Union. This, he said, would provide living space for the German race and destroy the fountainhead of world Communism at the same time.

Adolf Hitler had led his Nazi Party in a coordinated attempt to seize the German government on November 8, 1923. Known as the "Beer Hall

Putsch," it failed miserably and Hitler was put on trial for crimes of treason. Infamously, his judges at the trial were opponents of the Weimar Republic and allowed Hitler to make long political speeches during the trial. He was found guilty, but instead of a death sentence or life imprisonment (typical sentences for high treason), he was sentenced to five years in prison. Ultimately he only served nine months. Hitler served his sentence at Landsberg Prison along with some of his deputies, including his personal secretary at the time, Rudolf Hess. Hitler was allowed to receive visitors and talk politics, essentially running his political party from his prison cell. He became convinced, however, that he must use his time to write out his full story and to make clear to the German people his vision for their "historic destiny." He began focusing on dictating the book and for several months devoted himself almost exclusively to this task.

When the book was completed it was edited by Hess and others and published in two volumes. The first volume was released in 1925, the second in 1926. It was marginally popular during the 1920s, but increased greatly in popularity after the coming of the Great Depression in 1929. As conditions worsened in Germany, the Nazi Party grew in appeal with German voters, and Hitler's book sales grew as well. By 1933, when Hitler was made chancellor of Germany, *Mein Kampf* had sold approximately 240,000 copies, and generated more than a million Reichsmarks for its author. During the period that the Third Reich was in power, Hitler made *Mein Kampf* a mandatory gift for every new married couple, the marriage books coming in a wooden gift case. It was also issued for free to soldiers going into combat. It is estimated that by the time of Hitler's death in 1945 the book had sold close to 10 million copies worldwide.

In the book, Hitler discusses his childhood and adolescent years, including the relationships with his parents and his poor performance in school. He discusses at length his desire to become a trained artist, and his disappointment with his rejection from the Royal Academy in Vienna. He also recounts his days in Vienna as a young adult and his first encounters with Jews and with anti-Semitic politics. Initially indifferent to and tolerant of Jews, he says his exposure to them in Vienna helped him to understand their harmful and corrosive influence on German society. He goes on to identify the great enemies of Germany that had brought the nation to such utter destitution by the 1920s. He identifies the Jews as especially harmful and linked them to another of Germany's great enemies, the Marxists. Hitler explains his view—which was shared by other anti-Semites at the time—that the Jews were united in a world conspiracy to undermine the supposedly productive races for their own personal enrichment. Using control of the world's financial markets and, incongruously, control of the Marxist movements, Jews worked to destabilize society for purposes of their own profit and increasing world control.

Hitler also identified those in charge of the Weimar Republic immediately after the end of the First World War as the "November Criminals." He accused them of unnecessarily surrendering to the enemy and for making Germany a subordinate nation, doomed to live under the hostile conditions of the Treaty of Versailles. Finally, Hitler denounced the system of parliamentary democracy as a formula that simply would not work and which was leading the nation into growing levels of chaos and servitude.

As prescriptions to cure these ills and eliminate these enemies, Hitler advocated the policies of his Nazi Party. A Nazi government under his leadership would create an authoritarian system, ridding the land of the multitude of political parties and especially suppressing the Communists and Socialists. He also advocated policies that rejected the conditions of the Versailles Treaty and which would make Germany increasingly economically self-contained (therefore economically independent). Once in control of its own national destiny, Hitler went on, the German race would be free to fulfill its "historic destiny," of expanding its geographical borders. Hitler advocated German expansion into Eastern Europe and then on to a full conquest of the Soviet Union. This, he said, would provide the supposedly virile German race with the geographic space it needed to grow and expand, while providing the natural resources and food needed to make the German people powerful and independent.

Adolf Hitler acted upon the majority of the ideological principles he discussed and the policies he advocated in *Mein Kampf*. During the Hitler regime Marxist organizations were outlawed and their political parties eliminated. Jews were removed from politics, business, and cultural life, eventually losing their citizenship. Later they fell victim to blatant state-sponsored violence and mass murder. The system of liberal democracy was eliminated and a single-party dictatorship was established. Finally, despite making a temporary and dishonest Non-Aggression Pact with the Soviet Union in 1939, Hitler expanded Germany's borders into the East, taking Austria, Czechoslovakia, and Poland. Then, in 1941, he launched a full-scale invasion of the Soviet Union. For those who tried to come to terms with Nazism during the 1930s and wondered what exactly the Hitler regime planned to do, all of these principles and objectives had been clearly listed in *Mein Kampf*; the answers had been spelled out for those who cared to read it and to take it seriously.

See also: Hess, Rudolf; Hitler, Adolf; National Socialist German Workers' Party (Nazi Party).

Further Reading

Hitler, Adolf, *Mein Kampf,* translated by Ralph Manheim (Boston: Mariner, 1971 [1925–1926]).

Hitler, Adolf, *Hitler's Second Book: The Unpublished Sequel to Mein Kampf,* edited by Gerhard L. Weinberg (New York: Enigma, 2003 [1928]).

MOSLEY, SIR OSWALD (1896–1980)   Sir Oswald Mosley was a British politician who served in parliament from 1918 to 1931, and eventually founded the British Union of Fascists (BUF), the largest and most visible fascist party in Britain. As the "leader" of the British Union of Fascists, Mosley put together an extensive and coherent political program which he described in his book, *The Greater Britain,* published in 1932. His party experienced growth and popularity during 1933 and 1934, but then went into decline. When the Second World War broke out the BUF briefly continued to operate, but was legally banned by the British government in 1940 and most of its key membership was arrested and interned. Mosley made a political comeback after the war, founding the "Union Movement" Party, which advocated a Europe unified as a single state. This group never generated any significant support. Much vilified as the "British Hitler," Mosley left Britain in 1951 living most of the rest of his life in France.

Sir Oswald Mosely was born in London on November 16, 1896. He was raised by his mother and his grandfather. Later, as a young adult, he attended the Sandhurst Military Academy (although he was expelled) and joined the British Army during the First World War. He fought with the infantry on the Western Front, but later joined the Royal Flying Corps, where he was in a crash that permanently injured his leg. Being deeply affected by the horrors of the war, Mosley was particularly interested in building a newer and better Britain at war's end. In 1918 he stood for parliament at only 21 years of age and won the seat for Harrow as a member of the Conservative Party. He grew disillusioned with the Conservatives' policy in the Irish situation and their use of the oppressive "Black and Tans," and made the decision to switch parties. He was out of parliament from 1924 to 1926 when he was elected the Labour Party candidate from Smethwick. As a Labour politician, dealing with the economic "slump," he supported radical changes and had been an early subscriber to the economic theories of John Maynard Keynes. He advocated Keynesian economic policies such as deficit borrowing by the government and public works projects, all to stimulate consumption as the best way to heal the economy.

In 1929, a Labour government was elected, and the charismatic Mosley was given a minor position in the government as chancellor of the Duchy of Lancaster. He was, however, assigned to work under Cabinet member Jimmy

Thomas in creating a strategy to solve Britain's deep unemployment problem. Disappointed with Thomas' lack of energy and creativity, Mosley put together his own plan which included steps such as massive public works programs, creating a protected home market for British industries, and even for nationalizing some of Britain's heavy industries where labor unrest was at its worst. His plan was rejected by the Cabinet in favor of policies that went in the opposite direction of cutting social programs to balance the budget.

Mosley became fed up and—after making a famous speech in parliament on the matter—resigned from the government and then from the Labour Party altogether. He went on to form his own political party known as the "New Party." Only four Labour members of parliament (including his wife Cynthia Mosley nee Curzon) left the party with Mosley. Others joined from outside government, however, and put together a political campaign for the 1931 elections. The New Party advocated the Keynesian economic solutions of Mosley's earlier plan (known as the "Mosley Manifesto"), but the party also advocated a new parliamentary system based on industries (essentially the Corporative system of Fascist Italy), and a streamlined Cabinet with only a ruling committee of five. The New Party failed utterly in the 1931 elections with none of its candidates winning office, and Mosley himself even lost his seat.

Once out of politics, Mosley then began to tour the British Empire and the new states of Europe. He was especially moved by his visit to Fascist Italy where he spent a great deal of time with Benito Mussolini and became increasingly drawn to the Fascist system. Back home in Britain, Mosley wrote out his new political vision for a "Fascist Britain" in a political manifesto he titled *The Greater Britain*. At the same time, he changed the direction and the name of his political party to the British Union of Fascists which he launched in October 1932. This would emerge as Britain's largest and most influential fascist organization. During 1933 Mosley was able to secure official support from Viscount Rothermere and his popular newspaper the *Daily Mail*. Mosley launched his own party newspaper as well, first called the *Blackshirt* and later changed to *Action*.

Mosley's political agenda became the platform of the BUF. He advocated a dictatorship for Britain, with himself as "leader." The leader was to obtain power only by the vote. Once in power, however, Mosley would reorganize the parliamentary system to a "Corporative State," with members of parliament elected by and representing specific industries. He advocated a self-contained and self-sufficient economy in which Britain's domestic producers and imperial producers would enjoy a protected exchange, but foreign goods and credit would be excluded by law. He also promoted a revitalization of British agriculture to ensure the security of Britain's food supply. Connected with this, he advocated a massive rearmament program, particularly in the air, to make Britain absolutely secure in terms of national defense. To achieve these goals he advocated the use of the most modern industrial practices, scientific research, and new technologies—all to help insulate Britain from the economic and political instability of the world situation at the time.

His party would also use a uniformed paramilitary force, known as the "Blackshirts," to keep order at their political rallies and to intimidate anyone who might interfere with their marches on the streets. After a particularly violent incident at a meeting at Olympia Hall in London in 1934, support for the BUF began to fall off. By 1936, there was little support for the group, and Jewish organizations and groups of the labor left worked together to physically stop a march of the BUF in the East End of London. Known as the "Battle of Cable Street," this incident is remembered as a symbolically powerful moment in the fight against fascism in Britain. After this low point, Mosley's BUF had one last surge of popularity during 1938 and 1939, as war with Nazi Germany loomed on the horizon. In this tense environment, Mosley insisted that Britain should not go to war with Germany over any question in Eastern Europe.

When war did come, the BUF clearly supported the British government and many of its members went into the military. There were suspicions, however, that Mosley and the BUF were secretly defeatist and were hoping to be put in power if the Nazis invaded Britain. For such reasons the British government officially banned the BUF and other fascist groups and arrested their key membership, including Mosley and his second wife Diana. Mosley's first wife, Cynthia, had died in 1933 and Mosley had secretly married Diana Guiness (nee Mitford) in 1936 in the living room of Nazi propaganda minister Joseph Goebbels with Adolf Hitler present. The Mosleys were jailed and confined in separate facilities from 1940 to 1943.

Mosley was released in 1943, by which time the threat of a German invasion had all but passed. After the war Mosley attempted a political comeback and launched his "Union Movement," a political party advocating the unification of Europe into a single powerful state. The Union Movement never generated a great deal of support, and Mosley chose to leave Britain during the 1950s. He returned to run for Parliament in 1959 and in 1966 on an anti-immigration platform, but was soundly defeated in both races. In 1968 he published his memoir, *My Life*. Mosley died in France at his estate on December 3, 1980.

See also: British Union of Fascists.

Further Reading
Mosley, Oswald, Sir, *The Greater Britain* (London: BUF, 1932).

Mosley, Oswald, Sir, *Tomorrow We Live* (London: BUF, 1938).

Skidelsky, Robert, *Oswald Mosley* (New York: Holt, Rinehart & Winston, 1975).

Thurlow, Richard C., *Fascism in Britain: From Oswald Mosley's Blackshirts to the National Front* (London: I.B. Tauris, 1998).

MURDER OF GIACOMO MATTEOTTI The murder of Giacomo Matteotti in June 1924 was an international incident occurring during the first stages of Benito Mussolini's Fascist regime in Italy. Matteotti was an elected deputy in Italy's Chamber of Deputies (or parliament) representing the United Socialist Party. He was open in his denunciation of Mussolini's Fascists and particularly of their use of violence to achieve political power. After making two particularly fiery speeches against the Fascists in parliament he went missing. After a two-month search his body eventually was discovered in a ditch outside Rome; Matteotti had been brutally stabbed many times. Five members of the Fascist secret police were arrested and tried for the crime and three were found guilty, though they were granted amnesty by King Victor Emmanuel III. The international community was appalled and began to denounce the Mussolini regime, and Mussolini himself was quite worried his government might fall.

Having weathered the storm of public opinion after the murder, by 1925 Mussolini felt secure enough to make a famous speech in which he took sole responsibility for the "climate of violence" brought about by his regime, and maintained its necessity. Fascism, he said, would bring stability by any means necessary. This sounds like a possible admission of guilt by Mussolini for ordering the murder of Matteotti, but to this day Mussolini's direct involvement in the crime never has been proven.

Benito Mussolini was named prime minister by Italy's king Victor Emmanuel III on October 29, 1922. The early stages of his government were marked by inconsistent policies and some internal strain within the Fascist Party. Mussolini, however, had been able to convince the parliament to change the electoral laws so that any one party that won an election and achieved 25% or more of the total vote (this was a large number given the numerous political parties in Italy) would be granted two-thirds of the seats in parliament. These were the conditions created by the "Acerbo Law," passed in November 1923. This new electoral reality was in force for the elections of 1924. During those elections Mussolini directed his Blackshirts to use extraordinary means to generate votes for the Fascists. This could mean promises of grants to local politicians or it could mean simple intimidation in the streets. The result at the polls was that the Fascists gained a remarkable 65% of the total vote, giving them the right to two-thirds of the seats in parliament. It is from this point that the Italian Parliament increasingly became a simple Fascist Party congress as opposition parties gradually were suppressed and outlawed.

Immediately after the 1924 elections, however, one of the opposition politicians elected was the Socialist, Giacomo Matteotti. He had been elected in 1919 and 1921 previously, and had emerged as the leader of the United Socialist Party. He had also been hard at work on a book that exposed the violence and brutality of Mussolini and his Fascists. The book was published in early 1924 under the title *The Fascisti Exposed: A Year Under Fascist Domination*. He now had clearly defined himself as an implacable enemy of Mussolini's regime. That hostility would grow as he made two sensational speeches in parliament, laying out the violence and intimidation used by the Fascists to gain votes, and openly condemning them for their illegal violence against Socialists and any other opponents. His central point was that Mussolini's government was illegitimate because the elections were made invalid by Fascist thuggery. Mussolini was furious with him and publicly and privately suggested that Matteotti should be "gotten rid of," or that he should be "made to disappear secretly but finally."

Whether Fascist henchmen were acting on directives from Mussolini still is a controversial subject, but on June 10, 1924 Matteotti was seen to be seized on the streets of Rome and bundled into a car. He was stabbed multiple times with a woodworking knife and his body was dumped near Riano, 20 miles outside the city of Rome. After he was found to be missing, a massive manhunt was launched that lasted for two months. In August his body was found, setting off a wave of condemnations by the international press. Mussolini feared that his government might well collapse under the weight of popular outrage. There was no sizeable popular demonstration against the government, however. Even in the industrial towns—where Socialism was most powerful—the people were silent. Fascist violence and intimidation had terrified the people enough that they dared not take to the streets.

After a gradual period of political recovery there was an internal revolt within the Fascist Party itself during January 1925. A few of the party extremists looked to depose Mussolini using accusations of violence—including the Matteotti murder—against him. To this Mussolini responded by recalling parliament and making one of his most important speeches. In the speech he took personal responsibility for all the violence the Fascist regime had brought about. He made it clear that Italy needed stability, and that he and his Fascists would produce that stability by any means necessary. He challenged anyone else with the power and support to replace him to do so. No one did. The only two political liberals left in his government resigned, and Mussolini managed to make his position stronger than ever.

See also: Mussolini, Benito; National Fascist Party (PNF).

Further Reading
Bosworth, R. J. B., *Mussolini's Italy: Life Under the Fascist Dictatorship, 1915–1945* (New York: Penguin, 2006).
Canali, Mauro, "The Matteotti Murder and the Origins of Mussolini's Totalitarian Regime in Italy," *Journal of Modern Italian Studies* 14: 143–167 (2009).

MUSSOLINI, BENITO (1883–1945) Benito Mussolini was a leading journalist and political figure in Italy's Socialist Party and later the *Partito Nazionale Fascista* (National Fascist Party) (PNF), which he founded. As leader of the PNF he would become prime minister in 1922, and by 1925 he consolidated his position into a full dictatorship. He remained the head of government (known as the Duce) in Italy from October 1922 until he was officially deposed by Italy's king in July 1943. Mussolini was perhaps the most important single individual in the early development of Fascist ideology and was the first man to assume power in a fascist dictatorial regime.

Scholars have had difficulty reaching consensus as to a precise definition of fascism, and there have been numerous, quite complicated interpretations of the phenomenon as a wider political philosophy. Scholar R. J. B. Bosworth, however, suggests that defining "fascism" is as simple as identifying those movements that were attempting to imitate the policies, rhetoric, and government apparatus of Mussolini's regime in Italy. That regime would bring about a totalitarian system which eliminated all opposition political parties, eliminated all non-Fascist trade unions, limited personal freedoms, and glorified violence and war. During the 1930s Mussolini grew increasingly close to Adolf Hitler's Nazi regime in Germany and eventually, in 1940, Mussolini joined the Second World War on Hitler's side. Italian forces performed poorly during the war and in 1943 Mussolini was forcibly removed from power by his own party and the king of Italy, Victor Emmanuel III. After a brief period in prison, Mussolini was rescued by German commandoes and taken to Germany in safety. He was installed by Hitler in a small far northern area of Italy where he acted as the dictator of the Italian Social Republic. As Allied armies overwhelmed German forces, however, Mussolini went on the run and finally was captured by Italian Communist partisans. Mussolini and his mistress, Clara Patacci, were shot. Their bodies were transported to Milan the following day where their corpses were hung up in the city's main square as the crowds celebrated his demise.

Benito Amilcare Andrea Mussolini was born on July 29, 1883, in the town of Predappio in the province of Forli in northwest Italy. His mother, Rosa, was a deeply religious Catholic and a schoolteacher. His father, Alessandro, was a blacksmith by trade but a fervent follower of Socialism. He exposed young Benito to numerous Marxist ideas and writings and taught him about the famous Socialists and Anarchists of the Italian revolutionary tradition. As such, Benito grew up with a strong belief in Socialist ideals and in the need for violent revolution to bring about a better world. As a young man he excelled in his studies and was able to get work as a schoolmaster. He moved to Switzerland to avoid conscription and was able to work in the Socialist movement there, but then came home to Italy after several brushes with the police. He eventually served two years in the Italian military during 1905 and 1906 and when released returned to work as an elementary school teacher.

In these years and those that followed, Mussolini was a voracious reader of political philosophy. He was strongly influenced by Friedrich Nietzsche and the work of the Syndicalist, Georges Sorel, who advocated the use of the general strike to bring about revolutionary change, and who believed violence was admirable and purifying. Mussolini began writing his own political tracts and working in various Socialist newspapers around Italy, and thus earned a reputation for himself. He also got into trouble with his activism, however, once spending five months in prison for demonstrating against Italy's war of conquest in Libya. Eventually he would join the Italian Socialist Party and become the editor of its newspaper, *Avanti!* He was considered a rising star in the party, and the readership of the newspaper was expanded some five-fold under his editorship. Mussolini and the leadership of the party, however, clashed over the question of Italy's participation in the First World War.

After a period of indecision, the Italian Socialist Party declared its official position in opposition to the war. Initially Mussolini agreed. Over time, however, he increasingly came to advocate Italy's participation and eventually the conflict between he and the party's leadership became untenable. He was expelled from the party in 1914. He had already founded and edited his own newspaper called *Il Popolo d'Itlalia* (*People of Italy*). In it, he preached the need for Italy to help crush the reactionary Central powers of Germany and Austria, and carried an almost hysterically nationalist tone. Mussolini's own political ideas were evolving—he came to see war as a vehicle for erasing class differences, as it brought the nation together. After Italy's entry into the war on the side of the Allies (Britain, France, and Russia) in 1915, Mussolini would sign on for duty. He served in the trenches along the Austrian front during 1916 and 1917, but was wounded by an exploding grenade. Returning home from combat he continued to publish his newspaper, often receiving funding from large right-wing corporations and nationalist political supporters.

After the end of the war Mussolini's nationalist aspirations took on another dimension. With industry ramping down there was a wave of strikes and labor

union actions. Socialists began to be elected to the parliament in large numbers and soon held the majority of seats. Italian history remembers the period
of 1919 and 1920 as the *Biennio Rosso* or the "Red Two Years," and it generated fears that Italy was on its way to its own Socialist revolution. Mussolini
had come to reject Marxism, and decided to found his own nationalist political movement to combat the rise of Socialism. In 1919, he formed his initial
political group known as the *Fasci di Combattimento* (Fascist Combat Squads).
Many of the right-wing veterans returning from the war also were alarmed at
the expansion of Socialism and the chaos of the home front. They signed on
to Mussolini's groups—many of them keeping their military uniforms. The
Special Forces or *Arditi* wore a black shirt and breeches, and so the squadrons
of demobilized veterans under Mussolini earned the nickname the "Blackshirts." These squads moved into Italian towns that were under Socialist local
government and used violence and intimidation to terrorize the Socialist infrastructures. They smashed newspaper offices, burned labor exchanges, and
often kidnapped and brutally assaulted local Socialist politicians.

By 1921, Mussolini was anxious to enhance the organization of his Fascist
squads into a genuine political party. On November 9, 1921, Mussolini
founded the *Partito Nazionale Fascista* (National Fascist Party) (PNF). He
chose the ancient Roman symbol of the fasces for the party, a bundle of sticks
with a protruding axe blade. This symbolized the power of the totally unified
state, and the means of violent, decisive action. The party ran candidates in
the 1921 election, but won only 37 seats of 535. With increasing levels of violence and chaos, however, the Fascists were fast destabilizing Italian politics,
and the parliamentary system was faltering. Governments were named but
repeatedly fell because of a lack of support between parties. In October 1922,
Mussolini and his party took advantage of the situation by coordinating a
mass movement designed to seize the government by force—or at least to
threaten it. Tens of thousands of Mussolini's Fascist Blackshirts moved toward
Rome, some of them seizing telephone exchanges and railway stations along
the way. Under the pressure created by this "March on Rome," the king of
Italy decided the best way to bring stability was to offer the office of prime
minister to Mussolini himself.

In his early days in office, Mussolini was constrained by constitutionality
and could work only partially toward his goals of eliminating opposition parties. With elections set for 1924, however, the laws were changed by the Italian
parliament. The new electoral law (the Acerbo Law) stated that any party that
won a majority with more than 25% of the total vote would be entitled to
two-thirds of the seats in the Assembly. The Fascists (using intimidation at the
polls and street violence) were able to achieve the majority and took the two-
thirds majority. This gave Mussolini the power to pass any laws he liked. One

Socialist politician made two furious speeches denouncing the Fascist violence and intimidation and essentially declared the election results invalid. His name was Giacomo Matteotti, and days later he was went missing. His body later was discovered in a ditch outside Rome—with multiple stab wounds. Fascist henchmen had bundled him into a car and murdered him. The public was scandalized in Italy and worldwide, and for a period of weeks Mussolini was quite concerned he might be ousted, but eventually the emergency passed.

After 1925, Mussolini was able to eliminate all opposition parties, and close down all non-Fascist trade unions. He established detention camps for removing undesirable citizens and created a secret police unit known as the *Organizzazione per la Vigilanza e la Repressione dell'Antifascismo* (Organization for the Vigilance and Repression of Anti-Fascism) (OVRA), which was put in charge of internal security. Mussolini would also begin work on reorganizing Italian industry along the lines of a system known as the "Corporative" model. Here boards of experts, knowns as "Corporations," were formed from management, the Fascist Party, scientific experts, and labor. They would work together to manage and control entire sectors of industry. Individual companies would continue to be privately owned and managed and would compete just as they had, but the "Corporation" had the authority to implement policies across the entire industry and theoretically worked to maximize the benefits of industry for the entire nation. Mussolini received much credit from all over the world for this system which seemed to have solved the class war. But in working toward this new system, Mussolini also had outlawed trade unions and strikes. Although labor was represented on the Corporations, workers enjoyed little to no power at all.

In 1935, Mussolini launched a large-scale invasion of the Empire of Ethiopia, then known as Abyssinia. Abyssinia was a member of the League of Nations and the move was quite controversial. After faltering initially, the Italian military used poison gas on the Abyssinians and attained victory after about seven months of fighting. The Italians went on to occupy and colonize the region, which Mussolini celebrated as a returning to the days of the glorious Roman Empire. Other nations balked at this, however, and though not willing to intervene militarily, did levy economic sanctions on Italy. This prompted Mussolini to shift his economic policy toward the maximization of autarky and to move closer to Nazi Germany for alliance.

Through the 1930s Mussolini and Hitler grew closer. In 1938 Mussolini, who had earlier committed Italy to Austria's independence, withdrew that commitment. He allowed Hitler to annex Austria into the German nation without any objection. In the following year, Mussolini signed a military/diplomatic pact of alliance known as the "Pact of Steel," which gave Hitler the assurances he wanted for the invasion of Poland. With Mussolini's partnership, the

German Führer felt certain that if Germany invaded Poland no other nation would dare intervene. This proved to be a mistake, and after the invasion both Britain and France declared war on Germany. Italy, however, did not join the war initially. Mussolini did not think that Italy was ready for such a wide conflict. By the summer of 1940, however, after Hitler had swept through Europe, dismantling France, Mussolini felt he could now join the war safely. The Italians fought to take territory in the south of France, in Greece, and against the British in North Africa. Despite Mussolini's bluster and bragging about the Italian war machine, the Italians performed dismally on the battlefield. Nazi troops were required to assist the Italians nearly everywhere they fought.

By the summer of 1943, Allied troops had taken North Africa and were moving up the Italian peninsula toward Rome. During July the Grand Council of Fascism (the highest Fascist authority outside of Mussolini himself) met to review the situation. With the explanation of the Allied troop movements and the threat to the Roman capital, the members of the Council voted to remove Mussolini from his position and give full powers to the Italian king. Mussolini was arrested, and put in an Alpine mountain resort that was converted to a jail to ensure his safekeeping. Later, the Italian government switched sides, joining the Allies against Hitler. Adolf Hitler, however, planned a raid on the Italian jail and his special forces were able to break in and liberate Mussolini, bringing him back to Germany for safety. Hitler felt that Italy could not be lost, and sent a large army into Italy from the north. The north of Italy then was established as the Italian Social Republic, governed from the small city of Salo, with Mussolini acting as its dictator.

During 1944, however, the Allies continued to move northward up the Italian peninsula meeting and pushing back the German troops. By 1945, the north was overrun and Mussolini was forced to attempt to escape into neutral Switzerland. He was captured, however, by Italian Communist partisans. He was traveling with a group of officials from his Salo government and his mistress, Clara Patacci. The partisans made the decision to execute the entire group, including Mussolini, and shot them all in a small town called Dongo near Lake Como on April 28, 1945. The next day their bodies were driven to the city of Milan—where Mussolini had once founded his movement—and their corpses were hung upside down. The great Piazza filled with people who spat at the corpses, ripped their clothing, and rejoiced that the dictator was finally dead. Recent research suggests that a British secret agent sent by Winston Churchill to the Italian partisans may have been the key decision maker in the execution of Mussolini. The research suggests that Mussolini was carrying with him the correspondence between Mussolini and Churchill that would have been humiliating for the British leader if it was exposed. The agent insisted that Mussolini be shot, and then destroyed the evidence.

Although there are eyewitnesses whose testimony agrees with this new interpretation, this theory remains controversial. Today Mussolini's remains lie in
the family crypt at Predappio, where the tomb remains a site of pilgrimage for
extreme-right visitors.

See also: *Biennio Rosso*; Blackshirts; Corporatism (Corporative State); March
on Rome; Murder of Giacomo Matteotti; Organization for the Vigilance and
Repression of Anti-Fascism (OVRA); Pact of Steel; *National Fascist Party*
(PNF).

Further Reading

Bosworth, R.J.B., *Mussolini* (New York: Oxford University Press, 2002).
Bosworth, R.J.B., *Mussolini's Italy: Life Under the Fascist Dictatorship, 1915–1945*
    (New York: Penguin, 2006).
Finaldi, Giuseppe, *Mussolini and Italian Fascism* (Harlow, UK: Pearson, 2008).
Smith, Denis Mack, *Mussolini: A Biography* (New York: Vintage, 1983).

NATIONAL FASCIST PARTY (PNF) *(PARTITO NAZIONALE FAS-
CISTA)*   The *Partito Nazionale Fascista* (PNF) (National Fascist Party) of
Italy was the political party founded by Benito Mussolini in November 1921,
and was the governing party of Italy from 1922 until 1943. Mussolini had
formed an informal group of paramilitary bands based in Milan in 1919.
These groups were organized to fight back against the expansion of Socialism
and did so through the use of violence and intimidation. The formation of
the PNF represented Mussolini's effort to transform his paramilitaries into
a formal political party that would run candidates in the Italian elections. The
PNF organization was instrumental in coordinating the March on Rome
in October 1922, which helped pressure the Italian king into appointing
Mussolini as prime minister. The PNF also acted as the principal governing
instrument through which Mussolini ruled the country. After eliminating
all other political parties, the Italian Parliament reverted to a Fascist Party
congress with only PNF representatives present. Besides Mussolini's personal
authority, the highest authority in the PNF and the Italian government was
the Grand Council of Fascism, which controlled and regulated policy.

The PNF was founded on November 9, 1921, by Benito Mussolini and
immediately absorbed the corps of paramilitary groups known as the Blackshirts and their group leadership. The symbols of the party chosen by Mussolini were the bundled fasces with a protruding axe blade. This image was
superimposed upon the green, white, and red tricolor of the Italian flag. The
party also published a regular newspaper called *Il Popolo D'Italia* (*People of
Italy*) which ran until Mussolini was deposed in 1943.

The party ran candidates in the Italian elections in 1921 and polled approximately 19% of the national vote, but only won 37 seats out of 535 in the Italian Parliament. Mussolini was among the elected deputies. After the political chaos and violence of the following months, and the March on Rome in October 1922, King Victor Emmanuel III named Mussolini prime minister. By 1924, there were new elections but the Fascists had been able to change the election laws. The new "Acerbo Law" said that any party that won a majority with more than 25% of the total vote would be given two-thirds of all the seats in Parliament. The PNF was able to accomplish this and became the majority party in Italy. After this Mussolini was able to consolidate his power absolutely. Elections in 1929 and 1934 were merely public relations measures, as the PNF ran unopposed and won 535 of 535 seats in both elections.

In July of 1943, with the Allied armies advancing up the Italian peninsula from the south, the Grand Council of Fascism—the party's highest collective authority—voted to depose Mussolini and to turn over all political power to the king. Mussolini attempted to meet with the king and instead was arrested and imprisoned. The PNF officially was dismantled on July 27, 1943, and was reestablished later as the Republican Fascist Party. The party's leaders attempted to dissociate themselves from the dictatorship of Mussolini, who had taken Italy to war. This was in view of the advancing Allied armies—which Italy hoped would be more lenient given its rejection of Mussolini and dictatorship. Although other versions of fascist political groups have developed in Italy, the PNF never has been formally reestablished.

See also: Balbo, Italo; Blackshirts; Corporatism (Corporate State); Fasces; March on Rome; Mussolini, Benito; Organization for the Vigilance and Repression of Anti-Fascism (OVRA).

Further Reading

Bosworth, R. J. B., *Mussolini's Italy: Life Under the Fascist Dictatorship, 1915–1945* (New York: Penguin, 2006).

Germino, D. L., *The Italian Fascist Party in Power: A Study in Totalitarian Rule* (Baton Rouge: Louisiana State University Press, 1990).

Morgan, P., *Italian Fascism 1919–1945* (New York: St. Martin's Press, 1995).

NATIONAL SOCIALIST GERMAN WORKERS' PARTY (NAZI PARTY) (*NATIONALSOZIALISTISCHE DEUTSCHE ARBEITERPARTEI*)

The National Socialist German Workers' Party (*Nationalsozialistische Deutsche Arbeiterpartei*) (NSDAP), also called the "Nazi" Party, was the principal organizing structure though which Adolf Hitler and his National

Socialist followers created their revolutionary identity, entered German politics, gained power, and governed the German nation. The party initially was founded as the German Workers' Party (*Deutsche Arbeiterpartei*) (DAP) in early 1919. Its name was changed to the National Socialist German Workers' Party and it was reestablished on February 24, 1920. The party's general objectives attracted a young Adolf Hitler to join its ranks in September of 1919. Under Hitler's influence the party more clearly formed its political program, issuing a list of "25 Points."

During 1921 Adolf Hitler emerged as the party's clear and unquestioned leader, and from this point he provided the principal individual influence defining the party's objectives, structure, and activities. Top party members attempted to seize government in Munich during 1923 (the Beer Hall Putsch). The attempt was crushed by local troops and police, however, and Hitler was arrested. Despite this, the party ran in elections three times during the 1920s; however, it never tallied any significant results. After the 1929 stock market crash and the coming of the Great Depression, the Nazi Party began to win significant numbers of seats—even achieving a majority status by July of 1932. After Hitler was appointed chancellor in 1933, he outlawed opposition parties and the Nazi Party became the single political apparatus of the state. The German Parliament (*Reichstag*) was now merely a Nazi Party congress. The Nazi Party evolved a complex relationship to the organs of state government, retaining power over organizations including the SA (paramilitary force) and the SS (the elite state security force). At the end of World War II the Nazi Party was dissolved and outlawed.

The Nazi Party initially emerged from the chaotic political climate in Germany immediately following the First World War. A Communist uprising raged during 1918 and early 1919, and right-wing nationalists—in the form of the paramilitary *Freikorps* ("Free Corps")—fought against it, seeking to vanquish Marxism from Germany. The political far right also generally hoped to abolish the liberal-democratic system in place under the new Weimar Republic. Numerous political organizations espousing such claims appeared, including the German Workers' Party which was established by Anton Drexler on January 5, 1919. The party advocated state intervention to help the middle classes and the importance of preserving and strengthening the German (or Aryan) racial community. It fiercely condemned Communists and Jews.

The German Workers' Party was quite small, having only approximately 60 members by September 1919 when the German military sent a young Adolf Hitler to spy on it. Hitler allegedly engaged in a serious and complex political argument with one of the DAP members, and so impressed the party leadership that he was offered a place in the DAP soon after. Hitler became the party's 55th member, though his membership number was 555. The party did this to convince others of its size and importance. In February 1920 the DAP became the National Socialist German Workers' Party and Hitler soon emerged as the party's top orator. Hitler's almost hysterical speeches could bring an audience to its feet and whip it into a passionate fury. Because of this, and undoubtedly Hitler's fanatic belief in the NSDAP's agenda, he was able to position himself as the party's supreme leader. He was elected party chairman on July 28, 1921, and held the top party position until his death in April 1945.

The party's program remained consistent from its earliest years. It advocated self-sufficiency for Germany economically and politically. It emphasized the need for colonies for the expansion of the vital German race; its earlier programs pressed for the recovery of Germany's lost overseas colonies, but later Hitler insisted that Germany must carve out its colonial territory in Eastern Europe. The party philosophy equated the German racial community with the German political state and stressed that non-Aryans should not enjoy political participation or the rights of German citizens. The party was fanatically anti-Marxist and stood for the elimination of Socialism and Communism from the country. Connected to the principles of racial purity, the Nazi Party insisted that Jews were biologically separate and could not be assimilated into the German nation. Further, party rhetoric asserted that Jews were the root cause of most of Germany's serious problems—including economic, social, and even moral problems. The Nazi Party also was anti-democratic and advocated a single-party dictatorship under the leadership of Adolf Hitler who, they believed, embodied the will of the German people.

To broadcast this political program and promote the Nazi message, the Nazi Party produced a newspaper called the *Volkisher Beobachter* ("*Volkish* Observer") which was published from 1920 to May 1945. One Nazi Party official, Julius Streicher, published a second newspaper known as *Der Sturmer* ("The Attacker"), which was the chief outlet for Nazi anti-Semitic propaganda. It was a tabloid-style publication with grotesque cartoons and sensationalist headlines that attacked Jews, monarchists, capitalism, and Marxists of all hues. Both newspapers glorified Hitler as the savior of the nation.

Hitler also was an important influence in the party's use of symbols and political ceremony. He helped make the decision to use a black swastika in a white disc superimposed on a red flag. These were the colors of the old *Kaiserreich*, but with distinctly modern imagery. Later, in 1929, Horst Wessel—a Nazi Party member and leader of an SA division in Berlin—was killed by a Communist Party member. Hitler and his head of propaganda, Joseph Goebbels, created a song about the man (the "Horst Wessel Song") and it emerged as the Nazi Party anthem from 1930 until the party's dissolution in 1945. After Hitler became chancellor, he also constructed a massive parade ground at the city of Nuremburg which became the location for the annual Nazi Party rallies. The mass rallies usually were used for their awe-inspiring propaganda value and to make major announcements in political policy.

The Nazi Party ran candidates in six legitimate German elections. In 1924, with Hitler in jail after the Beer Hall Putsch, the party earned 6.5% of the popular vote and won 32 seats. The party declined after Hitler's release from prison, however, gaining only 3% of the vote in December 1924 and 2.6% in 1928. After the Great Depression began, however, the Nazi Party enjoyed a tremendous surge in popularity. In 1930 the party gained 107 seats in the *Reichstag*, in July 1932 it garnered 230 seats, and in November 1932 it won 196 seats. When Hitler was appointed chancellor in January 1933, the Nazis enjoyed a representation comparable with that of the German Communists.

During the years of the Hitler regime, after eliminating all opposition parties, the Nazi Party was the only political party in the nation and it often was necessary to belong to the party to be permitted to hold any prominent position in business, academia, or cultural life—for positions in government it was essential. Nazi Party officials often were placed in positions that enabled them to guide the activities of (and to spy upon) non-party organizations. Party members were placed on the boards of large businesses, in the decision-making boards of the Labor Front, and on the boards of museums, orchestras, and universities. This ensured the influence of Nazi ideology on all walks of life. The party remained in place during the years of the Second World War and often came into conflict with the traditional German military forces—the *Vermacht*—as military branches of the party such as the SS vied for ultimate authority in theaters of war.

After the conclusion of the Second World War, the Nazi Party was formally dissolved and outlawed by the Allied Powers as part of the process of "de-Nazification." The most prominent surviving party leaders were tried and sentenced for war crimes and crimes against humanity at the Nuremburg Trials. Though some neo-Nazi groups have attempted to reestablish the Nazis' racist policies, no official effort has succeeded in reestablishing the party.

See also: Anti-Semitism; Beer Hall Putsch; Goering, Hermann; Hess, Rudolf; Hitler, Adolf; *Mein Kampf*; Night of the Long Knives; Nuremburg Laws; *Schutzstaffel* (SS); *Sturmabteilung* (SA).

Further Reading

McDonough, Frank, *Hitler and the Rise of the Nazi Party* (New York: Pearson Longman, 2003).

Orlow, Dietrich, *The History of the Nazi Party* (Pittsburgh: University of Pittsburgh Press, 1969).

Shirer, William L., *The Rise and Fall of the Third Reich* (New York: Fawcett Crest, 1960).

NIGHT OF THE LONG KNIVES   The "Night of the Long Knives" is the term that developed to describe a series of political murders carried out by Adolf Hitler's Nazi regime during the period from June 30 to July 2, 1934. The Nazis murdered a group of officials from both the German government and the Nazi Party who either contested the regime or had fundamental disagreements with Hitler about the Nazi vision of Germany's future. The most prominent men murdered during this political purge were Kurt Von Schleicher, a conservative politician who had once been Germany's chancellor; Gregor Strasser, a member of the Nazi Party who envisioned a more socialist future for Germany; and Ernst Rohm, the leader of the Nazi *Sturmabteilung* (SA), the paramilitary force also known as the "Brownshirts." Although the international community was scandalized by this series of murders, the murders served to strengthen Hitler's position at home, particularly with the German military leadership.

Hitler was appointed chancellor in January 1933. In the aftermath of the *Reichstag* Fire, he was able to secure nearly absolute power. By 1934, Hitler had established the legal basis to eliminate all opposition political parties, and Germany had become a single-party state. There were areas where Hitler lacked legal power, however. The office of the president remained and at the time was occupied by Paul von Hindenburg; that office held power over Germany's armed forces. The armed forces—particularly the army—were extremely independent, and Hitler intended to find strategies to gain increased control over them. Hitler also recognized that the army leadership feared and despised the Nazi SA—the uniformed paramilitary forces used by the Nazis for street violence and intimidation. The army leadership, with some justification, saw the SA as preparing to replace the army as the core of Germany's national defense. Hitler understood that he needed the army for his dreams of future conquests and that he could help bring the army further under his power by eliminating the threat posed by the SA.

Hitler also had difficulty within his own Nazi Party. There remained a faction of the more "leftist" Nazis that envisioned a "second revolution" to follow Hitler's rise to power. This faction—led by Nazi political theorist Gregor Strasser—believed that after Hitler's successful "Nationalistic" revolution, there should follow a program to confiscate wealth from the nation's wealthy elite (particularly Jews) and then to redistribute it to the country's working classes. Open enemies of the capitalist system, the faction's vision also included the nationalization of vital industries. This agenda would alienate the leaders of Germany's industrial community whom Hitler needed to make Germany the world's most powerful nation. Therefore Hitler looked for opportunities to undermine or eliminate this "leftist" faction.

A further concern for Hitler within the Nazi Party was the leadership of the SA. During the 1920s and early 1930s, the SA had attacked Communists and Socialists in open street violence. The SA had smashed and burned left-wing newspaper offices and Jewish businesses, and had broken up political rallies of the leftist parties. The SA's constant initiation of violence and street battles provided the chaos and destabilization necessary to force the leaders of the German government to ask Hitler to become chancellor. Once Hitler actually was in power and had eliminated the political opposition, however, there remained only a limited role for the SA. With no opposition party to attack, the SA began to assault ordinary citizens, the police, and foreign visitors (even foreign diplomats). The commander of the SA, Ernst Rohm, was a veteran of the German army and the early days of the Nazi movement. He had worked to change the organization of the SA during the early 1930s making its "groups" accountable only to Rohm and then to Hitler. Rohm—with his virtually independent SA—was a prominent member of the leftist faction of the party along with Strasser.

Hitler also despised the so-called "conservative" elements of his government. When taking power, Hitler had been forced to include several conservative politicians in his government, including the former chancellor Franz von Papen, who became vice chancellor under Hitler. A number of such conservatives—who had no sympathy at all for Nazism—supported Papen and hoped for the day when Hitler's government would fall, and Papen could once again assume the chancellorship. With this they hoped that they could reestablish the full Liberal Democratic system. Hitler (correctly) saw such politicians in his government as enemies working for the downfall of the Nazi system.

Assessing this array of dilemmas, Hitler and his inner circle made the decision to solve them by eliminating the key individuals associated with those problems. In the early morning of June 30, 1934, Hitler and his close associates (including Hermann Goering, Rudolf Hess, Heinrich Himmler, and Reinhard Heydrich) flew to Munich. There had been a mass demonstration and street rioting by the SA on the evening before with several violent incidents. Hitler confronted the head of the Munich branch of the SA, relieved him, and then had him shot. The group then moved to a hotel where Ernst Rohm and several of his associates were staying and arrested them. Rohm was held for more than 24 hours before Hitler finally gave the order for Gestapo agents to execute him. Rohm was given the opportunity to shoot himself but refused, and so he was executed by Nazi secret police.

The purge continued throughout the country as SS and Gestapo agents arrested, imprisoned, and executed numerous members of the SA and of the government. Conservative followers of von Papen were shot, including General von Schleicher and his wife. Franz von Papen himself was arrested and imprisoned, but he later was released. The experience so terrified him that he never criticized the Nazi regime again, and became an enthusiastic diplomat for the Third Reich. Gregor Strasser and his brother Otto were shot. Leaders of the Catholic Action group were shot as were leaders of the Catholic Centre political party. In the end, nearly 100 people were arrested and executed, although there might have been many more. The Nazis kept few records of the incident and many records were destroyed deliberately.

Hitler justified his actions to the public by announcing there had been a plot on his life led by Ernst Rohm and others. As such, the German public's reaction was muted. It did have the effect of strengthening the relationship between Hitler's Nazi government and the German army, which was grateful for the elimination of the SA as a threat to its position. In time, all German soldiers took a personal oath to support Adolf Hitler. Even the very elderly President Hindenburg applauded the move, congratulating Hitler for "nipping treason in the bud."

See also: Hitler, Adolf; National Socialist German Workers' Party (Nazi Party); *Sturmabteilung* (SA).

Further Reading

Evans, Richard J., *The Third Reich in Power, 1933–1939* (New York: Penguin, 2005).

Gallo, Max, *Night of the Long Knives,* translated by Lily Emmet (New York: Harper & Row, 1972).

Kershaw, Ian, *Hitler 1889–1936: Hubris* (New York: W. W. Norton, 1998).

NUREMBURG LAWS   The "Nuremburg Laws" were two acts of legislation passed by the German government in September 1935 that expanded and intensified the existing persecution of Jews in Germany. Nazi ideology had been fanatically anti-Semitic from its origins and the Nazi state had taken actions to limit the rights of Jews since its establishment by Adolf Hitler in 1933. By 1935, however, there remained questions as to who actually qualified as being Jewish. There also were a number of areas of German life in which Jews had the legal freedom to mix with people considered racially "Aryan." These areas were addressed in the Nuremburg Laws; after their enactment, conditions for Jews in Germany deteriorated steadily. One key stipulation of the Nuremburg Laws was that which revoked Jews' German citizenship and gave them the legal status of "state subjects," with diminished legal rights.

From the earliest days of the Hitler regime in Germany, the Nazi Party pursued legal strategies to institutionalize their group's fanatical prejudice against and hatred of Jews. The first of these official state actions against Jews—the state "Boycott of Jewish Businesses"—was launched on April 1, 1933. Only a week later, on April 7, the government passed the "Law for the Restoration of the Professional Civil Service," which removed Jews from their positions in Germany's civil bureaucracy and banned them from holding such positions in the future. These and other measures served to gradually remove Jews from government, business leadership, and cultural life.

The most fanatical elements of the Nazi Party—known as the *Alte Kampfers* ("old fighters")—however, insisted that Jews still enjoyed too many rights and still played too great a role in German society. Their hysterical anti-Semitism convinced them that this meant that Jews were still able to corrode and corrupt German society from within. Because of this tension, by 1935 the Nazi organizations such as the *Sturmabteilung* (SA) began launching unofficial violent attacks on Jews. They formed barriers preventing consumers from entering Jewish businesses, they spray-painted the windows of Jewish businesses with hostile graffiti, and they bullied and intimidated Jews on the streets.

One member of the Nazi government spoke out about the negative effects of this constant campaign of disorganized violence against Jews. Hjalmar Schacht was the minster of economics in Hitler's government at the time, and was responsible for growing the German economy and finding the economic wherewithal to fund a giant program of rearmament. Schacht spoke out, saying that Jews ran several important businesses, had much to contribute to building the economy, and that this contribution was being undermined as Jewish businesses were wrecked or driven under. Schacht asserted that an organized, state-sponsored, and legal program must be put in place to accomplish the state's anti-Semitic goals. Such a legally based approach would remove rights from Jews without undermining the German economy in the short term. Based on Schacht's ideas, calls within the Nazi Party then increased for tough laws to be issued—especially those preventing biological mixing between Jews and Germans, which the Nazis believed contributed to "racial defilement."

Hitler's inner circle went to work on drafting such laws. As this was proceeding, however, Hitler experienced a public relations difficulty. The great party rally held every year at Nuremburg was scheduled for September 15. Hitler had been planning to give a tough speech on foreign policy, supporting Mussolini's invasion of Abyssinia, but at the last minute he was advised against it. He therefore found himself in need of a major announcement for the rally. He decided that the racial laws being discussed would make a dramatic announcement and therefore demanded they be accelerated to be ready for the rally. At the rally the German *Reichstag* met in formal assembly, and it was here that the Nuremburg Laws were announced, ratified, and made German law.

The first of the so-called Nuremburg Laws was the "Law for the Protection of German Blood and Honor," backdated to September 5, 1935. Its provisions included the following.

1. Marriages between Jews and citizens of "German blood" were forbidden.
2. Any such marriages, even if concluded abroad, were declared invalid.
3. Extramarital sexual relations between Jews and those of German blood were forbidden.
4. Jews were forbidden to employ Germans under the age of 45 as domestic workers.
5. Jews were forbidden to display the German flag or national colors.
6. The punishments for violations of the marriage or sex stipulations were imprisonment and hard labor.

The second of the Nuremburg Laws was the "Reich Citizenship Law." This law stipulated the following.

1. It provided legal definition for who was considered a Jew versus those considered German citizens.
2. Those people with four grandparents or three grandparents of Jewish descent were considered Jews outright. Those with two grandparents of Jewish descent and two of German descent were considered Jewish if they practiced the Jewish religious faith, but were considered German if they did not. Those with three or more German grandparents were considered German citizens.
3. Those of Jewish extraction (as determined by the criteria above) now had their legal status changed to *Staatsangehörige* or "state subjects." This was a status other than citizen or *Reichsburger*. Thus, by definition, Jews were stripped of their citizenship and were not entitled to the same legal rights as German citizens.

The passage of the Nuremburg Laws did placate the most anti-Semitic elements of the Nazi Party and the rash of disorganized violence against Jews declined. Although most of the German public decried the wild and chaotic violence, Germans generally were pleased with the organized institutional measures. This new legal environment created a permanent and official basis for removing Jews from German life and diminishing their access to the nation's resources. It also made it infinitely easier to pass further measures against Jews—with no legal status as citizens, they could hardly argue for the protection of their civic rights.

See also: Anti-Semitism; Hitler, Adolf; Holocaust; Racial Hygiene.

Further Reading

Evans, Richard J., *The Third Reich in Power, 1933–1939* (New York: Penguin, 2005).

Moeller, Robert G., *The Nazi State and German Society: A Brief History with Documents* (Boston: Bedford/St. Martin's, 2009).

Noakes, Jeremy and Geoffrey Pridham (eds.), "The Nuremburg Laws," in *Documents on Nazism, 1919–1945* (London: Jonathan Cape: 1974), 460–463.

ORGANIZATION FOR THE VIGILANCE AND REPRESSION OF ANTI-FASCISM (OVRA) (*ORGANIZZAZIONE PER LA VIGILANZA E LA REPRESSIONE DELL'ANTIFASCISMO*)

The Organization for the Vigilance and Repression of Anti-Fascism (*Organizzazione per la Vigilanza e la Repressione dell'Antifascismo*) (OVRA) was Mussolini's secret police organization. It chiefly was used to spy on the Italian public to identify anti-Fascist elements and purge them from Italian society. The OVRA used telephone taps and human spies in their efforts to track and prove anti-Fascist tendencies. Headed by Arturo Bocchini, OVRA eventually compiled a massive repository of files and dossiers on thousands of suspected subversives. Its practices of internal espionage, interrogation, torture, and collection of intelligence stood as models for the secret police organizations in other fascist regimes. The Nazi Gestapo, for instance, maintained close relations with OVRA and they often worked in collaboration.

In October 1926, an Italian Anarchist named Anteo Zamboni attempted to assassinate Italy's dictator, Benito Mussolini. Zamboni's shots missed their mark and he immediately was grabbed by Fascist Blackshirts and hanged. Mussolini was badly shaken by the incident and turned his fury upon the opponents of his regime by passing a succession of legislation cracking down on any political opposition. He was able to outlaw opposing political parties, and create provisions for special court tribunals to try so called "enemies of the state." The death penalty also was made a possible punishment for political dissidents.

As part of this rash of new legislation, provisions were passed creating a new organ of the government to identify and eliminate political opposition. A "Department of Political Police" was established with this brief, though this department was to remain clandestine—the Italian public was not officially made aware of its existence until 1930, when it was mentioned in articles in the official Fascist state news publications. The "Department of Political Police," would eventually adopt the name of the Organization for the Vigilance and Repression of Anti-Fascism. The man put in charge of the organization was Arturo Bocchini, who was a long-time veteran of the police force. He had been a Fascist supporter from the beginning of Mussolini's regime and had served as police prefect in Brescia, Bologna, and Genoa.

Bocchini's organization used espionage within Italy to root out the underground leaders of the opposition political parties, particularly the Socialists and Communists. Among the most famous figures arrested by OVRA was Communist intellectual Antonio Gramsci, who languished in Fascist prisons until he was released for health reasons. Gramsci died in a Roman hospital in 1937. Gramsci and most of the other supposedly anti-Fascist elements were confined on remote Mediterranean islands that were maintained as prisons by the OVRA. The most significant of these was the island of Ustica, located off the north coast of Sicily. Political opponents, homosexuals, chronic criminals, and others were removed from Italian society and isolated on the island in prisons resembling concentration camps. It is estimated that nearly 15,000 people were sentenced to *confino* in this manner (Finaldi, 58).

Bocchini's activities, however, could stretch beyond those who posed genuine political threats. The spy activities are reported to have become so wide ranging that at one point Bocchini was monitoring the telephone activity of Mussolini himself. Bocchini died of a stroke very soon after the Italians joined the Second World War on the side of Nazi Germany. As that war progressed, however, OVRA contributed to the war effort by handling, interrogating, and isolating Yugoslavian prisoners of war.

After the removal of Mussolini in 1943, the Italian government officially disbanded OVRA. After the war, however, many of its agents and its entire volume of secret information were appropriated by the newly formed intelligence services of the Italian Republic.

See also: Gestapo; Mussolini, Benito.

Further Reading

Bosworth, R. J. B., *Mussolini's Italy: Life Under the Fascist Dictatorship, 1915–1945* (New York: Penguin, 2006).

Finaldi, Giuseppe, *Mussolini and Italian Fascism* (Harlow, UK: Pearson, 2008).

PACT OF STEEL   The "Pact of Steel" is the public name given to a diplomatic treaty of alliance between Nazi Germany and Fascist Italy, which was signed on May 22, 1939. The formal title of the treaty is the "Pact of Friendship and Alliance Between Germany and Italy," but Benito Mussolini used the title "Pact of Steel" for propaganda purposes. Mussolini had intended to use the title "Pact of Blood" but became convinced this was problematic given notions of racial differences between the two peoples. Made up of seven specific articles, the treaty served to strongly ally the two nations and to produce new levels of coordination in the following four areas.

1. The coordination of military activities and policies.
2. The coordination of foreign policy between the two governments.
3. The coordination of military aid—if war was declared on either nation the other was obligated to come to its military assistance.
4. The coordination of press and propaganda particularly as related to diplomatic issues and relations with foreign governments.

Originally, the treaty had been intended to include the Empire of Japan, but the Japanese government wanted the treaty to be oriented toward defense against the Soviet Union. Italy and Germany were more focused on orienting the treaty against the European democracies of Britain and France. As such, their alliance with Japan would be formalized in a subsequent treaty, the Tri-Partite Pact, signed in September 1940. The signatories of the Pact of Steel were the German foreign minister Joachim von Ribbentrop and the Italian foreign minister Galeazzo Ciano. The text stipulated that the treaty's duration was 10 years, expiring in May 1949.

The formation of the Pact of Steel was conceived by Adolf Hitler as he prepared for further expansion in central Europe. Hitler had rearmed Germany into a formidable military force, violating the Treaty of Versailles' extreme limits on the size of the German military. He sent his military troops into the Rhineland, also in violation the Versailles Treaty. Hitler then lent significant assistance to Francisco Franco's Nationalist cause in the Spanish Civil War, violating the agreement of nonintervention reached with Britain and France. In 1938, Hitler annexed Austria and made it part of the German Reich. Later in 1938 he annexed the Sudetenland area of Czechoslovakia, and finally proceeded to claim the rest of that nation through military occupation. All Europe by this time was nervous about falling back into war. It had become clear to Hitler that a further expansion he intended to launch in Poland might trigger that war. To intimidate the democracies (chiefly France and Britain) he decided to make a formal and public military alliance with Mussolini's Italy. This would make the democracies less willing to intervene militarily if Germany invaded Poland, as they would have to fight two nations and not just one. This was, in essence, the motivation for the Pact of Steel.

The Italians, however, were not prepared for war. Italy's foreign minister Ciano was especially concerned about Italy's lack of modern weaponry. The German diplomats, however, assured him (falsely) that this treaty had no relevance to Poland. Ribbentrop told Italian diplomats that "a strong and independent Poland constitutes a vital necessity for Germany," and that Germans "understand very well that Warsaw is not Prague." With such assurances, Mussolini and Ciano agreed to the creation of the alliance, and alarmingly left all of the drafting of its language to the German diplomats. Italy had said it would not be ready for war until 1943, and the German contingent explained that this was in line with Germany's schedule.

In the end, Germany invaded Poland in September 1939 triggering the Second World War. Italy indeed was not ready and did not yet enter the conflict. That nation would enter the war on the side of Germany and Japan in 1940, but by 1943 Italy had been overcome by the Allies and had changed sides. As a direct result of this, the Pact of Steel formally was dissolved in September 1943.

See also: Ciano, Count Gian Galeazzo; Hitler, Adolf; Mussolini, Benito.

Further Reading

Overy, Richard, *The Origins of the Second World War* (New York: Longman, 1998).

Taylor, A. J. P., *The Origins of the Second World War*. New York: Athenaeum, 1962).

Toscano, Mario, *The Origins of the Pact of Steel* (Baltimore: Johns Hopkins Press, 1968).

PARIS PEACE CONFERENCE   The Paris Peace Conference was the assembly organized by the victorious countries of the Frist World War to determine the conditions for peace and future relations with the defeated Central Powers. The Conference lasted from January 1919 to January 1920. Although there were several other participants, the principal decisions of the conference were made by a group of the four heads of government from the largest Allied powers. These included President Woodrow Wilson of the United States, Prime Minister David Lloyd-George of Great Britain, Prime Minister Georges Clemenceau of France, and Prime Minister Vittorio Orlando from Italy. The chief accomplishments of the conference included the establishment of the League of Nations, the reconfiguration of national boundaries within Europe and the Middle East, the redistribution of imperial territories, and the creation of individual peace treaties which imposed conditions on the defeated nations. Several of the decisions of the conference concerning Italy, Austria, and especially Germany, caused severe national humiliation within those countries and contributed to the specific Nationalist objectives of their respective fascist movements.

On January 8, 1919, American president Woodrow Wilson gave a speech in which he listed a group of reasons he believed had contributed to the start of the Great War and included a number of remedial policies that he believed would prevent such a conflict from ever happening again. His list of items became known as the "Fourteen Points," and several of its principles became influential guiding policies of the subsequent Paris Peace Conference. Wilson traveled to Paris to be directly involved in the negotiations, marking the first time a U.S. president traveled overseas for such an extended period. In Europe, popular opinion generally was positive and Wilson attained something like celebrity status. European politicians, however, were less enthusiastic and viewed the Fourteen Points with some skepticism.

Among the Fourteen Points were included the following assertions, which became the guiding principles of the conference.

- There should be an organ of world government—an "Association of Nations" through which diplomatic crises could be managed collectively.
- There should be no more secret diplomacy or treaties.
- Territorial disputes and nationalist tensions should be resolved through the "self determination of peoples."
- All nations should work together to reduce their armaments.
- There should be freedom of navigation on the open seas.

There also were a number of recommendations concerning specific national boundaries and economic issues. The British flatly rejected the issue of freedom of the seas and it played no meaningful role in the negotiations at Paris.

In the early days of the conference a council of 10 formed for key discussions and decision making, but this proved cumbersome and ineffective. By March, the representatives of the victorious powers had settled on a council of the four heads of government with a few assistants. This group became known in the press as the "Big 4." Although this council—Wilson, Lloyd-George, Clemenceau, and Orlando—generally was acknowledged to be the chief organ of decision making it was, in reality, a council of three. Orlando spoke very little English and had difficulty in participating or making his views known. Later, arguments over Italian territorial issues compelled him and his Italian delegation to walk out of the talks.

The first major accomplishment of the conference was the agreement to establish a "League of Nations" in accordance with Wilson's recommendation. A "Covenant" was drawn up and the arrangements were made for the inauguration of this diplomatic institution. It would begin operations in the early 1920s in the city of Geneva, Switzerland. Communist Russia was not made a member (nor was a Russian delegation invited to the Paris Peace Talks). Some of the defeated nations, such as Germany, initially were not admitted, although provisions were made for their eventual membership. In a stunning development that reflected the new isolationist tendency in the

United States, the U.S. Congress voted against that nation's membership. Despite it having been the conception of Wilson and his advisors, the United States would never join the League of Nations during its existence.

The conference leaders also made a number of major decisions on national boundaries and imperial territories. The map of Europe was redrawn. Among other moves, the modern nation of Poland was created as was the nation of Czechoslovakia. The nation of Yugoslavia was created in response to the demands of the Pan-Slavist movement. The Austro-Hungarian Empire was dissolved in this process, with Austria reduced to a smaller nation with Vienna as its capital. The Ottoman Turkish Empire was dissolved and the modern nation of Turkey established, but much of the Ottoman imperial territory was divided up amongst other European empires.

The Treaty of Saint-Germain-en-Laye was signed on September 10, 1919, and imposed the conditions for peace on the defeated Austria. This treaty stipulated that Austria accepted its responsibility as a key initiator of the Great War. It formally dissolved the Austro-Hungarian empire and established the new Republic of Austria in the German-speaking territories of the former empire, just south of the German nation and to the north of Italy. The treaty imposed limitations on the size of the Austrian military, restricting its army to only 30,000 men. Finally, the treaty also prohibited Austria from union with the German nation, a move for which some Pan-Germanists in the Austrian Empire had been advocating for generations. Such a union—known to Pan-Germanists as an *Anschluss*—was prohibited without the approval of the League of Nations. This would lay the foundations of a conflict that would later see Adolf Hitler's Nazi regime annex the Austrian nation into Germany in 1938.

Italy had joined the war on the side of the Allied powers in 1915 despite its membership in the Triple Alliance, the defensive treaty alliance between Germany, Austria-Hungary, and Italy. Italy decided to do this as a result of secret negotiations with the British. These talks produced the secret Treaty of London in 1915, which promised the Italians significant tracts of Austrian territory should Italy join the Allies, and should they emerge victorious. Because of this, Italian prime minister Orlando and his Italian delegation were anxious to claim those territories as part of the Paris Peace Conference. Particularly due to the insistence by Wilson that there should be no further secret diplomacy in the future, however, the other members of the "Big 4" were not willing to honor the conditions of the secret Treaty of London. Italy was awarded some small territories on the Adriatic coast, but nothing like the territories they had expected. As a result Orlando and the Italians walked out of the conference. In Italy this was an outrage and was considered a betrayal of the Italians by the larger powers. It prompted the poet and nationalist

Gabriele D'Annunzio to lead an Italian contingent to attack and occupy the city of Fiume on the Adriatic coast in defiance of the conference's decisions. It would also help inspire defiant Nationalism across Italy and contributed to the level of support for Mussolini's Fascist Party.

Finally, the leaders of the Paris Peace Conference produced the Treaty of Versailles which imposed the conditions for peace on the defeated Germany. Although Wilson had advocated a gentler treatment of Germany to encourage its "rehabilitation," the other leading council members were determined to see Germany pay for its crimes. France had lost nearly two million people and its national infrastructure was devastated. Britain had lost nearly six hundred thousand men. Lloyd-George and Clemenceau knew that their respective populations expected harsh treatment of Germany—Lloyd-George promised the British electorate in a campaign speech that he would squeeze Germany "until the pips squeak."

The Treaty of Versailles was signed by the stunned and angry German delegation on June 28, 1919, at the Palace of Versailles in the Hall of Mirrors. It stipulated that Germany "and her allies" bore all responsibility for the eruption of the Great War. Based on this premise then, the treaty went on to remove Germany's overseas colonies in Africa, East Asia, and the Pacific. These colonies were later turned over to other imperial powers as "mandates." The treaty imposed severe arms limitations on Germany, limiting its army to 100,000 men and its navy to a token number of battleships. A submarine force was now prohibited. Additionally, the treaty entirely prohibited Germany from establishing a military air force. Finally, the treaty outlined a schedule of reparations payments over a significant period of time at the level of 20 billion gold marks. Germany also would be forced to turn over significant levels of raw materials and industrial produce to the Allies, including iron, steel, timber, and coal. This level of financial and industrial payment would put inordinate economic pressure on Germany in the years to come. To ensure the payments were made, the treaty also outlined the arrangements for British and French troops to occupy German territories in the Rhineland.

Germany lost significant portions of its national territory at the conference, it lost its overseas colonies, saw the German-speaking population broken up into several different nations, its national defense was reduced to a token force, and Germany was saddled with crushing reparations payments. On top of all of this, foreign powers were put in place to continually apply pressure and force Germany to meet its obligations. All of these issues inspired a fearsome Nationalist reaction in Germany, as many ordinary Germans longed to throw off such burdens, recover their territory, recover their arms, and recover their self-determination. Such longings found expression in the movement known as Nazism, and under the pressures of the interwar years Adolf Hitler's Nazi Party would come to power. In power, Hitler and his government sought—among many other initiatives—to reverse the conditions of the Treaty of Versailles, avenge Germany's defeat, and renew German independence.

See also: First World War; Treaty of Versailles.

Further Reading
Dockrill, M. L., *The Paris Peace Conference: Peace Without Victory?* (New York: Palgrave, 2001).
Fromkin, David, *A Peace to End All Peace: Creating the Modern Middle East 1914–1922* (New York: Holt, 1989).
Macmillan, Margaret, *Paris 1919: Six Months That Changed the World* (New York: Random House, 2003).

PETAIN, HENRI PHILIPPE (1856–1951)   Henri Philippe Petain was one of France's leading generals during the First World War and the interwar years. After the defeat of France by Nazi Germany, Petain was made the virtual dictator of the Vichy French State. During the period from 1940 to November 1942, the Vichy French State maintained close relations with Nazi Germany and provided aid in several key areas to the Nazi war effort. These included industrial production, raw materials, labor, and cooperation in the atrocities of the Holocaust. It remains a matter of debate whether Petain's regime in Vichy France was fully fascist, but that nation's cooperation with the other fascist governments is beyond question. After the defeat of Germany in 1945, Petain was among those key officials found to be guilty of "collaboration" with the Nazis. He was tried and sentenced to death for his crimes against France. Because of his advanced age, however, Petain's sentence was commuted to life imprisonment. Petain stands as the most prominent figure associated with the so-called "collaborators," and arguably the most controversial and polarizing figure in 20th century French history.

Philippe Petain was born in Cauchy-a-la-Tour in northern France in 1856. As a child, Petain was an avid follower of the tales of Napoleon's glory. Petain enrolled in France's Saint Cyr Military Academy and attended the Army War College. By 1878, he had matriculated and taken a commission in the French army. He served as an officer in multiple infantry brigades through the late 19th century. In the summer of 1914, 58-year-old Petain was preparing for retirement when the Great War broke out. Petain was rapidly promoted to brigadier general and then to corps commanding general. He played key roles at the Battle of the Marne and at Verdun. Later, as commander and chief of the French army Petain successfully negotiated a peaceful end to the massive mutiny of French soldiers on the Western Front.

After the Great War, Petain made an unsuccessful run for president. He later was made inspector general of the French army. In these years he vigorously supported the creation of a separate military air force and was briefly made inspector general of that air force. Petain also was a firm supporter of the building of the Maginot Line—a great line of forts along the German borderlands intended to make a future German invasion of France impossible. In 1939, as war loomed again in Europe, Petain—at the advanced age of 82—was made ambassador to Spain.

During the spring of 1940, Adolf Hitler's Nazi forces invaded France and drove a successful campaign through the north in only six weeks' time. The Nazis occupied Paris by mid-June of 1940, by which time the French government had left and set up its operations in Bordeaux. Petain had returned from Spain to join the government and worked with the other members of the government, led by Prime Minister Paul Reynaud. French resistance, however, was not sufficient to repel the Nazis, and communications from Britain and the United States made it clear that the Allies could not commit to any serious military aid in the short term. Faced with the reality that no foreign aid was coming—and the horror of more needless death and destruction—Reynaud resigned and recommended Petain as his successor.

As prime minister, Petain on the 15th of June formed a government and began the process of reaching peace terms with the Germans. On June 22 the French signed an armistice document that surrendered direct control of all of northern France and the western seaboard to Germany. These lands were occupied and governed by Germany until the summer of 1944. The nation of France, however, was allowed to continue to exist, but with much smaller boundaries and its seat of government moved to the small spa town of Vichy. On July 10, 1940, the remaining deputies that could be found met to ratify the armistice agreement. In doing so, they dissolved the Third Republic and granted virtual dictatorial power to Petain as "Head of State."

Petain then created a strongly conservative government that some scholars argue was fascist in its essence; it certainly adopted characteristics of fascist regimes. Petain quickly passed legislation that abolished the position of president, and then gave himself the power to pass laws without parliament and to appoint his own ministers. He changed the national motto from its revolutionary credo of *Liberte, Egalite, Fraternite* ("Liberty, Equality, Fraternity") to *Travail, Famille, Patrie* ("Work, Family, Fatherland"). All trade unions were eliminated and labor strikes were made illegal. Petain also began the process of converting French industrial organization to a Corporative structure along the lines of that pioneered in Fascist Italy. This process, however, never was fully completed. Petain passed a number of laws reflecting the fascist obsession with family and birthrate. Abortion was outlawed and the divorce laws were made quite stringent. Contraception was suppressed but never outlawed. Pregnant women were given priority in the rationing programs. The Vichy government under Petain also gave material aid to Nazi Germany in a number of ways: 40% of all the industrial output of Vichy France went to the Germans, as well as 15% of all food production. Petain also allowed 76,000 Jews to be rounded up and eventually sent to the German network of death camps during the Holocaust.

After the Allies had liberated French territory in early September 1944, Petain was removed to Germany, but he later requested to be allowed to return to France. Back in France he faced accusations of treason. A provisional government had been established under Charles De Gaulle and that government arrested Petain and placed him on trial. Petain defended himself by explaining that he had no choice but to have taken the actions he did, if the integrity and independence of France was to have been maintained. The three judges at his trial all recommended he be acquitted of any treason charges, but the jury found him guilty and sentenced him to death. Because of his advanced age the court commuted the sentence to life imprisonment. Petain lived most of the rest of his life in the prison on the Ile d'Yeu, a small island off France's Atlantic coast. He died there on July 23, 1951, at age 95, and was buried near the prison.

See also: Vichy France.

Further Reading

Griffiths, Richard, *Marshal Petain* (London: Constable, 1970).

Paxton, Robert O., *Vichy France: Old Guard, New Order, 1940–1944* (New York: Columbia University Press, 1972).

Williams, Charles, *Petain: How the Hero of France Became a Convicted Traitor and Changed the Course of History* (New York: Palgrave Macmillan, 2005).

PRIMO DE RIVERA, JOSE ANTONIO (1903–1936) Jose Antonio Primo de Rivera—son of Spain's military dictator, General Miguel Primo de Rivera—was the founder and former president of the *Falange Espanola* ("Spanish Phalanx"), the most important fascist party in Spain during the 1930s. Primo de Rivera constructed a formal political program for his group and did run candidates in the 1936 general election, although no fascists won any seats. In the early stages of the Spanish Civil War Primo de Rivera was taken into custody by the Republican government, tried, and then executed in 1936. With the establishment of Francisco Franco's regime after the Civil

War, Primo de Rivera's fascist organization was merged into a single far-right coalition party called the *Falange Espanola Tradicionalista y de las JONS.*

Jose Antonio Primo de Rivera was born on April 24, 1903, in Madrid. His mother died when he was very young and he was raised primarily by his father's sister, outside of the household. He received most of his early education as "home schooling," but enrolled at the University of Madrid in 1917, where he studied law. He was an outstanding student and graduated in 1923 with both a bachelor's degree and a graduate degree. Primo de Rivera then enlisted in the Spanish army and was stationed at Barcelona. By this time, his father, a top general in the army, had seized control of the Spanish government and was ruling as a military dictator. In 1924, Primo de Rivera was involved in an incident where he assaulted a superior officer for open criticism of his father's government and other family members. He was court martialed for this incident but suffered only minor punishment. He was released from his military service by 1925 and began practicing law in Madrid. Primo de Rivera was quite successful and by 1931 he even ran for a seat in Spain's new parliament—which had emerged from the collapse of his father's dictatorship—but he was not elected.

Primo de Rivera had developed a strange mix of political views during the 1920s and early 1930s. He maintained strong devotions to traditional elements of Spain's national identity—such as the military, its empire, and the Catholic Church—but he also embraced modernist ideas, believing that liberal democracy had run its course and that a new modern system had to be found. He came to believe in the emerging political system of fascism as the best way forward. To that end, on October 29, 1933, he founded Spain's first explicitly fascist political party. In his speeches to the party faithful he made clear his beliefs that Liberal Democracy was doomed and that Spain needed a dictatorship; in his "Twenty-Seven Points," Primo de Rivera called it a "totalitarian instrument to defend the integrity of the fatherland." He also repudiated the capitalist system, and insisted on a Corporative system for Spain, with boards established to regulate entire industries for the benefit of the nation as a whole. He advocated the nationalization of the banking services and the major public utilities, but otherwise defended private property and vigorously attacked Marxism. Primo de Rivera also advocated the use of violence as necessary to defend national integrity and to advance the agenda of his *Falange Espanola.* Like other fascist movements, Primo de Rivera's developed a paramilitary arm with a uniformed guard—the "Blueshirts"—that engaged in violent demonstrations, street brawls, and attacks on political enemies.

In November 1933, Primo de Rivera was elected to Spain's parliament—the Congress of Deputies—as part of the broad right-wing coalition known as the Spanish Confederation of Autonomous Right-Wing Groups (the

Confederación Española de Derechas Autónomas) (CEDA). He maintained his seat until 1936. In that year, new elections were held and brought a new government to power. Joseph Stalin in the Soviet Union had called for all the parties of the Marxist left to cooperate and vote together in a "Popular Front" against the rise of fascism. As such, Spain's newly elected government contained a number of prominent left-wing members and stood for a reforming agenda that appalled the most conservative right-wing elements of the country.

For some of the top generals in the Spanish army the reforming agenda was unacceptable. The generals secretly began organizing a rebellion to seize the government by force. Even before the rebellion could be launched (and thus start the Spanish Civil War), the new Republican government arrested Primo de Rivera—ostensibly for illegally carrying firearms. There was no question, however, that the government wanted Primo de Rivera interned to limit his political agitation. He eventually was imprisoned in Alicante and from there was able to communicate with some of the conspirators involved in launching the coup attempt. In July 1936, the "Nationalist" coup was launched and the Spanish Civil War began. At that time, authorities found firearms and ammunition in Primo de Rivera's jail cell. He then was tried on charges of "conspiracy against the Republic"—essentially treason—which carried a death sentence. He was found guilty on November 18, 1936, and executed by firing squad on November 20, 1936. After the start of the Spanish Civil War and then the execution of Primo de Rivera, huge numbers of Spanish youths signed on for the *Falange Espanola*. The party that once had struggled to reach 5,000 members now burgeoned to nearly 40,000.

After his death, Primo de Rivera came to occupy a special place of reverence in the memory of Spain's conservative right. As the Civil War came to an end in 1939, Francisco Franco, the leader of the Nationalist cause, formed a single-party coalition of the far right-wing groups—the *Falange Espanola Tradicionalista y de las JONS*. The *Falange Espanola* was among the groups included and this ensured that that political organization retained elements of fascism even well into the post-war era. Franco, whose regime lasted until his death in 1975, built a massive monument to the Nationalist forces, known as the "Valley of the Fallen." In 1959, the Franco regime exhumed the remains of Jose Antonio Primo de Rivera and reinterred them at the Valley of the Fallen basilica.

See also: *Falange Espanola*; Spanish Civil War.

Further Reading
Payne, Stanley G., *Falange: A History of Spanish Fascism* (Stanford: Stanford University Press, 1961).

Payne, Stanley G., *Fascism in Spain, 1923–1977* (Madison: University of Wisconsin Press, 1999).

RACIAL HYGIENE "Racial hygiene" is the term used to describe a belief system that advocates the need for maintaining the purity of a racial community, and the practices used to achieve this objective. The concept grew out of the development of the eugenics movement which was prominent in the late 19th and early 20th centuries. The eugenics movement—founded by racial theorists such as Sir Francis Galton and Arthur de Gobineau—advocated calculated strategies for keeping racial communities distinct and physically vigorous.

Adolf Hitler and the Nazi movement he led believed that the Nordic or "Aryan" race was superior and had the obligation to keep itself pure to be fit enough to fulfill its "historic destiny." In Nazi ideology, that destiny included the domination of other races and nations and the development of a superior culture. The Nazi regime—with racial hygiene as its guiding principle—enacted policies that restricted marriages between racial and ethnic groups, promoted the mating of those considered racially optimal, and euthanized groups considered unfit. After the end of the Second World War in 1945, the concept of racial hygiene generally was discredited as harmfully racist and based on unscientific principles.

The eugenics movement had itself grown out of the theories of evolution and natural selection as put forward by Charles Darwin in his famous books, *On the Origin of Species* (1859) and *The Descent of Man, and Selection in Relation to Sex* (1871). Believing that human populations around the globe had been shaped by the same forces of natural selection that created the diversity of the animal kingdom, many western intellectuals became convinced that certain racial groups were at different levels of evolutionary adaptation. Almost without exception, such thinkers believed that white European-descended peoples constituted a superior racial group relative to the other races on the planet. Further, racial theorists such as Arthur De Gobineau believed that strong "racial health" produced superior culture. According to these principles, so the thinking ran, European racial communities had to avoid reproducing with different races as this would eventually produce cultural chaos. Even more importantly, the mixing with supposedly inferior races had to be prevented in order to avoid the physical and mental deterioration of the white European racial community.

These pseudoscientific ideas reached their most destructive destination in the German Third Reich, created by Adolf Hitler and his Nazi Party. Hitler had come to be a fanatic believer that race was the most important element behind the progression of history. Marxists believed that the struggle between *classes* was the preeminent stimulator of events, but Hitler and Nazi ideology said that it was the struggle between racial groups that drove human history. The Nazis also took for granted that the Aryan race—as best represented by the German national community—was the most developed and dominant race among the world's peoples. As such, Nazi ideology said the German race had a "historic destiny." This destiny was to conquer the inferior races, to exterminate and enslave them, and to forcibly take their geographical territory from them for the expansion of the German race and its culture.

Under this racially based ideology and political program, Hitler and his Nazis were determined to preserve German racial superiority for its eventual mission. This meant that the state would have to promote the propagation of the most desirable racial traits in its population and prevent any dilution or deterioration. To accomplish this, the Nazi state enacted a number of policies. To stimulate the "positive" propagation of racial strength the Nazi state established the *Lebensborn* program in 1935, run by the SS. This program built facilities for men and women of supposedly superior racial stock to use for breeding. Some young adult women went to these facilities and took pride in having extramarital children for the benefit of the state. After the children were born, they were removed and placed with racially appropriate families that wanted to adopt. The state also created awards and honors for those exemplifying Aryan racial tendencies in their physiology or in activities such as athletics.

On the "negative" side of racial hygiene policy were the programs which sought to eliminate "harmful elements" from the racial community, and those that prevented any mixing with foreign elements. In the early days of the Nazi regime, concentration camps were set up to hold those removed from German society as undesirables. Those purged from German society included Marxists, chronic alcoholics, chronic criminals, Jews, and homosexuals. This not only meant that these people were purged from German society, it also meant that they could not reproduce and spread their supposedly inferior genetics.

As early as 1933, the German government passed the Law for the Prevention of Genetically Diseased Offspring or the "Sterilization Law." This provided the legal basis for programs that sterilized groups that were believed to be racially unfit. In 1935, the Nazi state passed the "Nuremburg Laws." These laws stripped Jews (considered to be the most harmful of the foreign racial groups) of their rights and their German citizenship. The Nuremburg Laws established a legal basis for determining who was Jewish, and made both sex and marriage between Jews and non-Jews illegal. By 1939 other programs had been established enabling German doctors to end the lives of patients considered to be "incurably sick." This included a program to kill mentally handicapped children. By 1941, 70,000 children and adults had been killed by their doctors for the purposes of racial hygiene—for keeping the German race "pure" (Proctor, 177).

See also: Anti-Semitism; Hitler, Adolf; Holocaust; Nuremburg Laws.

Further Reading

Ehrenreich, Eric, *The Nazi Ancestral Proof: Genealogy, Racial Science, and the Final Solution* (Bloomington: University of Indiana Press, 2007).

Evans, Richard J., *The Third Reich in Power, 1933–1939* (New York: Penguin, 2005).

Gotz, Aly, Peter Chroust, and Christian Pross, *Cleansing the Fatherland: Nazi Medicine and Racial Hygiene,* translated by Belinda Cooper (Baltimore: Johns Hopkins, 1994).

Proctor, Robert N., *Racial Hygiene: Medicine Under the Nazis* (Cambridge, MA: Harvard University Press, 1988).

REARMAMENT (GERMAN)   Rearmament was a policy carried out by Adolf Hitler's German Reich from 1933 to 1939 to expand and modernize the German armed forces. This massive economic and military program was conducted in direct violation of the conditions of the Treaty of Versailles, which had imposed stringent limitations on the size of the German military. Hitler used the open declaration of rearmament as a demonstration of Germany's defiance of the Treaty, and its self-determination. Rearmament, however, was more than just an assertion of German national self-determination. The state direction of industrial production greatly stimulated Germany's economy and by 1938 brought the nation to virtual full employment. The massive war machine created by 1939 was the instrument of terror Hitler used to fulfill what he believed was Germany's "historic destiny"—the military conquest of Eastern Europe and the Soviet Union.

After Germany's defeat in the First World War, the Allied Powers constructed the Treaty of Versailles to impose conditions on Germany to ensure that again nation never would be the cause of war. That Treaty, signed in 1919 at the Paris Peace Conference, removed Germany's overseas colonies, reconfigured its traditional borders, and imposed a rigorous schedule of reparations payments that squeezed the German economy until the rise of the Hitler's Nazi regime. It also imposed strict limitations on the size of Germany's military forces. It limited Germany's army to a force of only 100,000 men, limited its navy to a small number of battleships and cruisers, and forbade a submarine fleet. Germany also was forbidden to maintain a military air force. The governments of the Weimar Republic (from 1918 to 1932) carried out some programs of secret industrial production, such as the building of civilian aircraft that could be converted for military purposes in the event of war, but these programs were small in scale.

Upon taking power in January 1933, Adolf Hitler began the process of building Germany's infrastructures through large-scale public works programs. Some of this work was devoted to secretly building military facilities. In 1935, the Nazi regime announced that it was expanding the number of men in its army and that it had created the *Luftwaffe*, the German air force. That same year, Germany reached a negotiated settlement with Britain to increase the size of its navy to a ratio of 35% of the tonnage of the British Royal Navy.

In 1936, Hitler announced his new economic strategy for Germany, which he called the "Four Year Plan." This was a plan to achieve economic self-sufficiency or autarky by 1940. The Four Year Plan was deeply integrated with rearmament as Hitler's ministers now coordinated German industry toward arms production on a massive scale, and at the same time demanded the exclusive use of domestic materials and labor. German industry thrived in this environment as the majority of the nation's industrial producers now worked on the basis of government contracts with guaranteed production levels and prices.

Hitler began using his massive new armed forces by providing military aid to Franco's Nationalist forces in the Spanish Civil War in 1936. By 1938 Hitler used his growing armed forces to intimidate the governments of Austria and Czechoslovakia and annex them into the German Reich. By 1939, Hitler believed that his military forces were sufficiently powerful to launch the invasion of Poland—which started the Second World War. As Hitler was poised to launch his invasion of Poland, the German army had reached the level of nearly 3 million men and had nearly 4,000 tanks available. Over the course of the war, approximately 12.5 million men served in the German army.

See also: Hitler, Adolf; Paris Peace Conference; Treaty of Versailles.

Further Reading

Carr, William, *Arms, Autarky, and Aggression: A Study in German Foreign Policy, 1933–1939* (New York: Norton, 1973).

Overy, Richard, *The Origins of the Second World War* (New York: W. W. Norton, 1998).

Whaley, Barton, *Covert German Rearmament 1919–1939: Deception and Misperception* (Frederick, MD: University Publications of America, 1984).

REICHSTAG FIRE   The *Reichstag* was the German Parliament Assembly, and on the evening of February 27, 1933, the *Reichstag* building in downtown Berlin was set on fire in what is agreed to have been an act of arson. The building burned intensely from just after 9:00 p.m. to 11:30 p.m., and was completely destroyed as a useful assembly. This fire would prove to be a crucial event in the process that made Adolf Hitler a dictator with virtually absolute power in Germany. A small group of individuals were arrested for setting the fire, and were known Communists. Depicting the *Reichstag* fire as the first violent act in a Communist plan to seize power, Hitler asked for—and received—full powers from the German Parliament and from its president. With those political powers in place Hitler used them to eliminate the Communist Party as a political force, and to pass laws making his position as dictator permanent and legal.

When German president Paul von Hindenburg in January 1933 appointed Adolf Hitler as chancellor, Hitler's Nazi Party and the German Communist Party were the two largest parties represented in the German Parliament. Hoping to change the composition of the *Reichstag*, Hitler asked President von Hindenburg to use his powers (under article 48 in the Weimar Republic's Constitution) to close down the *Reichstag* and call for new elections. Hindenburg agreed, and a national election was set for March 5, 1933.

On the evening of February 27, however, the Berlin Fire Brigade received reports that the *Reichstag* building in the center of town was on fire. The firemen were able to bring the blaze under control before midnight, but by that point the interior was a complete loss. Adolf Hitler and some of his chief ministers arrived toward the end of the evening and were advised by Hermann Goering that the blaze had been set by members of Germany's Communist Party. Nazi security services found unused bundles of arsonists' materials at the scene as well as one individual—Marinus van der Lubbe, a Dutchman who had just moved to Germany in 1933. A member of the Dutch Communist Council, van der Lubbe planned to work with German Communists and possibly to immigrate to the Soviet Union at a later date. There seems to be no question that van der Lubbe was involved in setting the fire, but debate continues as to whether he acted alone or was part of a coordinated Nazi plot. There has also been controversy as to whether van der Lubbe was psychologically disturbed or even mentally handicapped, however there is no clear evidence for this claim. Under torture, van der Lubbe confessed to the crime and revealed names of other members of the Communist leadership. Acting on this information, Nazi authorities later arrested four Communist leaders suspected of complicity in the crime, including Georgi Dimitrov, a Bulgarian Communist leader who went on to be the head of the Soviet Comintern (Communist International). Van der Lubbe and the others stood trial in Germany's highest court, but only van der Lubbe was found guilty. He was sentenced to death and executed by guillotine on January 10, 1934.

After the fire, Hitler asked President Hindenburg to use his Article 48 powers again to place full power in the hands of the chancellor, specifically to deal with the supposed Communist threat. Hindenburg agreed and drafted the *"Reichstag* Fire Decree," which gave Hitler full power to act against the Communist political organizations. Hitler used the party press to announce to the country that the fire represented a first violent act in a widespread Communist plot to take over the country. He followed up with speeches in parliament making the same claim (after the *Reichstag* Fire, the deputies met in the city's opera house).

Hitler used the decree to remove all Communist deputies from the *Reichstag* and eventually to legally outlaw the Communist Party. With the Communist Party gone, the Nazis became the majority party in the parliament. The Nazis used this majority to pass a major piece of legislation known as the "Enabling Act" on March 23, 1933. The law placed unlimited power in the hands of the German chancellor (Adolf Hitler), and allowed him to initiate and make laws without consulting the *Reichstag*. In essence, the Enabling Act made Adolf Hitler the absolute dictator of Germany. In the following year, the *Reichstag*— with its Nazi majority still intact—made Adolf Hitler chancellor for life. After Hindenburg's death in 1934, the Nazis eliminated the office of the president, making the chancellor the highest office in the land.

See also: Enabling Act of 1933; Hitler, Adolf.

Further Reading

Evans, Richard J., *The Third Reich in Power, 1933–1939* (New York: Penguin, 2005).

Kershaw, Ian, *Hitler 1889–1936: Hubris* (New York: W.W. Norton, 1998).

Tobias, Fritz, *The Reichstag Fire*, translated by Arnold J. Pomeranz (New York: Putnam, 1964).

REMILITARIZATION OF THE RHINELAND   After Germany's surrender in the First World War, the Treaty of Versailles—signed at the end of the Paris Peace Conference—stipulated that the region in Germany between the French border and the Rhine River, known as the "Rhineland," could have no German military presence. This area indeed was occupied by Allied troops until 1930. Adolf Hitler's German Reich remilitarized the Rhineland. This was Hitler's first foreign policy action that stood in open violation of the Treaty of Versailles, and represents the first in a chain of expansionist actions that ultimately led to the commencement of the Second World War.

Although the demilitarization policy had been accepted and adhered to by the leaders of the Weimar Republic, Adolf Hitler saw it as an intolerable repressive measure against his German nation. On March 7, 1936, Hitler moved German troops into the area, establishing barracks and permanent military installations. Neither the League of Nations nor Europe's democracies made a serious effort to stop Hitler's action. Because of the lack of response, Hitler came to believe that the European democracies were too weak to interfere with his expansionist moves planned for the coming years.

The demilitarization of the Rhineland was a stipulation imposed on Germany by the signatories of the Treaty of Versailles, which was signed in 1919 at the end of the Paris Peace Conference. France was especially insistent upon its inclusion, because the central objective of French policy at the conference was to prevent any future German ground invasion. The treaty further stated that if Germany introduced any military presence into the area or built any type of military fortification that this would be interpreted by the Allied Powers as "a hostile act . . . calculated to disturb the peace of the world." To ensure the initial enforcement of the policy, the Allied Powers stationed British and French troops in the area throughout the 1920s.

In 1925, an important diplomatic conference was held at Locarno in Italy, and the nations of Europe tried to reach a more stable settlement of European border issues. As a part of the Locarno agreements Germany agreed to continue the policy of a demilitarized Rhineland permanently. This was considered significant, as the policy no longer was being imposed upon Germany by force, and had the stamp of German agreement. The Treaty of Versailles had dictated that Allied troops remain in the Rhineland until 1935. In 1929, however, a conference was held at The Hague to discuss the modification of German reparations as imposed by the Versailles Treaty. The schedule of payments was eased and the British and French agreed to remove their troops from the Rhineland. All British and French troops had been removed before the end of 1930.

Adolf Hitler became the chancellor of Germany in January 1933. His Nazi Party stood for a number of policies which aimed at reasserting German independence and national self-determination. Eliminating the various conditions of the Versailles Treaty was among the most prominent of these policy priorities. In pursuit of these objectives, Adolf Hitler removed Germany from the League of Nations and began plans for moving German military troops into the Rhineland region in violation of the treaty. Hitler gave a speech on May 21, 1935, announcing that his government planned to adhere to the policy of demilitarization, as consistent with the Locarno agreements. Germany would continue to honor the Locarno policies, however, only "so long as the other parties are, on their side, ready to stand by that pact." Hitler was alluding to an agreement already being negotiated between France and the Soviet Union, which was signed in May 1935 and was ratified by the French government by February 1936. The Franco-Soviet Treaty of Mutual

Assistance was used by Hitler as justification for his remilitarization of the Rhineland.

On March 7, 1936, Hitler ordered 19 battalions of his army and a small squadron of airplanes to deployed to the Rhine River. Three of those battalions then crossed the Rhine into the Rhineland region. As this operation proceeded, the French began to mass troops on the German border and the potential for a major engagement loomed. Some Nazi generals advised Hitler to pull out his troops to avoid any such engagement. Hitler was determined not to do so unless the French forces crossed the border into Germany. They never did.

Concerned about the massive costs of mobilizing its entire army and worried about the scale of the conflict that might follow, the French did not move into the Rhineland region. German documents and testimony, however, make clear that if the French *had* moved into the area then Hitler would have had to immediately pull his forces out. In 1936, the German war machine was not yet powerful enough to win such a conflict with France.

The British government did not make any formal protest, and many of its top politicians thought that Germany simply was moving its own resources into its own territory. The League of Nations released a declaration saying that the move violated the treaties of Versailles and Locarno, but it did not take any preventative or punitive actions. Even the passage of economic sanctions was rejected by the League Council. Reassured by the inactivity of the League, Britain, and France, Hitler became increasingly convinced that the democracies had become weak and decadent. This gave him the confidence to embark on a series of further encroachments that by September 1939 led to the beginning of the Second World War.

See also: Hitler, Adolf; Treaty of Versailles.

Further Reading

Emmerson, James Thomas, *The Rhineland Crisis: 7 March, 1936—A Study in Multilateral Diplomacy* (Ames: Iowa State University Press, 1977).

Evans, Richard J., *The Third Reich in Power, 1933–1939* (New York: Penguin, 2005).

Overy, Richard, *The Origins of the Second World War* (New York: Longman, 1998).

Taylor, A. J. P., *The Origins of the Second World War* (New York: Athenaeum, 1962).

SALAZAR, ANTONIO OLIVEIRA DE (1889–1970)   Antonio de Oliveira Salazar was a Portuguese university professor and politician who established a dictatorship in the fascist style in Portugal lasting from the late 1920s to 1968. He served as Portugal's finance minister after a military coup d'état in 1926 and again in 1928. By 1932, he was appointed prime minister and emerged as a virtual dictator. Salazar constructed a right-wing ultra-Nationalist regime, which he called the *Estado Nuovo*, and which would remain in place until 1974. Although Salazar personally disliked the demagoguery and aggression of Benito Mussolini and Adolf Hitler, his state did bear resemblance to the most repressive regimes in its adoption of Corporatism and especially its repressive policies and use of secret police.

Salazar was born on April 28, 1889, in the town of Vimiero in northeastern Potugal. He was raised as a devout Catholic, and proved himself very early to be a gifted student. After a stint in a seminary he enrolled at the University of Coimbra in 1910. By the time he left school, he had obtained a doctorate and had been hired as a professor of political economy. He was deeply committed to Portugal's traditional institutions of monarchy and Church. In 1910, the same year that Salazar began his studies, Portugal's monarchy was overthrown by the republican elements in the government. The republican system, however, did not bring Portugal stability or prosperity. From 1910 to 1926, Portugal's young Republic was in a fluid and chaotic state. There were no less than 45 different cabinets during that period. Salazar and other ultra-conservatives were appalled at the situation. As a result, Portugal's military in 1926 made a series of attempts to seize the government. General Oscar de Fragoso Carmona eventually took power.

Salazar had been elected to parliament in 1921, but he had detested the parliamentary process and thus resigned. Although Salazar had an academic reputation and only a smattering of political experience, Carmona asked him to be the finance minister in his government. Salazar accepted the position on the condition that he be awarded exceptional powers.

As finance minister Salazar pulled off miracles. He cut social spending, raised taxes, and required certain crops to be grown for export. The eventual result was that he created not only balanced budgets, but even budget surpluses for Portugal from 1928 to 1932. In 1932, Carmona moved into the more symbolic position of "president" and made Salazar prime minister with the responsibilities of running the day-to-day government of the nation. The office of president would not have a meaningful political role again and Salazar, as prime minister, emerged as an individual dictator with virtually absolute power.

Salazar's series of governments became known as the *Estado Nuovo* ("New State"). He moved to unify the parties of the conservative right into a single party that he called the "National Union." This became the dominant party in Portugal and Salazar picked his cabinet members only from this party. Unlike other Fascist dictators, however, Salazar did not forcefully outlaw opposition parties, nor did he make it mandatory to belong to the National Union. He was, however, a believer in the "Corporatist" system pioneered by Mussolini's Italy and he reorganized the Portuguese parliament along these lines. In doing this, he created a group of "Corporations" which represented entire industries.

Salazar's dictatorship was similar to other fascist regimes of the period in that he outlawed trade unions and made labor strikes illegal. In place of trade unions he created state-run workers' organizations that heard grievances about labor issues and sponsored entertainment and sports leagues. This program was called the "National Foundation for Joy at Work"—reminiscent of the similar program in Nazi Germany, known as the "Strength Through Joy" program. Salazar also organized a uniformed paramilitary force along fascist lines, known as the Portuguese Legion. The force was used to keep order at party meetings and speeches, and provided muscle and intimidation against political rivals on the streets. Salazar also established a frightening order of secret police, which by 1945 was known as the *Polícia Internacional e de Defesa do Estado* (International and State Defense Police) (PIDE). The PIDE used internal espionage to root out political opposition, and used arrest and torture to remove opposition leaders. It also moved to break up or prevent any public demonstrations by the political opposition. The PIDE even spied on the military, and in 1946 dissolved a plot to overthrow Salazar.

Salazar retained a suspicion of the "liberal west," throughout his life, attempting to shelter Portugal from the supposedly corrosive influences of Liberal Democracy, a free press, and (especially) any influences of Marxist ideas. He never traveled any further from Portugal than neighboring Spain. Despite these prejudices, he engineered Portugal's entry into the United Nations and negotiated that nation's early membership in the North Atlantic Treaty Organization. Salazar suffered a stroke on September 27, 1968, which put him into a coma lasting nearly two years. He died on July 27, 1970.

Debate still continues as to the extent to which Salazar's regime was a true fascist dictatorship. Although he used many of the same techniques associated with regimes generally accepted as fascist, he vigorously opposed racism, demagoguery, and especially the celebration of war. He constructed multiple organizations to regiment Portuguese society, and used genuine repression to do so; however, he also is credited with bringing order and economic stability to a nation that was mired in chaos before Salazar's rise to power. Although the question of whether Salazar was a "true" fascist dictator is the topic of continued debate, his *Estado Nuovo* was certainly inspired by key elements of fascist ideology.

Further Reading
Hugh, Kay, *Salazar and Modern Portugal* (London: Eyre & Spottiswode, 1970).
Meneses, Filipe, *Salazar: A Political Biography* (New York: Enigma Books, 2009).
Raby, D. L., *Fascism and Resistance in Portugal* (New York: St. Martin's, 1988).

***SCHUTZSTAFFEL* (SS)**   The *Schutzstaffel* or "SS," as it came to be known, was an elite organization within the Nazi Party in Germany that emerged as the primary group in charge of state security and the execution of Adolf Hitler's racial policy. The group was formed in 1923—just as the Nazi Party was emerging—as a small security force to protect the party's top leadership. The group evolved into the personal bodyguard for the Nazi leader Adolf Hitler. After Hitler and the Nazis took power in 1933, the SS grew dramatically, taking on responsibility for all of the police functions within Germany, and later for the administration of its network of concentration camps. After the commencement of the Second World War, the SS was put in charge of the planning and operations for the "resettlement" of Germany's occupied territories and infamously the planning and execution of the horrors of the Holocaust, which killed nearly six million Jews and nearly as many others (Gilbert, 245). In the months immediately after the end of the war in Europe, the Allied Powers declared the SS to be a criminal organization and many of its members were arrested and tried for war crimes and crimes against humanity.

The SS was a fairly small and insignificant organization within the *Sturmabteilung* (SA) when its future leader, Heinrich Himmler, joined it in 1925. Himmler eventually took full leadership of the group in 1929 and made it one the most powerful organizations in Nazi Germany. Himmler began this process by ensuring that the SS was staffed only by those considered the elite of Germany in racial and ideological terms. Any applicant had to demonstrate pure "Aryan" heritage going back more than a century, and had to demonstrate a fanatical enthusiasm for the racial and national ideology of Nazism. Each member took a special oath committing himself to total obedience of Adolf Hitler and the German people.

In 1934, just a year after Hitler came to power, Himmler's SS was able to gain authority over most of the police force in Germany. With the security forces then, the SS played a crucial role in the "Night of the Long Knives," when Hitler had several party rivals murdered to consolidate his power. Having proved their abilities in this episode, Hitler granted the SS independence from any other organization, making Himmler and his entire organization accountable only to the Führer. Additionally, the SS was given legal jurisdiction over its own members, meaning that members of the SS were not subject to the civilian judicial system of Germany. The SS was above the law.

During the 1930s, the central agencies of the SS were the police forces which included the civilian uniformed police (the "Orpo"), the criminal police force (the "Kripo"), and infamously the agency for internal state security known as the "Gestapo." The Gestapo's mission was to identify and eliminate all influences harmful to the Aryan nation. Using the techniques of espionage, wiretapping, and a network of citizen informers the Gestapo rooted out spy rings, resistance groups, and thousands of individuals it deemed to be harmful—including leaders of opposition political parties, trade union leaders, religious leaders, homosexuals, chronic criminals, and alcoholics. Once arrested by the Gestapo, these people were sent to live in "concentration camps," where many died from the restrictive conditions.

When the Second World War began, the SS took on an even wider role. First, a very large unit of the SS called the "Waffen-SS" trained regiments of elite combat soldiers who fought alongside Germany's traditional armed forces (the *Wehrmacht*). The SS, however, also was given enormous responsibilities in implementing the Nazi racial and ideological policies in the conquered territories. This included moving huge numbers of non-German populations including Poles, Czechs, Lithuanians, and Latvians out of areas designated for settlement by ethnic Germans. The SS also administered the process of moving ethnic Germans into those vacated areas. In this process the SS identified any non-Germans who possessed "German racial elements" and relocated them to Germany to be raised by the state. Those people who were deemed unfit racial stock were sent to concentration camps for detention and very often for use as slave labor.

In this overarching role of managing the racial policy of the conquered territories, the SS was given its most vital job. It moved Jewish populations to concentrated relocation areas (such as the Ghettos of cities such as Warsaw or Riga). As part of this process, however, the SS formed special squads to begin the process of exterminating these Jews. These earliest squads, operating before 1942, were known as the *Einsatzgruppen* ("police squads" or "death squads"). They identified and consolidated Jewish people of a region into large groups and executed them, mostly using firing squads. In early 1942, after this process proved to be problematic and slow, Hitler called for a more thorough and efficient system. The result was the planning and implementation of the death-camp system.

Concentration camps were converted from detention centers to camps where the inmates were systematically killed. These camps were linked by a calculated transit system from the west of Europe to the east. When Jews were moved from the west or from Ghettos in the east to the death camps, they most often were herded into gas chambers where they met a gruesome death. It was the SS security chief Reinhard Heydrich who conceived the greater part of the logistics plan of the Holocaust and it was Himmler's organizations which subsequently carried it out.

After the war, the role of the SS in the Holocaust was exposed and SS members were hunted and arrested. Many stood trial and were executed for their crimes against humanity. Several, however, were able to escape to nations whose leaders were sympathetic to the Nazi cause, such as Spain, Egypt, and Argentina. From these foreign outposts, the SS members worked to build a secret network that helped fellow former SS members in the postwar world. The organization was known as *the Organisation der ehemaligen SS-Angehörigen* (Organization of Former Members of the SS) (ODESSA), and ODESSA worked to obtain new identities for the ex-members and help them reenter civilian life while hiding their true identities and their past actions.

See also: Hitler, Adolf; Holocaust; National Socialist German Workers' Party (Nazi Party).

Further Reading

Gilbert, Martin, *The Routledge Atlas of the Holocaust* (London: Routledge, 2002).
Hoehne, Heinz Zollin, *The Order of the Death's Head: The Story of Hitler's SS* (New York: Penguin, 2001).
Koehl, Robert Lewis, *The Black Corps: The Structure and Power Struggles of the Nazi SS* (Madison: University of Wisconsin Press, 1983).

SPANISH CIVIL WAR   The Spanish Civil War was an armed conflict between the forces of a democratically elected Republican government and the forces of the Spanish military which were attempting to oust that government and seize control of the country. The war lasted from July 1936 to April 1939. Most of the armed support for the Republican government came from the working classes of Spain and support was coordinated by the various workers' trade union organizations such as the Socialist *Unión General de Trabajadores* ("General Union of Workers") (UGT) and the Anarchist *Confederación Nacional del Trabajo* ("National Confederation of Labor") (CNT). Later, groups of ordinary citizens came to Spain from all over the world to defend the government in battalions known as the "International Brigades."

The Spanish military was supported by those who supported the political right and feared that the Republican government would lead to outright Socialism in Spain. After reaching a stalemate, the Spanish generals, led by Francisco Franco, appealed to Nazi Germany and Fascist Italy, and both of these regimes gave significant assistance to Franco's "Nationalists." The Republican side appealed to the western democracies Britain and France, but neither nation agreed to help. Only the Soviet Union agreed to help Spain in its fight against fascism. The war ended in April 1939 with General Francisco Franco able to establish his own fascist dictatorship that lasted until his death in 1975.

Spain was ruled by a military dictatorship for most of the 1920s but threw off this regime in the early 1930s. The Spanish people elected to eliminate their monarchy and to create the Second Spanish Republic. The first government established in the new Republic was left-leaning and had a lengthy agenda of liberal reforms, including granting the vote to women, making divorce legal, and expanding secular schooling. To those on the far right this was unacceptable, and the forces of the conservatives worked together to form a coalition called the *Confederación Española de Derechas Autónomas* ("Spanish Confederation of Autonomous Right-Wing Groups) (CEDA). Elections in 1933 brought a right-wing government to power. This, in turn, set off a number of strikes and workers revolts, including a 1934 coal miner's revolt in the north in Asturias. The revolt was brutally crushed by General Francisco Franco. It was becoming clear, however, that Spain was so polarized politically that civil war was looming.

In 1936, Joseph Stalin of the Communist Soviet Union called for all parties of the left to unite in elections in a "Popular Front" to fight the spread of fascism. This strategy was successful, and another election in Spain that year brought a left-leaning government to power. This government prepared to carry on the agenda of progressive reforms, which would now include land reform. The political right once again feared that Spain was moving toward a Socialist revolution.

A group of Spain's top generals was unwilling to accept this and began to plan for a seizure of the government. Spain had seen such military seizures in the past and they came to be known as *pronunciamientos*. In mid-July the army moved in a coordinated effort bringing several of its island and North African forces to Spain. General Jose Sanjurjo was the nominal figurehead of the military uprising and it was assumed that he would take control of the government once control of the capital had been secured. Just as the rebellion was getting started, however, Sanjurjo was killed in a plane crash as he attempted to fly to Spain from his exile in Portugal. After the death of Sanjurjo there was a brief period of uncertainty about the Nationalist leadership. Eventually General Francisco Franco emerged as the supreme leader of the military forces.

The multi-pronged advances of the Spanish armies, however, were stalled and eventually halted by the efforts of ordinary Spanish working-class people and the small numbers of the Spanish military that remained loyal to their government. The Nationalists took the cities of Cadiz and Seville, but no others. The workers' defense forces were coordinated mostly by the trade union organizations of the left, including the Socialist UGT and the Anarchist CNT. They used weapons stores that had been hidden since the workers' uprisings of 1934. By the end of the summer the Republican forces held on to the entire Mediterranean coast, with the exception of the area around Cadiz, and the most of the north coast as well. The Nationalist forces had been able to secure territory through the north and northwest but not the capital, Madrid. Thus the war was fought on multiple fronts.

The Nationalists, led by Franco, appealed to the Hitler regime in Germany and the Mussolini regime in Italy. Both agreed to help and sent significant numbers of troops, airplanes, tanks, and supplies. Facing this, the Republican government appealed to both Britain and France, but neither nation was willing to intervene and rejected all appeals. The diplomats of the democracies did, however, attempt to stop any outside intervention in Spain by setting up a Non-Intervention Committee that would ensure that no major power interfered in the Spanish situation. Germany and Italy were represented on the committee, but ignored its mandates. The committee did nothing to stop German and Italian intervention, but made efforts to stop anyone else from participating. It was a diplomatic fiasco. In the end, the only nation that was willing to lend meaningful aid to the Republic was the Soviet Union. By 1937, the Soviets began shipping large volumes of troops and equipment, but also gradually began to insist on a greater level of command and control. The Republican government was in no condition to resist, and over time the Spanish trade union leadership was ousted. Many people were arrested and even executed by Communist organizations.

Through 1937 and 1938 Nationalist forces slowly captured territory in the north and tightened the circle around Madrid. During April 1937, a Nazi air squadron known as the "Condor Legion" carried out a planned mass bombing on the Basque city of Guernica, killing hundreds. It was the first example of massive "carpet bombing" and the German military used it to gain experience for Hitler's planned invasions in Europe later. By 1939, Barcelona had been taken by the Nationalists and the Republican forces were weakening. The Soviets were tiring of the campaign and began to withdraw aid. With the situation rapidly deteriorating for the Republic, both Britain and France formally recognized the Franco regime on February 27, 1939. Even so, the capital remained in Republican hands. In Madrid, however, Republican military officers rose against Prime Minister Juan Negrin and ousted him, forming a military government of their own. The leaders of the coup hoped to be able to negotiate a peace with Franco. Instead of negotiating, however, Franco launched an all-out offensive against Madrid in late March. It was successful and by March 31 Franco held Madrid and all other major Spanish cities. The following day, Franco proclaimed victory for the Nationalists in a radio address he made to the country.

Franco by this time had consolidated all the far-right political organizations into a single party organization with himself as leader. The party was known as the *Falange Espanola Tradicionalista y de las JONS* and included the *Falange Espanola,* the most explicitly fascist of Spain's parties. Its founder and leader, the Spanish fascist Jose Antonio Primo de Rivera, had been imprisoned by the Republican government immediately when the rebellion began. Franco did nothing to secure his release and he was tried and executed in November 1936. Jose Antonio's party apparatus, however, continued to influence the dictatorship of Franco into the future. Franco established himself with absolute power, eliminated all opposition political parties, and outlawed trade unions and strikes. He also implemented a stringent regime of trade laws that made Spain a virtually autarkic or self-contained economy. In the aftermath of the war Franco rounded up thousands of political opponents and Republican fighters. They were subject to arrest, forced labor, and approximately 200,000 were killed by firing squad (Beevor, 405). As a final insult, Franco used Republican war prisoners to build a great monument to the Nationalists which still stands today and is known as the *Valle de los Caidos* ("Valley of the Fallen").

See also: *Falange Espanola*; Franco, Francisco; Guernica (Bombing of); Primo de Rivera, Jose Antonio.

Further Reading

Beevor, Antony, *The Battle for Spain: The Spanish Civil War 1936–39* (London: Wiedenfield and Nicolson, 2006).

Howson, Gerald, *Arms for Spain: The Untold Story of the Spanish Civil War* (New York: St. Martins, 1998).

Jackson, Gabriel, *The Spanish Republic and the Civil War, 1931–1939* (Princeton: Princeton University Press, 1965).

Payne, Stanley G., *The Spanish Civil War* (New York: Cambridge University Press, 2012).

STURMABTEILUNG **(SA) ("STORM TROOPERS")**   The *Sturmabteilung* (literally "Storm Troopers") also known as the SA and the "Brownshirts," was the uniformed paramilitary branch of the Nazi Party. Established by 1921, this paramilitary organization provided violent force and intimidation in advancing the agenda of the Nazis. It provided security and prevented any protests or heckling at Nazi rallies, engaged in street violence with similar bands of other parties of the far left, and used general intimidation and bullying against groups like Slavs, Gypsies, and Jews. The SA was vital to causing chaos and violence around Germany in the early 1930s which eventually led President Paul von Hindenburg to appoint Adolf Hitler chancellor. After Hitler took power, however, the power and independence of the SA became a concern (especially to the German army), and Hitler moved to execute its leader and significantly reduce its size and role. Still, the SA continued to exist until the collapse of the Nazi state at the end of World War II.

Adolf Hitler joined the young political group called the *Deutsche Arbeiterpartei* ("German Workers' Party") (DAP) in September 1919 as one of its earliest members. The party's name later was changed to the *Nationalsozialistische Deutsche Arbeiterpartei* ("National Socialist German Workers' Party") (NSDAP) or Nazi Party. During 1920 the party—and Hitler himself—discovered his exceptional power as a speaker and as a galvanizing force for the party's political agenda. Eventually any visitors to Nazi speeches or meetings were coming especially to hear Hitler. He used this leverage to make himself absolute leader of the party by 1921.

One thing Hitler and other party leadership discovered was the need for some type of security force, as political opponents often attempted to break up their meetings and these confrontations sometimes deteriorated into brawls. Such an event happened on the evening of February 24, 1920, as Hitler was announcing the formalization of the party's political agenda (the Nazi "25 Points"). Opponents in the crowd shouted down the speakers and the meeting turned into a violent bar fight—it was held in one of Munich's largest beer halls. Many of the Nazi party's ex-soldiers fought together to beat up and throw out the hecklers, and as a result Hitler began to see the need for a permanent force for such activities.

As a model, he looked to the legions formed by Benito Mussolini in Italy, known as the "Blackshirts." The German group formally was launched under the name "Gymnastic and Sports Group," but as the men continued to fight political opponents in violent ways their activities became increasingly reminiscent of the battlefield. By 1921, they adopted the name of "Storm Troopers," borrowing the name from a group of Germany's Special Forces during World War I. As they adopted a formal uniform, they found there was a great surplus of brown uniforms available from the army, which had overbought the uniforms anticipating putting together new divisions from the German colonies. The Nazi SA made these uniforms their own (thus the name, "Brownshirts") and created their own insignia. The SA expanded in 1922 by creating a division specifically for German youth. Youths were indoctrinated with the virtues of devotion to the state and military discipline. This group eventually evolved into the *Hitlerjungend* or "Hitler Youth." It was maintained and administered by the leadership of the SA until 1932.

From the early 1920s until late 1932, the SA engaged in a variety of conflicts providing violence and intimidation toward enemies of the Nazi Party. The SA most regularly fought the forces of Germany's Communist Party and those who fought for the Social Democratic Party. The organization routinely broke into and smashed up the offices of Marxist party publications, and regularly beat up and intimidated Jews and other minorities—sometimes in an organized fashion and sometimes just for "fun." The group's numbers swelled as well, and the SA reached nearly a million members by January 1933, when Adolf Hitler took power.

By the late 1920s the undisputed leader of the SA was Ernst Rohm, and he was still in command when Adolf Hitler became chancellor of Germany in 1933. Rohm had the delusion that the SA would come to supersede the traditional German armed forces in providing the lethal security forces for the Nazi state. He increasingly attempted to override the authority of the highest officers on Germany's General Staff, and had gotten himself named to the nation's General Defense Council. The top leadership in the army began working with members of the Nazi government on a plan to eliminate Rohm and to reduce the power and independence of the SA. Adolf Hitler became convinced that Rohm had to go and that the SA had to be diminished. To this end, Hitler launched a wave of political murders committed from June 30 to July 2, 1934, to eliminate all those within the party that stood as obstacles to Hitler's eventual objectives. This bloodbath became known as the "Night of the Long Knives," and nearly 100 people were executed. Ernst Rohm and other key leaders of the SA were murdered in the purge.

Thereafter the SA assumed a much reduced role in the party; however, it still was called upon routinely to provide street violence and abuse by the government, particularly against Jews. The Nazi boycott of Jewish businesses in early 1933 used the SA to block entrance to Jewish-owned businesses and to commit such vandalization as mark the windows of Jewish shops with spray paint. The SA also played a vital role beating and torturing Jews during the state-sponsored program known as *Kristallnacht* in 1938. The SA committed brutal violence against Jewish people, smashed windows of Jewish homes and businesses, and set fire to hundreds of Jewish Synagogues.

See also: Beer Hall Putsch; Hitler, Adolf; National Socialist German Workers' Party (Nazi Party).

Further Reading

Evans, Richard J., *The Coming of the Third Reich* (New York: Penguin, 2003).
Hancock, Eleanor, *Ernst Roehm: Hitler's SA Chief of Staff* (New York: Palgrave Macmillan, 2008).

TREATY OF VERSAILLES   The Treaty of Versailles was one of the treaties concluded at the Paris Peace Conference in the summer of 1919 held to settle the conditions of peace after the end of the First World War. The official title of the document was the "Treaty of Peace Between the Allied and Associated Powers and Germany." It was drafted to list the conditions and provisions the Allied Powers were to impose upon the defeated nation of Germany. Though there is scholarly debate on the matter, the conditions of the treaty generally were considered to be extremely harsh for Germany and likely to lead to economic distress and a collective sense of hatred and resentment on the part of the German populace. The treaty included articles that removed geographic territory from Germany, removed its overseas colonies, imposed arms limitations, and imposed a schedule of steep reparations payments.

Fighting in the First World War ended on November 11, 1918, with Germany signing an "armistice" agreement. To resolve the dizzying array of issues that remained at war's end, however, a great conference was called at the city of Paris. The Paris Peace Conference was held from January 1919 until January 1920. Most of the major issues discussed at the conference ultimately were decided by a Council of Four which was made up of the political leaders of the four most powerful of the Allied nations. The members of that council were United States president Woodrow Wilson, British prime minister David Lloyd-George, France's prime minister Georges Clemenceau, and Italy's prime minister Vittorio Orlando.

Among the most difficult problems with which the victorious powers wrestled was the question of how to treat the defeated nation of Germany. That nation generally was acknowledged to have been guilty of militarist aggression and provocations leading to the Great War. In nations such as Britain and France—each of which had experienced horrifying numbers of dead and wounded—the public demanded that Germany pay the price for the global nightmare it had wrought. In Britain, during the general election which immediately followed the cessation of hostilities, David Lloyd-George had promised in his campaign speeches to squeeze the Germans "until the pips squeaked." Woodrow Wilson and the U.S. contingent, however, did not seek such harsh treatment of Germany, fearing that such a policy would create a new set of national tensions that would last into the future. Wilson was not able to convince the others of his views on this matter, and was placated by the rest of the "Big 4" agreeing to his dream of establishing the League of Nations.

When it was finalized, the treaty contained a number of articles that imposed a crushing peace on the Germans. In Article 231, such devastating measures were justified by declaring that Germany and its allies bore all responsibility for the First World War. The treaty reads, "The Allied and Associated Governments affirm and Germany accepts the responsibility of Germany and her allies for causing all the loss and damage to which the Allied and Associated Governments and their nationals have been subjected as a consequence of the war imposed upon them by the aggression of Germany and her allies." Having established this premise, the treaty made clear the intent to strip Germany of the ability to cause such a conflict again. It did so in a number of ways.

Germany's geographic territory first was modified. Before the end of the war, Germany had taken from Russia considerable territory that was rich with industry and natural resources. The separate peace signed between Russia and Germany was known as the Treaty of Brest-Litovsk, but Germany's defeat voided that treaty and Germany was forced to return that territory to the Russians. The Poles also had declared an independent nation during 1918, and this was honored by the Paris Peace Conference. Poland was officially re-established as a sovereign nation and given a narrow finger of formerly German territory that extended to the Baltic Sea coast. This gave Poland some access to the sea at the port city of Danzig, but it had the consequence of dividing the German nation into two non-contiguous sections.

Additionally, the region of Germany west of the Rhine River extending to the French border was designated a demilitarized zone, and German military presence and fortifications were prohibited there. Both Britain and France maintained troops in that region until 1930 to enforce this article.

Article 119 of the treaty stripped Germany of its overseas colonies. These colonies were declared "Mandates," by the Council of Four and were distributed among the victorious powers. German colonies in Africa were assigned to France, Belgium, Portugal, and Britain. Germany's small possessions in the Pacific were distributed to Japan, Australia, and New Zealand.

The Treaty of Versailles also imposed stringent limitations on the German military to disable Germany's ability to threaten its neighbors and to encourage general disarmament. Germany's army, henceforth, was to be a force of no more than 100,000 men and its general staff was dissolved. A number of other stipulations dismantled Germany's military infrastructure, such as the provision that reduced Germany's officer schools to three. The German navy was limited to a small number of ships, including 6 light cruisers, 6 battleships, and 12 destroyers. Its submarine fleet was eliminated. Article 198 of the treaty forbade the Germans from developing a military air force.

The Treaty of Versailles also imposed upon Germany a crushing schedule of reparations payments. Germany was to pay a total of 20 billion marks (in gold) to the various victorious powers. These payments could be paid in other forms such as currency or commodities. Additionally, Germany was forced to turn over great amounts of industrial produce and raw materials such as coal, steel, and timber.

The leading politicians of Germany's newly established Weimar Republic were forced to accept the conditions of the treaty. Despite their efforts at negotiation, the leaders of the Paris Peace Conference threatened to re-open hostilities if the Germans did not sign. With little choice, the German contingent signed on June 28, 1919. Predictably, the treaty produced an ultra-nationalist backlash in Germany. The German public felt a sense of outrage and national humiliation over the conditions of the treaty—particularly its enforcement by foreign powers on German soil. The rejection of the treaty and its dissolution was one of the leading principles of the NSDAP (Nazi Party) led by Adolf Hitler. After three years in power, in 1936 Hitler began a series of violations of that treaty that eventually contributed to the outbreak of the Second World War.

See also: First World War; Paris Peace Conference; Rearmament; Remilitarization of the Rhineland.

Further Reading

Elcock, H. J., *Portrait of a Decision: The Council of Four and the Treaty of Versailles* (London: Eyre & Methuen, 1972).

Keynes, John Maynard, *The Economic Consequences of the Peace* (Rahway, NJ: Quinn & Bodin, 1920).

Macmillan, Margaret, *Paris 1919: Six Months That Changed the World* (New York: Random House, 2002).

VICHY, FRANCE   "Vichy France" is the term used to describe the French State after its defeat by Nazi Germany forces in June 1940. While the Germans occupied and governed northern France and the Atlantic coastal lands, there remained a section of France designated as an unoccupied zone and an independent state. The seat of government was moved to the spa town of Vichy and a fascist-style regime was established under the leadership of Premier Marshal Philippe Petain. The Petain regime maintained France as an independent state from 1940 to November 1942, when the Nazis moved into the southern regions as well. From that point Petain's regime was a mere puppet government under constant control by Nazi officials. The Vichy French regime represented the most right-wing, reactionary elements of the country and assembled a group of policies that have earned it a reputation as a fascist, or at least quasi-fascist, regime. Controversially, the government and people of Vichy France lent assistance to the Nazis in numerous ways which created accusations of "collaboration." As France gradually was liberated through 1944 and 1945, there were savage reprisals against active and open collaborators.

On May 10, 1940, Adolf Hitler's German armies marched in an invasion of France and the Low Countries. France had invested most of its defense budget in fortifications on the German border known as the "Maginot Line," but had stopped building at the border of the Ardennes Forest, believing that the great forest presented too great an obstacle for an effective invasion. German forces, however, were increasingly mechanized and moved easily through the Ardennes forest and thus around the Maginot Line. French forces—even with the aid of the British Expeditionary Force—were defeated in a matter of weeks.

The French government fled Paris for Bordeaux, but soon realized that there was no hope of rallying its armies. On June 22, 1940, an armistice was signed between France and Germany that designated most of the north of France for direct German control and designated the southern section of the country to remain the "rump" of the French State. As France fell and negotiations with the Germans were imminent, the French president Albert Lebrun appointed Marshal Henri Philippe Petain as premier with full powers. Petain, a legendary hero of the First World War, and his staff signed the armistice and soon after began assembling a government to begin governing the "Free Zone," of southern France.

Petain assembled a collection of politicians sympathetic with the values and policies of the far right. In a symbolically powerful move, he changed the nation's motto from *Liberte, Egalite, Fraternite* ("Liberty, Equality, Fraternity") (derived from the French Revolution of 1789), to *Travail, Famille, Patrie* ("Work, Family, Fatherland"). Petain's government took on many of the aspects of acknowledged fascist governments, including the attempted reorganization of French industry along the lines of the "Corporative" model pioneered by Benito Mussolini in Italy. Boards of experts known as "Occupational Associations" monitored and regulated entire industries, theoretically for the benefit of the nation. All trade unions were disbanded and outlawed and all strike activity was made illegal. Petain also began his regime with several new measures intended to return French workers to the soil. These measures proved to be unworkable, as the demands by the Nazis for war material made industrial production a constant priority.

Other Vichy laws, which resembled fascist programs, reflected the obsession with the growth of the French race and increasing the birth rate. Abortion was outlawed, divorce was made almost impossible to secure, and contraception suppressed. Pregnant women were issued "priority cards," which allowed them to obtain first claim on groceries and other consumer products. The measures, however, which have most condemned the Vichy regime are those in which it significantly lent aid to the Nazi war effort. The Vichy French government turned over 85% of all vehicles produced to the Nazis; and 15% of all food production went to the Nazis. In all, 40% of all Vichy French industrial output was turned over to the Hitler regime (Davies, 110).

Vichy also sent legions of French laborers to work in German factories. Most chilling of all, both in the north and south of France a network of concentration camps was established. This was part of a wide-ranging plan to identify and detain French Jews in segregated camps. Later, these Jews were shipped to Eastern Europe where the Nazis had established their death camps as part of the Holocaust. In all, approximately 76,000 French Jews were rounded up and sent to their deaths with the cooperation of the Vichy regime (Davies, 110).

Away from the continent, Charles de Gaulle had formed a government of Free France, based in London. The Free French worked to assemble a military force and to take control of French colonial areas in Africa, the Middle East, and the Caribbean. This produced an ongoing struggle as Vichy forces fought to retain control of these areas, but it gradually lost them. The Free French also worked to create an active French Resistance inside France. To fight against such activities the Vichy regime established the *Milice Francaise* ("French Militia") which was a secret police and internal security force. This organization used espionage, detainments, and torture to root out and eliminate any subversion. To this end it worked closely with the Nazi Gestapo.

The Allies staged the massive invasion of the continent at Normandy, known as Operation Overlord, on June 6, 1944. After the deadly struggle to establish a new front on the north coast of France, Allied armies pushed eastward toward Paris. They liberated Paris on August 25, 1944. With this, Petain and the other officials of the Vichy French government were evacuated to Germany where they were expected to act as an official government in exile. As the Allies and Free French gradually took back control of the country, they announced that the Vichy regime had been unconstitutional and hence none of its legislation was valid. What followed was a period of unrestrained violence and recriminations against those who had actively collaborated with the Nazis. This took the form of hangings, firing squads, and public humiliations.

Petain and many of the Vichy officials eventually were tried for treason. They generally defended themselves with the argument that in the situation they were faced with, forming such a government and actively working with the Nazis was absolutely necessary to protect the French people from further death and destruction. For Petain and Pierre Laval (Petain's prime minister) this argument was not sufficient, and French courts sentenced both men to death. Laval was found guilty and executed by firing squad. Petain also was found guilty but because of his heroic war record in earlier years and his advanced age, his sentence was commuted to life in prison.

See also: Petain, Henri Philippe.

Further Reading

Burrin, Philippe, *France Under the Germans: Collaboration and Compromise* (New York: The New Press, 1995).

Davies, Peter, *The Extreme Right in France, 1789 to the Present* (London: Routledge, 2002).

Fogg, Shannon Lee, *The Politics of Everyday Life in Vichy France* (New York: Cambridge University Press, 2009).

Paxton, Robert O., *Vichy France: Old Guard, New Order, 1940–1944* (New York: Columbia University Press, 1972).

Sweets, John F., *Choices in Vichy France: The French Under Nazi Occupation* (New York: Oxford University Press, 1986).

Primary Documents

"THE FUTURIST MANIFESTO"

Written by FILIPPO TOMMASO MARINETTI

**Published in *Le Figaro* as "Manifeste du Futurisme,"
February 20, 1909**

The "Futurist Manifesto," by F. T. Marinetti (published in February 1909) sought to make public—in shocking language—the principles defining a new movement in the arts. It emphasizes a number of the frustrations and anxieties that had been growing within Italy, especially among the younger generations. Marinetti stridently rejects the values and the aesthetics of the past—the museums, cemeteries, professors, and antiquaries. He embraces instead a rather stark type of modernity, glorifying technology, speed, power, factory production, and masculinity. Marinetti also emphasizes the benefits of violence and warfare. This all reflects a growing anger with Italy's national backwardness, its failure to assert itself among the "Great Powers," and the belief of younger citizens that the institutions of the past must be obliterated. Benito Mussolini was deeply influenced by Marinetti, and Marinetti himself later became a rabid follower of Mussolini and eventually a Fascist group leader. The Fascist movement seems to have been the political expression of that set of national frustrations. As Italian Historian Benedetto Croce wrote in 1924, "For anyone who has a sense of historical connections, the ideological origins of Fascism can be found in Futurism. . . ."

1. We want to sing the love of danger, the habit of energy and rashness.
2. The essential elements of our poetry will be courage, audacity and revolt.
3. Literature has, up to now, magnified pensive immobility, ecstasy and slumber. We want to exalt movements of aggression, feverish sleeplessness, the double march, the perilous leap, the slap and blow with the fist.
4. We declare that the splendor of the world has been enriched by a new beauty: the beauty of speed. A racing automobile with its bonnet adorned with great tubes like serpents with explosive breath . . . a roaring motor car which seems to run on machine gun fire, is more beautiful than the Victory of Samothrace.
5. We want to sing the man at the wheel, the ideal axis of which crosses the earth, itself hurled along its orbit.
6. The poet must spend himself with warmth, glamour and prodigality to increase the enthusiastic fervor of the primordial elements.
7. Beauty exists only in struggle. There is no masterpiece that has not an aggressive character. Poetry must be a violent assault on the forces of the unknown, to force them to bow before man.
8. We are on the extreme promontory of the centuries! What is the use of looking behind at the moment when we must open the mysterious shutters of the impossible? Time and Space died yesterday. We are already living in the absolute, since we have already created eternal, omnipresent speed.
9. We want to glorify war—the only cure for the world—militarism, patriotism, the destructive gesture of the anarchists, the beautiful ideas which kill, and contempt for women.
10. We want to demolish museums and libraries, fight morality, feminism and all opportunist and utilitarian cowardice.
11. We will sing of great crowds agitated by work, pleasure and revolt; the multi-colored and polyphonic surf of revolutions in modern capitals: the nocturnal vibration of the arsenals and the workshops beneath their violent electric moons: the gluttonous railway stations devouring smoking serpents; factories suspended from the clouds by the thread of their smoke; bridges with the leap of gymnasts flung across the diabolic cutlery of sunny rivers; adventurous steamers sniffing the horizon; great-breasted locomotives, puffing on the rails like enormous steel horses with long tubes for bridle; and the gliding flight of aeroplanes whose propeller sounds like the flapping of a flag and the applause of enthusiastic crowds.

It is in Italy that we are issuing this manifesto of ruinous and incendiary violence, by which we today are founding Futurism, because we want to deliver Italy from its gangrene of professors, archaeologists, tourist guides and antiquaries.

Italy has been too long the great second-hand market. We want to get rid of the innumerable museums which cover it with innumerable cemeteries.

The oldest among us are not yet thirty, and yet we have already wasted treasures, treasures of strength, love, courage and keen will, hastily, deliriously, without thinking, with all our might, till we are out of breath.

Look at us! We are not out of breath, our hearts are not in the least tired. For they are nourished by fire, hatred and speed! Does this surprise you? It is because you do not even remember having been alive! Standing on the world's summit, we launch once more our challenge to the stars!

Source: James Joll, *Three Intellectuals in Politics* (New York: Pantheon, 1960), 179–184.

CLARIFICATION SPEECH

BENITO MUSSOLINI

Delivered to the Italian Chamber of Deputies, January 3, 1925

In 1923, Italy had passed a new electoral law, known as the "Acerbo Law," that allowed the winning party to take two-thirds of all the seats in parliament, so long as the winner obtained at least 25% of the total vote. The Fascists accomplished this in the 1924 elections and took two thirds of the seats in the parliament. In response, one United Socialist deputy, Giacomo Matteotti, spoke out, condemning the Fascist victory. He was murdered soon after, which caused a significant controversy. The Socialists in the parliament walked out in protest, refusing to acknowledge the election as valid. This walkout earned the nickname the "Aventine Secession" (after a political event in Ancient Rome).

Accused of violence, murder, and intimidation of the voters, Mussolini feared he might be deposed by Italy's king Victor Emmanuel III. To answer the controversy, he addressed the parliament and defiantly took responsibility—and challenged anyone who thought they had enough the power to attempt to depose him. This was his "Clarification Speech," in which he defended any violent steps his Fascists might have taken and announced his plans to move forward with his Fascist agenda unless the opposition could stop him. This speech is considered the moment when Mussolini declared his dictatorship. From this point the Socialist parties were outlawed, the Fascist Grand Council was established, and the Italian Parliament turned into a Fascist Party congress.

Gentlemen, the speech that I am about to deliver should not perhaps be classified, strictly speaking, as a parliamentary address. . . . A speech of this sort may or may not lead to a vote on policy. Let it be known that in any case I do not seek such a vote on policy. . . . My speech therefore will be very clear and such as to bring about absolute clarification.

. . . It is said that I have created a *Cheka*.[1] Where? When? How? No one can answer! . . . If I had created a *Cheka*, I would have done so according to the criteria that I have always imposed on that degree of violence which cannot be eliminated from history.

[There follows discussion of the political aftermath of the Matteotti affair.]

. . . It was at the end of that month . . . that I said "I want peace for the Italian people." I wanted to bring political life back to normalcy.

But, what was the reply to this principle of mine? First of all, there was the Aventine secession, an unconstitutional secession that was clearly revolution-ary. [Lively approval.] Then there followed a press campaign that lasted through June, July, and August; a filthy and wretched campaign that dishonored us for three months. . . the most fantastic, most horrendous, most macabre lies were widely published in all the papers! . . . In the meanwhile, this campaign bore fruit. On September 11 someone sought to avenge the dead man and shot one of our best people, a man who died in poverty. . . . Nevertheless, I contin-ued my effort at normalization. I repressed illegal acts . . . I proposed a reform of the electoral law.

And how did they respond to all this? They responded with an intensified campaign. They said that Fascism is a horde of barbarians encamped in the country, a movement of bandits and marauders!

Very well, I now declare before this assembly and before the entire Italian people that I assume, I alone, full political, moral, and historical responsibility for all that has happened.

[Very vigorous and repeated applause. Shouts of "*We are with you! All with you!*"]

. . . If Fascism has been nothing more than castor oil and the rubber trun-cheon, instead of being a proud passion of the best part of Italian youth, then I am to blame! [Applause] If fascism has been a criminal association, then I am the chief of this criminal association!

. . . When two irreducible elements are locked in a struggle, the solution is force. In history there never has been any other solution and there never will be.

. . . Gentlemen, Italy wants peace, tranquility, calm in which to work. We shall give her this tranquility and calm, by means of love if possible but by force if necessary. [Lively applause]

---

1. The Cheka was the murderous secret police organization founded by Vladimir Lenin in Russia during the days of the Russia Civil War from 1918 to 1922. It was notorious for inter-nal espionage, torture, and murder in the name of eliminating the enemies of the people.

You may be sure that within the next forty-eight hours after this speech, the situation will be clarified in every field. [Vigorous, prolonged applause; comments] Everyone must realize that what I am planning to do is not the result of personal caprice, of a lust for power, or of an ignoble passion, but solely the expression of my unlimited and mighty love for the fatherland.

[Vigorous, prolonged and reiterated applause. Repeated shouts of "*Long live Mussolini!*" . . . The meeting is ended.]

Source: Charles Delzell (ed.), *Mediterranean Fascism, 1919–1945* (New York: Harper & Row, 1971), 57–61. Introduction, editorial notes, translations by the editor, and compilation copyright 1970, Charles F. Delzell. Reprinted by permission of HarperCollins Publishers.

"FASCISM: DOCTRINE AND INSTITUTIONS"

Written by BENITO MUSSOLINI and GIOVANNI GENTILE

Published in the *Enciclopedia Italiana*, 1932

The document reproduced here is the text of an article written by Benito Mussolini and the Italian philosopher Giovanni Gentile. It is an attempt to clearly define and describe the new political philosophy of Fascism as it had developed in Italy. The article was first published in the *Enciclopedia Italiana* in its 1932 edition as part of an even longer entry describing the Italian Fascist system. The entry is notoriously verbose and difficult to follow, and does not, in the end, produce a concrete or coherent definition. The entry does, however, make a few major points.

One such point is that Fascism is the political embodiment of a national collectivism—a nationalist philosophy that has the power to bring together entire national communities. To be a member of the actual or the spiritual community one must be prepared to labor, contribute, and sacrifice for it. Another point is the role of action and violence in the philosophy. A Fascist community or a Fascist state must be an entity of power and virility, willing to expand through action, enterprise, and violent conquest if necessary. Pacifism is completely rejected, and war is celebrated as bringing out the best and hardest qualities in the national community. Mussolini gives a brief nod to religion, acknowledging its importance to ordinary people and assuring readers that Fascism protects and defends traditional religion. He also makes clear, however, that the Fascist State has no religious commitment.

Mussolini and Gentile spend a great deal of time discussing European historical development to explain how Fascism fits into that development. They explain that Liberal Democracy, Socialism, and individualism were conceptions based in the 19th century and that they had become obsolete. They see

Fascism as having grown out of these obsolete systems but emerging as a distinctly modern system for the 20th century.

> Like all political conceptions, Fascism is action and it is thought; action in which doctrine is immanent, and doctrine arising from a given system of historical forces in which it is inserted, and working on them from within. . . .
>
> Thus many of the practical expressions of Fascism—such as party organization, system of education, discipline—can only be understood when considered in relation to its general attitude toward life. A spiritual attitude. Fascism sees in the world not only those superficial, material aspects in which man appears as an individual, standing by himself, self-centered, subject to natural law which instinctively urges him toward a life of selfish momentary pleasure; it sees not only the individual but the nation and the country; individuals and generations bound together by a moral law, with common traditions and a mission which, suppressing the instinct for life closed in a brief circle of pleasure, builds up a higher life, founded on duty, a life free from the limitations of time and space, in which the individual, by self-sacrifice, the renunciation of self-interest, by death itself, can achieve that purely spiritual existence in which his value as a man exists. . . .
>
> Fascism wants man to be active and to engage in action with all his energies; it wants him to be manfully aware of the difficulties besetting him and ready to face them. It conceives of life as a struggle in which it behooves a man to win for himself a really worthy place . . . first of all by fitting himself (physically, morally, intellectually) to become the implement required for winning it. . . . The Fascist disdains an "easy" life.
>
> And above all, Fascism, the more it considers and observes the future and the development of humanity quite apart from political considerations of the moment, believes neither in the possibility nor the utility of perpetual peace. It thus repudiates the doctrine of Pacifism—born of a renunciation of the struggle and an act of cowardice in the face of sacrifice. War alone brings up to its highest tension all human energy and puts the stamp of nobility upon the peoples who have the courage to meet it. All other trials are substitutes. . . .

[The article goes on to discuss European historical development at length]

> . . . But the Fascist negation of Socialism, Democracy, and Liberalism must not be taken to mean that Fascism desires to lead the world back to the state of affairs before 1789, the date which seems to be indicated as the opening year of the succeeding semi-Liberal century; we do not desire to turn back. . . . Given that the nineteenth century was the century of Socialism, Liberalism and Democracy, it does not necessarily follow that the twentieth century must also be a century of Socialism, Liberalism, and Democracy: political doctrines pass, but humanity remains; and it may rather be expected that this

will be a century of authority, a century of the Right, a century of Fascism. For if the nineteenth century was a century of individualism it may be expected that this will be the century of collectivism, and hence the century of the State. . . .

The Fascist State is not indifferent to the fact of religion in general, or to that particular and positive faith which is Italian Catholicism. The State professes no theology, but a morality, and in the Fascist State religion is considered as one of the deepest manifestations of the spirit of man; thus it is not only respected but defended and protected. . . .

The Fascist State is an embodied will to power and government; the Roman tradition is here an ideal of force in action. . . . For Fascism, the growth of empire, that is to say the expansion of the nation, is an essential manifestation of vitality, and its opposite a sign of decadence. Peoples which are rising, or rising again after a period of decadence, are always imperialist: any renunciation is a sign of decay and death.

Fascism is the doctrine best adapted to represent the tendencies and the aspirations of a people, like the people of Italy, who are rising again after many centuries of abasement and foreign servitude. But empire demands discipline, the coordination of all forces and a deeply felt sense of duty and sacrifice. . . . If every age has its own characteristic doctrine, there are a thousand signs which point to Fascism as the characteristic doctrine of our time. For if a doctrine must be a living thing, this is proved by the fact that Fascism has created a living faith. . . .

Source: Charles Delzell (ed.), *Mediterranean Fascism, 1919–1945* (New York: Harper & Row, 1971), 91–106. Introduction, editorial notes, translations by the editor, and compilation copyright 1970 by Charles F. Delzell. Reprinted by permission of HarperCollins Publishers.

THE TWENTY-SIX-POINT PROGRAM OF THE *FALANGE ESPANOLA*

1937 Edition

Jose Antonio Primo de Rivera, the son of Spain's deposed dictator General Miguel Primo de Rivera, founded the *Falange Espanola* as an explicitly fascist political party in 1933. The party's statement of policies was called the "Twenty-Seven Points." As the Spanish Civil War began, Jose Antonio Primo de Rivera was arrested and then executed by the Republican government. His organization, however, would side with the military rebellion led by Francisco Franco. Franco later combined the various extreme-right organizations into a single political party, the *Falange Espanola Tradicionalista y de las JONS*. The *Falange Espanola* was a significant part of the new entity, and Franco retained its political statement, but reduced it slightly. The result was the document

included below—the "Twenty-Six Points." The policies listed are consistent
with those of most fascist groups in Europe at the time. These included a
belief in the nation as the supreme entity, the need for extraordinary military
strength, a Corporative-style economic organization, and protected and enhanced agricultural production. The list also advocates a nationalizing of the
banking system, and ensuring the right (and duty) of Spaniards to work. The
partnership of the Catholic Church is included in glowing terms although
its precise role is left vague, and it makes clear that the Church will not have
the ability to dictate to the State. Interestingly, there is no clear reference
here to race or the need to purge "foreign" elements (though there is a reference to finance capital and moneylenders, which often referred to Jews).
Although purging the nation of Marxist and Anarchist influences, and the
denunciation of separatist movements are listed as urgent priorities, no such
comments are made referring to the biological basis of the nation nor the
need to purge corrosive biological elements (as is made plain in many early
Nazi declarations).

Nation—Unity—Empire

1. We believe in the supreme reality of Spain. The strengthening, elevating,
   and magnifying of this reality is the urgent collective goal of all Spaniards.
   Individual, group, and class interests must inexorably give way in order to
   achieve this goal.
2. Spain has a single destiny in the world. Every conspiracy against this common unity is repulsive. Any kind of separatism is a crime which we shall
   not pardon.

   The existing Constitution, to the degree that it encourages disintegration, weakens this common destiny of Spain. Therefore we demand its
   annulment in a thundering voice.
3. We have the determination to build an Empire. We affirm that Spain's
   historic fulfillment lies in Empire. We claim for Spain a pre-eminent position in Europe. We can tolerate neither international isolation nor foreign
   interference.

   As regards the countries of Hispanic America, we favor unification of
   their culture, economic interests, and power. Spain will continue to act as
   the spiritual axis of the Hispanic world as a sign of her pre-eminence in
   worldwide enterprises.
4. Our armed forces—on land, sea, and in the air—must be kept trained
   and sufficiently large to assure Spain at all times its complete independence and a status in the world that befits it. We shall bestow upon
   our Armed Forces of land, sea, and air all the dignity they merit, and we
   shall cause their military conception of life to infuse every aspect of Spanish life.

5. Spain shall once more seek her glory and her wealth on the sea lanes. Spain must aspire to become a great maritime power, for reasons of both defense and commerce.

   We demand for the fatherland equal status with others in maritime power and aerial routes.

State—Individual—Liberty

6. Our State will be a totalitarian instrument to defend the integrity of the fatherland. All Spaniards will participate in this through their various family, municipal, and syndical roles. There shall be no participation in it by political parties. We shall implacably abolish the system of political parties and all of their consequences—inorganic suffrage, representation of clashing groups, and a Parliament of the type that is all too well known.

7. Human dignity, integrity, and freedom are eternal, intangible values. But one is not really free unless he is a part of a strong and free nation.

   No one will be permitted to use his freedom against the nation, which is the bulwark of the fatherland's freedom. Rigorous discipline will prevent any attempt to envenom and disunite the Spanish people or to incite them against the destiny of the fatherland.

8. The National-Syndicalist State will permit all kinds of private initiative that are compatible with the collective interest, and it will also protect and encourage the profitable ones.

Economy—Labor—Class

9. Our conception of Spain in the economic realm is that of a gigantic syndicate of producers. We shall organize Spanish society corporatively through a system of vertical syndicates for the various fields of production, all working toward national economic unity.

10. We repudiate the capitalist system which shows no understanding of the needs of the people, dehumanizes private property, and causes workers to be lumped together in a shapeless, miserable mass of people who are filled with desperation. Our spiritual and national conception of life also repudiates Marxism. We shall re-direct the impetuousness of those working classes who today are led astray by Marxism, and we shall seek to bring them into direct participation in fulfilling the great task of the national State.

11. The National-Syndicalist State will not cruelly stand apart from man's economic struggles, nor watch impassively while the strongest class dominates the weakest. Our regime will eliminate the very roots of class struggle, because all who work together in production shall comprise one single organic entity. We reject and we shall prevent at all costs selfish interests from abusing others, and we shall halt anarchy in the field of labor relations.

12. The first duty of wealth—and our State shall so affirm—is to better the conditions of the people. It is intolerable that enormous masses of people should live wretchedly while a small number enjoy all kinds of luxuries.
13. The State will recognize private property as a legitimate means for achieving individual, family and social goals, and will protect it against the abuses of large-scale finance capital, speculators, and moneylenders.
14. We shall support the trend toward nationalization of banking services and, through a system of Corporations, the great public utilities.
15. All Spaniards have the right to work. Public agencies must of necessity provide support for those who find themselves in desperate straits.

    As we proceed toward a totally new structure, we shall maintain and strengthen all the advantages that existing social legislation gives to workers.
16. Unless they are disabled, all Spaniards have the duty to work. The National-Syndicalist State will not give the slightest consideration to those who fail to perform some useful function and who try to live as drones at the expense of the labor of the majority of the people.

Land

17. We must, at all costs, raise the standard of living in the countryside, which is Spain's permanent source of food. To this end, we demand an agreement that will bring to culmination without further delay the economic and social reforms of the agricultural sector.
18. Our program of economic reforms will enrich agricultural production by means of the following: [There follows a lengthy list of specific measures to protect and improve food production which includes points 19, 20, 21, and 22].

National Education—Religion

23. It shall be the essential mission of the State to attain by means of rigorous disciplining of education a strong, united national spirit, and to instill in the souls of future generations a sense of rejoicing and pride in the fatherland.

    All men shall receive preliminary training to prepare them for the honor of being enlisted in the National and Popular Army of Spain.
24. Cultural life shall be organized so that no talent will be undeveloped because of insufficient economic means. All who merit it shall be assured ready access to a higher education.
25. Our Movement incorporates the Catholic meaning—of glorious tradition, and especially in Spain—of national reconstruction.

    The Church and State will co-ordinate their respective powers so as to permit no interference or activity that may impair the dignity of the State or national integrity.

National Revolution

26. The *Falange Espanola Tradicionalista y de las JONS* demands a new order, as set forth in the foregoing principles. In the face of the resistance from the present order, it calls for a revolution to implant this new order. Its method of procedure will be direct, bold and combative. Life signifies the art and science of warfare (*milicia*) and must be lived with a spirit that is purified by service and sacrifice.

Source: Charles Delzell (ed.), *Mediterranean Fascism, 1919–1945* (New York: Harper & Row, 1971), 273–277. Introduction, editorial notes, translations by the editor, and compilation copyright 1970 by Charles F. Delzell. Reprinted by permission of HarperCollins Publishers.

THE GREATER BRITAIN

Written by SIR OSWALD MOSLEY,
Leader of the British Union of Fascists

Published in October 1932

Sir Oswald Mosley had emerged as one of Britain's most dynamic politicians by 1931, but he also had quit both the Conservative Party and the Labour Party by that year. He went on to found his own party called the New Party. That party suffered a humiliating defeat in the 1931 election and Mosley himself lost his seat in parliament. He became increasingly attracted to the fascist dictatorships and went to work on a plan for making Britain a fascist state. He relaunched his political party in October 1932 as the "British Union of Fascists" (BUF) and at that same time published his very thorough political program, a book titled *The Greater Britain*. The excerpts below discuss some of the BUF's principal points and objectives. First, Mosley emphasized that modern science and technology had changed the economic world so drastically that Liberal-Democracy no longer was an effective political system. A new, modern system (fascism) was needed. He also stressed that Britain should focus on developing its own economy within its own borders, using the exclusion of foreign competitors' goods to protect the home industries. In exchange for the protection from such competition, employers would have to commit to keeping product costs down and to paying high wage levels. To control this system Mosley was particularly determined to see the "Corporative" system implemented as it was in Italy. He intended to create Corporations (boards of experts) to regulate entire industries. He also was determined to change the electoral system of Britain to one in which voters elected parliamentary representatives from within whatever industry they worked. The British Parliament would change from electoral districts to electing members of parliament by industry. He repeatedly emphasized creating a self-sufficient, self-contained imperial economic system or "Autarky" for Britain. Also important was the need to rearm Britain to the maximum capacity. All of this, he said, would help ensure that Britain was "insulated from world chaos." The BUF also rejected racism and anti-Semitism (the Nazi model), initially, making the point that the British Empire was full of different races and ethnicities and that such policies would be disastrous. After 1934, however, the BUF increasingly turned to overt anti-Semitism. Finally, Mosley makes the point that the BUF did not seek violence but would be prepared to defend itself from the Communists, and if the State went into collapse, his Fascists would be prepared to seize control of the state by violent force.

From the "Introduction"

In Great Britain during the past ten years there have never been less than a million unemployed, and recently unemployment has fluctuated over a two million figure. . . . We have tragic proof that economic life has outgrown our political institutions. Britain has failed to recover from the war period; and this result, however complicated by special causes, is largely due to a system of Government designed by, and for, the nineteenth century. . . . I believe that under the existing system, Government cannot be efficiently conducted.

The object of this book is to prove, by analysis of the present situation and by constructive policy, that the necessity for fundamental change exists. Our political system dates substantially from 1832. The intervening century has seen the invention and development of telegraph, telephone and wireless . . . motor transport on modern roads. . . [t]he modern process of mass production. Within the last century science has multiplied by many times the power of man to produce. . . .

From the standpoint of a century ago, all these changes are revolutionary. . . . It is hardly surprising that the political system of 1832 is wholly out of date today. . . . Our problem is to reconcile the revolutionary changes of science with our system of government, and to harmonize individual initiative with the wider interests of the nation.

Fascism—the Modern Movement

Hence the need for a New Movement, not only in politics, but in the whole of our national life. The movement is Fascist, (i) because it is based on a high conception of citizenship—ideals as lofty as those which inspired the reformers of a hundred years ago (ii) because it recognizes the necessity for an authoritative state, above party and sectional interests. . . . We seek to organize the

Modern Movement in this country by British methods in a form which is suitable to and characteristic of Great Britain. We are essentially a national movement, and if our policy could be summarized in two words, they would be "Britain First."

From Chapter II—"The Corporate State"

The main object of a modern and Fascist movement is to establish the Corporate State. In our belief it is the greatest constructive conception yet devised by the hand of man. It is almost unknown in Britain; yet it is, by nature, better adapted to the British temperament than to that of any other nation. . . . The producer, whether by hand or brain or capital will be the basis of the nation. The forces which assist him in his work of rebuilding the nation will be encouraged; the forces which thwart and destroy productive enterprise will be met with the force of national authority. The incalculable powers of finance will be harnessed in the service of national production.

The task of such industrial organizations (Corporations) will certainly not be confined merely to the settlement of questions of wages and of hours. They will be called upon to assist, by regular consultation, in the general economic policy of the nation. The syndicates of employers' and workers' organizations in particular industries will be dovetailed into the corporations covering larger and interlocking spheres of industry. These corporations in their turn will be represented in a national corporation or council of industry, which will be a permanent feature in cooperating with the Government for the direction of economic policy.

Occupational Franchise

Such a combination of new and effective instruments in Government will enable Fascism in the lifetime of the first Fascist Parliament to carry through immense changes in the national life. . . . At the end of that Parliament a new election will be held on an Occupational Franchise—a steel worker will vote as a steel worker; a doctor as a doctor, a mother as a mother, within their appropriate corporation. Party warfare will come to an end in a technical and non-political Parliament which will be concerned not with the Party game of obstruction, but with the national interest of construction.

From Chapter VI "Building Up the Home Market"

It is submitted in our policy that Protection (meaning the outright exclusion of foreign goods rather than through tariffs) must be conditional upon industrial efficiency. That efficiency we define broadly as low prices to the consumer and good wages to the worker. . . . Protection should only be given in return for definite conditions as to wages and prices.

From Chapter VII "The Export Trade"

Autarchy

The policy at which we aim is Autarchy, or that of the self-contained Nation and Empire, which I described as "Insulation." . . . It recognizes that modern nations can produce almost any goods they require with present machinery. . . . The problem is no longer whether the goods can be produced at the least possible cost, but whether they can be produced at all. To enable goods to be produced we must plan and regulate the industrial area covered by our own race, which is capable of supplying in abundance all the goods we need.

Once we free our economic system from the disruptive forces of world competition and can release the full power of our own potential production for a regulated Home market we can enjoy a standard of life far higher than we have known in the past without any dependence at all upon the chaos of world markets.

From Chapter VIII "The Empire"

. . . No effort should be spared to weld together by consent into a great economic entity the largest and most economically self-contained area in the world, bound together as it is by a common loyalty to the Crown.

If this can be achieved, we are indeed on the high road to an insulated system which could be immune from the chaos of present world conditions. No matter what happened in the rest of the world, this great structure of economic and political interests could weather the storm.

From Chapter IX "Fascism and Its Neighbors"

It will be the task of Fascist Europe to eliminate the risk of war by removing the causes of war. The economic causes of war, which are by far the most powerful factors in that disaster, will be reduced to the vanishing point by the policy already described. . . . Disarmament has so far proved impracticable. . . . The arrival of the Air factor has altered fundamentally the position of these Islands, and the consequences of that factor have never yet been realized by the older generation of politicians. We will immediately raise the air strength of Britain to the level of the strongest power in Europe. Successive governments have criminally weakened our air force and exposed this country to the gravest danger. I have never ceased to attack this mad policy since the war and under Fascism it will immediately be revised.

In general, we would seek peace and conciliation, and are prepared to take the lead in these subjects. [But], our main policy quite frankly is a policy of "Britain First."

From Chapter XII "Conclusion"

We are accused of organizing to promote violence. That accusation is untrue. It is true that we are organized to protect our meetings as far as possible from violence . . . when we are confronted by red terror, we are certainly organized to meet force by force, and will always do our utmost to smash it. The bully of the streets has gone too long unchallenged. . . . Emphatically this does not mean that we seek violence. . . . Whether our British Union of Fascists will arrive at power through the parliamentary system or whether it will reach power in a situation far beyond the control of parliament no one can tell. . . . If the situation develops rapidly . . . something like collapse may come before any new movement has captured parliamentary power.

In that case, other and sterner measures must be adopted for the saving of the State in a situation approaching anarchy. . . . In no case shall we resort to violence against forces of the Crown; but only against the forces of anarchy if and when the machinery of state has been allowed to drift into powerlessness.

Source: Sir Oswald Mosley, *The Greater Britain* (London: BUF, 1932). Published with permission of The Friends of Oswald Mosley (F.O.M.) London, and Black House Publishing Ltd.

PROGRAM OF THE NATIONAL SOCIALIST GERMAN WORKERS' PARTY

Announced February 24, 1920

The twenty-five-point program of the National Socialist German Workers' Party (Nazi Party) was assembled by the party's early leadership. This included the founder of the movement, Anton Drexler, Adolf Hitler, and the economist Gottfried Feder. The program was announced during a speech made by Adolf Hitler at a beer hall in Munich, Germany, on February 24, 1920. Though detailed, the program emphasizes a number of general principles, including the need for Germany to become politically independent by overturning the Treaty of Versailles; the desire to "reunite" all Germans into a single political state; making German racial stock the basis of the political nation (and excluding all others); basing income and wealth on productive activities that benefit the nation, rather than on investment income or war profits; and, throughout, Jews are overtly singled out as representing a harmful element that must be suppressed and purged. Many of the program's objectives imply a powerful and authoritarian state, and the final point (25), declares the Nazi desire for a strong and decisive central government. The point is vague, however, and even mentions a parliament—which would suggest the continuation of universal suffrage. This program was held in place by Hitler in the years to follow, and many of its principles remained central to the Nazi Party and to the Hitler regime. Many of its pro-labor suggestions of curbing big profits for business, however, proved unrealistic with the later priorities of rearmament and war.

1. We demand the union of all Germans in a Greater Germany on the basis of the right of national self-determination.
2. We demand equality of rights for the German people in its dealings with other nations, and the revocation of the peace treaties of Versailles and Saint-Germain.
3. We demand land and territory (colonies) to feed our people and to settle our surplus population.
4. Only members of the nation may be citizens of the State. Only those of German blood, whatever their creed, may be members of the nation. Accordingly, no Jew may be a member of the nation.
5. Non-citizens may live in Germany only as guests and must be subject to laws for aliens.
6. The right to vote on the State's government and legislation shall be enjoyed by the citizens of the State alone. We demand therefore that all official appointments, of whatever kind, whether in the Reich, in the states or in the smaller localities, shall be held by none but citizens.
7. We demand that the State shall make it its primary duty to provide a livelihood for its citizens. If it should prove impossible to feed the entire population, foreign nationals (non-citizens) must be deported from the Reich.
8. All non-German immigration must be prevented. We demand that all non-Germans who entered Germany after 2 August 1914 shall be required to leave the Reich forthwith.
9. All citizens shall have equal rights and duties.
10. It must be the duty of every citizen to perform physical or mental work. The activities of the individual must not clash with the general interest, but must proceed within the framework of the community and be for the general good.

We demand therefore:

11. The abolition of incomes unearned by work.

The breaking of slavery of interest

12. In view of the enormous sacrifices of life and property demanded of a nation by any war, personal enrichment from war must be regarded as a crime against the nation. We demand therefore the ruthless confiscation of all war profits.
13. We demand the nationalization of all businesses which have been formed into corporations (trusts).
14. We demand profit-sharing in large industrial enterprises.

15. We demand the extensive development of insurance for old age.
16. We demand the creation and maintenance of a healthy middle class, the immediate communalizing of big department stores, and their lease at a cheap rate to small traders, and that the utmost consideration shall be shown to all small traders in placing of State and municipal orders.
17. We demand a land reform suitable to our national requirements, the passing of a law for the expropriation of land for communal purposes without compensation; the abolition of ground rent, and the prohibition of all speculation in land.
18. We demand the ruthless prosecution of those whose activities are injurious to the common interest. Common criminals, usurers, profiteers, etc., must be punished with death, whatever their creed or race.
19. We demand that Roman Law, which serves a materialistic world order, be replaced by a German common law.
20. The State must consider a thorough reconstruction of our national system of education (with the aim of opening up to every able and hard-working German the possibility of higher education and of thus obtaining advancement). The curricula of all educational establishments must be brought into line with the requirements of practical life. The aim of the school must be to give the pupil, beginning with the first sign of intelligence, a grasp of the notion of the State (through the study of civic affairs). We demand the education of gifted children of poor parents, whatever their class or occupation, at the expense of the State.
21. The State must ensure that the nation's health standards are raised by protecting mothers and infants, by prohibiting child labor, by promoting physical strength through legislation providing for compulsory gymnastics and sports, and by the extensive support of clubs engaged in the physical training of youth.
22. We demand the abolition of the mercenary army and the formation of a people's army.
23. We demand legal warfare on deliberate political mendacity and its dissemination in the press. To facilitate the creation of a German national press we demand:
    a. That all editors of, and contributors to newspapers appearing in the German language must be members of the nation;
    b. That no non-German newspapers may appear without the express permission of the State. They must not be printed in the German language;
    c. That non-Germans shall be prohibited by law from participating financially in or influencing German newspapers, and that the penalty for contravening such a law shall be the suppression of any such newspaper, and the immediate deportation of the non-Germans involved.
       The publishing of papers which are not conducive to the national welfare must be forbidden. We demand the legal prosecution of all those

tendencies in art and literature which corrupt our national life, and the suppression of cultural events which violate this demand.

24. We demand freedom for all religious denominations in the State, provided they do not threaten its existence nor offend the moral feelings of the German race.

The Party, as such, stands for positive Christianity, but does not commit itself to any particular denomination. It combats the Jewish-materialist spirit within and without us, and is convinced that our nation can achieve permanent health only from within on the basis of the principle: The common interest before self-interest.

25. To put the whole of this program into effect, we demand the creation of a strong central state power for the Reich; the unconditional authority of the political central Parliament over the entire Reich and its organizations; and the formation of Corporations based on estate and occupation for the purpose of carrying out the general legislation passed by the Reich in the various German states.

The leaders of the Party promise to work ruthlessly—if need be to sacrifice their very lives—to translate this program into action.

Source: Jeremy Noakes and Geoffrey Pridham (eds.), *Documents on Nazism, 1919–1945* (London: Jonathan Cape, 1974), 37–40.

CLOSING SPEECH FROM THE TRIAL OF ADOLF HITLER

Delivered March 27, 1924

The Nazi Party in Munich launched an armed attempt to seize the local government on November 8, 1923, remembered as the "Beer Hall Putsch." Led by Adolf Hitler, the Nazi Party's inner circle seized a group of top city officials, and then sent legions of the SA ("Storm Troopers") to march toward the government buildings in the city center. They were stopped by armed police, and a brief gun battle ensued. Hitler was arrested and put on trial for high treason against the German government. His trial, however, was presided over by two right-wing judges who were sympathetic to the movement's high nationalism and its disgust with the Weimar Republic. The judges allowed Hitler to make very long speeches that harangued those that the Nazis saw as enemies of the true German race. It was, in fact, the national newspaper coverage of the trial which made Hitler a national figure, expanding interest in his movement beyond Munich. After delivering the speech provided below, Hitler, in the end, was found guilty. His sympathetic judges, however, gave him the minimum sentence of only five years in prison, with the opportunity for early release. He was formally sentenced on April 1, 1924. Hitler only spent nine months in Landsberg prison before being released on December 20, 1924, and returning to work as head of the Nazi Party.

(After speaking about those accusing Hitler of merely trying to get a government position for himself in the "Beer Hall Putsch," Hitler continued.)

How petty are the thoughts of small men! You can take my word for it, that I do not consider a ministerial post worth striving for . . . [f]rom the very first I have aimed at something more than becoming a Minister. I have resolved to be the destroyer of Marxism. This I shall achieve and once I've achieved that, I should find the title of "Minister" ridiculous. When I first stood in front of Wagner's grave, my heart overflowed with pride that here lay a man who had forbidden any such inscription as "Here lies State Councilor, Music Director, His Excellency Richard von Wagner." I was proud that this man and so many others in German history have been content to leave their names to posterity and not their titles. It was not through modesty that I was willing to be a "drummer" at that time for that is the highest task: the rest is nothing.

Mr. Public Prosecutor! You emphasize in the indictment that we had to wait with clenched teeth until the seed ripened. Well we did wait and when the man came, we cried "The seed is ripe, the hour has come." Only then, after long hesitation, did I put myself forward. I demanded for myself the leadership of the organization, for which we all longed and for which you inwardly long just as much, should go to the hero who, in the eyes of the whole German youth is called to it.

. . . What did we want on the evening of 8 November? . . . We wanted to create in Germany the precondition which alone will make it possible for the iron grip of our enemies to be removed from us. We wanted to create order in the state, throw out the drones, take up the fight against international stock exchange slavery, against our whole economy being cornered by trusts, against the politicizing of the trade unions, and above all, for the highest honorable duty which we, as Germans, know should be once more introduced—the duty of bearing arms, military service. And now I ask you: Is what we wanted high treason?

. . . The army which we have formed grows from day to day; it grows more rapidly from hour to hour. Even now I have the proud hope that one day the hour will come when these untrained bands will grow to battalions, the battalions to regiments and the regiments to divisions, when the old cockade will be raised from the mire, when the old banners will once again wave before us: and the reconciliation will come in that eternal last Court of Judgment, the Court of God, before which we are ready to take our stand. Then from our bones, from our graves, will sound the voice of that tribunal which alone has the right to sit in judgment upon us. For, gentlemen, it is not you who pronounce judgment upon us, it is the eternal Court of History which will make its pronouncement upon the charge which is brought against us. The verdict that you will pass I know. But that Court will not ask of us, 'Did you commit high treason or did you not?' That Court will judge us . . . as Germans who wanted the best for their people and their fatherland, who wished to fight and to die. You may pronounce us guilty a thousand times, but the Goddess who presides over the Eternal Court of History will, with a smile, tear in pieces the charge of the Public Prosecutor and the verdict of this court. For she acquits us!

Source: Jeremy Noakes and Geoffrey Pridham (eds.), *Documents on Nazism, 1919–1945* (London: Jonathan Cape, 1974), 61–63.

THE "ENABLING LAW"

Passed in the German *Reichstag*, March 24, 1933

Adolf Hitler took office as chancellor of Germany on January 30, 1933. Soon after, on February 27, the *Reichstag* building (German parliament) in Berlin was destroyed by fire. Nazi police rounded up suspects who were known Communists and used this fire to proclaim that the Communists had commenced a large-scale, coordinated attack on the nation. Hitler was able to use the arrests to evict the Communist Party deputies from the *Reichstag*, and suppress their party. Without the Communist Party deputies to vote against it, Hitler realized he could now pass a law that would grant him absolute power. He began drafting a law that would give him such dictatorial powers and the ability to override any stipulations in the existing German Constitution. The law was brought to a vote on March 24, and as the deputies arrived at the Kroll Opera House building (the old *Reichstag* building still was unusable), crowds of SA Brownshirts and Nazi Party members chanted and shouted outside, demanding the passage of the bill. Inside the chamber, SA henchmen lined the corridors hissing at and intimidating any politicians who spoke against passage of the bill. When the vote finally took place, only the 94 deputies of the Social Democratic Party (SDP) voted against it. The final vote was 444 approving the measure and 94 voting against it. With the "Enabling Act" in place, Hitler and his top ministers had the authority to make law themselves and rule by decree. They immediately used it to outlaw all opposition parties and to eliminate the Democratic system completely. Brief though it is, the law provided below made Hitler the dictator of Germany with virtually absolute power.

The *Reichstag* has passed the following law, which is, with the approval of the *Reichsrat*, herewith promulgated, after it has been established that it satisfies the requirements for legislation altering the Constitution.

Article 1—In addition to the procedure for the passage of legislation outlined in the Constitution, the Reich Cabinet is also authorized to enact Laws. This applies equally to the laws referred to in Article 85, paragraph 2, and Article 87 of the Constitution.

Article 2—The national laws enacted by the Reich Cabinet may deviate from the Constitution provided they do not affect the position of the *Reichstag* and the *Reichsrat*. The powers of the President remain unaffected.

Article 3—The national laws enacted by the Reich Cabinet shall be prepared by the Chancellor and published in the official gazette. They come into effect, unless otherwise specified, upon the day following their publication. Articles 68–77 of the Constitution do not apply to the laws enacted by the Reich Cabinet.

Article 4—Treaties of the Reich with foreign states which concern matters of domestic legislation do not require the consent of the bodies participating in legislation. The Reich Cabinet is empowered to issue the necessary provisions for the implementing of these treaties.

Article 5—This law comes into effect on the day of its publication. It ceases to be valid on 1 April 1937: it also ceases to be valid if the present Reich Cabinet is replaced by another.

Source: Jeremy Noakes and Geoffrey Pridham (eds.), *Documents on Nazism, 1919–1945* (London: Jonathan Cape, 1974), 195.

THE "NUREMBURG LAWS"

Law for the Protection of German Blood and German Honor
Passed September 15, 1935

First Regulation under the Reich Citizenship Law, Issued November 14, 1935

From the earliest days of the Nazi regime, Adolf Hitler had implemented laws and policies to remove Jews from participation in German society. This had proved somewhat problematic as questions arose as to who actually qualified as a Jew. It also emerged that there were a great number of non-Jews married to Jews, or children with a variety of relationships to Jewish parents and grandparents. There also were those people who did not practice Judaism as a religion, but were considered part of the Jewish ethno-racial group. To deal with such complexities, Nazi officials assembled two acts of legislation which passed during the autumn of 1935. They were announced at the Party Conference at

Nuremburg that year, and became known as the "Nuremburg Laws." The first, the "Law for the Protection of German Blood and German Honor," made clear that German biological or racial origins were the basis for citizenship in the German State. This law also sought to discourage racial Germans from "polluting" German blood by outlawing the mixing of races through sex or marriage. The next act of legislation was the "Reich Citizenship Law" (not included below), which made clear that only those deemed full German citizens could enjoy the full rights of German citizenship, including participating in the political nation. An addendum to that law, however, was issued on November 14 which dealt expressly with the question of Jewish citizenship and political participation. This addendum (included below) stipulated that no one deemed a Jew could enjoy the rights of German citizenship, and Jews could not vote or hold political office. Any Jew already holding a government position was forced out. The addendum also documented the criteria for determining who was considered to be Jewish via a dizzying set of stipulations. Parents, grandparents, and religious practice all figured in this absurd matrix of conditions that determined who would be considered a Jew—and hence be excluded from German citizenship.

Law for the Protection of German Blood and German Honor

Entirely convinced that the purity of the German blood is essential to the further existence of the German people, and inspired by the uncompromising determination to safeguard the future of the German nation, the *Reichstag* has unanimously resolved upon the following law, which is promulgated herewith:

Section I

1. Marriages between Jews and citizens of German or kindred blood are forbidden. Marriages concluded in defiance of this law are void, even if, for the purpose of evading this law, they were concluded abroad.
2. Proceedings for annulment may be initiated only by the Public Prosecutor.

Section 2

Sexual relations outside marriage between Jews and nationals of German or kindred blood are forbidden.

Section 3

Jews will not be permitted to employ female citizens of German or kindred blood as domestic servants.

Section 4

1. Jews are forbidden to display the Reich and national flag or the national colors.
2. On the other hand they are permitted to display the Jewish colors. The exercise of this right is protected by the State.

Section 5

1. A person who acts contrary to the prohibition of Section 1 will be punished with hard labor.
2. A person who acts contrary to the prohibition of Section 2 will be punished with imprisonment or with hard labor.
3. A person who acts contrary to the prohibition of Section 3 or 4 will be punished with imprisonment up to a year and with a fine, or with one of these penalties.

Section 6

The Reich Minister of the Interior in agreement with the Deputy Fuhrer and the Reich Minister of Justice will issue the legal and administrative regulations required for the enforcement and supplementing of this law.

Section 7

The law will become effective on the day after its promulgation; Section 3, however, not until 1 January, 1936.

First Regulation Under the Reich Citizenship Law

Article 1

Until further regulations regarding citizenship papers are issued, all subjects of German or kindred blood, who possessed the right to vote in the *Reichstag* elections at the time the Citizenship Law came into effect, shall for the time being possess the rights of Reich citizens. . . .

Article 2

1. The regulations in Article 1 are also valid for Reich subjects of mixed Jewish blood.
2. An individual of mixed Jewish blood is one who is descended from one or two grandparents who were racially full Jews, in so far as he or she does not count as a Jew according to Article 5, paragraph 2. One grandparent shall be considered as full-blooded if he or she belonged to the Jewish religious community.

Article 3

Only the Reich citizen, as bearer of full political rights, exercises the right to vote in political affairs or can hold public office. . . .

Article 4

1. A Jew cannot be a citizen of the Reich. He has no right to vote in political affairs and he cannot occupy public office.
2. Jewish officials will retire as of 31 December 1935. If these officials served at the front in the world war, either for Germany or her allies, they will receive in full, until they reach the age limit, the pension to which they were entitled according to the salary they last received; they will, however, not advance in seniority. . . .
3. The affairs of religious organizations will not be affected.
4. The conditions of service of teachers in Jewish public schools remain unchanged until new regulations for the Jewish school system are issued.

Article 5

1. A Jew is anyone who is descended from at least three grandparents who are racially full Jews. Article 2, paragraph 2, second sentence will apply.
2. A Jew is also anyone who is descended from two full Jewish parents, if (a) he belonged to the Jewish religious community at the time this law was issued, or joined the community later, (b) he was married to a Jewish person, at the time the law was issued, or married one subsequently, (c) he is the offspring of a marriage with a Jew, in the sense of Section I, which was contracted after the Law for the Protection of German Blood and German Honor became effective, (d) he is the offspring of an extramarital relationship with a Jew, according to Section I, and will be born out of wedlock after 31 July 1936.

Article 6

Requirements for the pureness of blood as laid down in Reich Law or in orders of the NSDAP and its echelons—not covered in Article 5—will not be affected. . . .

Article 7

The Fuhrer and Reich Chancellor can grant exemptions from the regulations laid down in the law.

Source: Jeremy Noakes and Geoffrey Pridham (eds.), *Documents on Nazism, 1919–1945* (London: Jonathan Cape, 1974), 463–465.

THE "HOSSBACH MEMORANDUM"

Notes Taken by Colonel Friedrich Hossbach at a Meeting of the Nazi High Command

November 5, 1937

Adolf Hitler called a special meeting of the heads of the three branches of the German military, and the Foreign Office on November 5, 1937. In that meeting he revealed his ultimate plans for the German nation. Hitler was so adamant about this announcement that he went so far as to insist that his plans should be taken as his last will and testament should he die in the near future. Notes of the meeting were taken by Hitler's military adjutant, Colonel Friedrich Hossbach. The meeting proceeded with Hitler reviewing the possibilities for the long-term prospects of the German people. First, he reviewed the possibility of achieving political and economic independence from the rest of the world through a policy of economic autarky. If Germany did not have to depend on any other nation, it could pursue its own political agenda without concern. He announced, however, that research had shown complete autarky to be impossible for Germany to achieve. Hitler then reviewed the prospects of Germany's achieving long-term growth through participation in the global economy. This too was rejected as a strategy, as Germany did not possess the appropriate level of resources, infrastructures, or sea lanes to emerge as a dominant player. With these two options eliminated he revealed what he believed was required as the third option—Germany must obtain enormous tracts of territory by force. This would provide the necessary natural resources—land for agriculture and food production—and the "living space" for the expansion of the Germanic population. He then laid out a basic plan which included the military seizure of Austria and Czechoslovakia and the estimated timing. Hitler's territorial expansion which occurred during the late 1930s had in fact been part of a considered plan.

Present:

The Führer and Chancellor
Field Marshall von Blomberg, War Minister
Colonel-General Baron von Fritsch, Commander in Chief, Army
Admiral Dr. R. C. Raeder, Commander in Chief, Navy
Colonel-General Goering, Commander in Chief, Luftwaffe
Baron von Neurath, Foreign Minister
Colonel Hossbach

The Fuhrer began by stating that the subject of the present conference was of such importance that its discussion would, in other countries, be a matter

for a full Cabinet meeting. . . . He wished to explain to the gentlemen present
his basic ideas concerning the opportunities for the development of our position in the field of foreign affairs and he asked . . . that his exposition be
regarded, in the event of his death, as his last will and testament.

The aim of German policy was to make secure and to preserve the
racial community [*Volksmasse*] and to enlarge it. It was therefore a question of
space.

The German racial community comprised over 85 million people and, by
reason of their number and the narrow limits of habitable space in Europe, it
constituted a tightly packed racial core . . . such as implied the right to a greater
living space than in the case of other peoples. . . . Germany's future was therefore wholly conditional upon the solving of the need for space, and such a solution could be sought, of course, only for a foreseeable period of about one to
three generations.

Before turning to the question of solving the need for space, it had to be
considered whether a solution holding promise for the future was to be reached
by means of autarky or by means of an increased participation in world
economy.

Autarky

Achievement possible only under strict National Socialist leadership of the
State, which is assumed; accepting its achievement as possible, the following
could be stated as results:

A. In the field of raw materials only limited, not total, autarky.
B. In the field of food the question of autarky was to be answered by a flat
   "No." Hand in hand with the general rise in the standard of living compared with that of thirty to forty years ago, there has gone an increased
   demand and an increased home consumption even on the part of the
   producers, the farmers. The fruits of the increased agricultural production
   had all gone to meet the increased demand.
       . . . It was not possible over the long run, in a continent enjoying a
   practically common standard of living, to meet the difficulties of food
   supply by lowering that standard and by rationalization. . . . Thus autarky,
   in regard both to food and to the economy as a whole, could not be
   maintained.

Participation in World Economy

To this there were limitations which we were unable to remove. The establishment of Germany's position on a secure and sound foundation was obstructed
by market fluctuations, and commercial treaties afforded no guarantee for their
actual observance.

The boom in world economy caused by the economic effects of rearmament could never form the basis of a sound economy over a long period, and the latter was impeded above all by the economic disturbances resulting from Bolshevism. There was a pronounced military weakness in those States which depended for their existence on foreign trade.

(With neither autarky nor participation in world trade seen as viable alternatives, Hitler continued. . . .)

The only remedy, and one which might seem to us visionary, lay in the acquisition of greater living space—a quest that has in every age been the origin of the formation of States and of the migration of peoples. . . . If, then, we accept the security of our food situation as the principal point at issue, the space needed to ensure it can be sought only in Europe, not, as in the liberal-capitalist view, in the exploitation of colonies. It is not a matter of acquiring population, but of gaining space for agricultural use. Moreover, areas producing raw materials can be more usefully sought in Europe, in immediate proximity to the Reich, than overseas.

The question for Germany was: Where could she achieve the greatest gain at the lowest cost?

(There follows extensive discussion about the power and antagonism of the British Empire and France)

. . . If the resort to force with its attendant risks is accepted as the basis

Contingency 1: Period 1943–45

The equipment of the Army, Navy, and Luftwaffe, as well as the formation of the officer corps, was nearly completed. Equipment and armament were modern; in further delay there lay the danger of their obsolescence. . . . Nobody knew today what the situation would be in the years 1943–45. One thing was certain, that we could wait no longer.

On the one hand there was the great *Wehrmacht*, and the necessity of maintaining it at its present level, the ageing of the movement and its leaders. . . . If the Fuhrer was still living, it was his unalterable determination to solve Germany's problem of space by 1943–45 at the latest. The necessity for action before 1943–45 would arise in contingencies 2 and 3.

Contingency 2:

If internal strife in France should develop into such a domestic crisis as to absorb the French army completely and render it incapable of use for war against Germany, then the time for action against the Czechs would have come.

Contingency 3:

> If France should be so embroiled in war with another State that she could not "proceed" against Germany.
>
> For the improvement of our politico-military position our first objective, in the event of our being embroiled in war, must be to overthrow Czechoslovakia and Austria simultaneously in order to remove the threat to our flank in any possible operation against the West. . . .
>
> . . . The time for our attack on the Czechs and Austria must be made dependent on the course of the Anglo-French-Italian war and would not necessarily coincide with the commencement of military operations by these three States. . . . He wanted, while retaining his own independence of action, to exploit this favorable situation, which would not occur again, to begin and carry through the campaign against the Czechs. This descent upon the Czechs would have to be carried out with lightning speed.

Source: *Documents on German Foreign Policy 1918–1945*, Series D, Volume 1, "From Neurath to Ribbentrop (September 1937–September 1938)" (Washington, DC: U.S. Government Printing Office, 1949), 29–39.

THE PACT OF FRIENDSHIP AND ALLIANCE BETWEEN ITALY AND GERMANY OR THE "PACT OF STEEL"

Signed May 22, 1939

Adolf Hitler's Nazi state made a number of expansionist moves after 1935, including the reoccupation of the Rhineland, lending assistance to Franco's Nationalists in the Spanish Civil War, annexing Austria into the German Reich, and seizing virtually all of Czechoslovakia. Hitler had further plans for expansion, though, including the invasion of Poland and the eventual conquest of the Soviet Union. By 1939, however, Hitler was concerned that any further expansionist moves might trigger war with the western democracies (Britain and France). To intimidate the democracies, Hitler urged the signing of a public and extensive reaffirmation of the political and military alliance between Germany and Fascist Italy. Hitler wanted the democracies to believe that if they intervened they would be facing war against both nations. This, he felt sure, would convince Britain and France to not intervene. Benito Mussolini was enthusiastic about the Pact's increasing coordination of diplomatic, military, and propaganda relations between Germany and Italy. Mussolini also was under the impression that Germany did not plan to go to war for another three years. After the signature of the Pact of Steel, however, Hitler felt secure enough to invade Poland in September 1939, which set in motion the Second World War.

The German Chancellor and His Majesty the King of Italy and Albania, Emperor of Ethiopia, deem that the time has come to strengthen the close relationship of friendship and homogeneity, existing between National Socialist Germany and Fascist Italy, by a solemn Pact.

Now that a safe bridge for mutual aid and assistance has been established by the common frontier between Germany and Italy fixed for all time, both Governments reaffirm the policy, the principles and objectives of which have already been agreed upon by them, and which has proved successful, both for promoting the interests of the two countries and also for safeguarding peace in Europe.

Firmly united by the inner affinity between their ideologies and the comprehensive solidarity of their interests, the German and Italian nations are resolved in [the] future also to act side by side and with united forces to secure their living space and to maintain peace.

Following this path, marked out for them by history, Germany and Italy intend, in the midst of a world of unrest and disintegration, to serve the task of safeguarding the foundations of European Civilization. . . .

Article 1—The High Contracting Parties will remain in continuous contact with each other in order to reach an understanding on all questions affecting their common interests or the general European situation.

Article 2—Should the common interests of the High Contracting Parties be endangered by international events of any kind whatsoever, they will immediately enter into consultations on the measures to be taken for the protection of these interests.

Should the security or other vital interests of one of the High Contracting Parties be threatened from without, the other High Contracting Party will afford the threatened Party full political and diplomatic support in order to remove this threat.

Article 3—If, contrary to the wishes and hopes of the High Contracting Parties, it should happen that one of them became involved in warlike complications with another Power or Powers, the other High Contracting Party would immediately come to its assistance as an ally and support it with all its military forces on land, at sea, and in the air.

Article 4—In order to ensure in specific cases the speedy execution of the obligations of alliance undertaken under Article 3, the Governments of the two High Contracting Parties will further intensify their collaboration in the military field, and in the field of war economy.

In the same way the two Governments will remain in continuous consultation also on other measures necessary for the practical execution of the provisions of this Pact.

For the purposes indicated in paragraphs 1 and 2 above, the two Governments will set up commissions which will be under the direction of the two Foreign Ministers.

Article 5—The High Contracting Parties undertake even now that, in the event of war waged jointly, they will conclude an armistice and peace only in full agreement with each other.

Article 6—The two High Contracting Parties are aware of the significance that attaches to their common relations with Powers friendly to them. They are resolved to maintain these relations in the future also and together to shape them in accordance with the common interests which form the bonds between them and these Powers.

Article 7—This Pact shall enter into force immediately upon signature. The two high Contracting Parties are agreed in laying down that its first term of validity shall be for ten years. In good time before the expiry of this period, they will reach agreement on the extension of the validity of the Pact.

In witness whereon the Plenipotentiaries have signed this Pact and affixed thereto their seals.

Done in duplicate in the German and the Italian languages, both texts being mutually authoritative.

Secret Additional Protocol to the Pact of Friendship and Alliance Between German and Italy

At the time of signature of the Pact of Friendship and Alliance, both Parties have reached agreement on the following points:

1. The two Foreign Ministers will reach agreement as quickly as possible on the organization, headquarters and working methods of the commissions for military questions and questions of war economy to be set up under their direction as provided for in Article IV of the Pact.
2. In execution of Article IV, paragraph 2, of the Pact the two Foreign Ministers will as quickly as possible take all necessary steps to ensure continuous collaboration in the fields of the press, information, and propaganda in accordance with the spirit and aims of the Pact.

   For this purpose each of the two Foreign Ministers will assign to his country's Embassy, in the capital of the other, one or more specially qualified experts who, in direct collaboration with the Foreign Ministry there, will continually consult on the steps which are suitable for promoting the policy of the Axis and counteracting the policy of opposing Powers in the fields of the press, information and propaganda.

Berlin, May 22, 1939—in the XVIIth year of the Fascist Era.

Signed: Joachim von Ribbentrop   Signed: Galeazzo Ciano

Source: Charles Delzell (ed.), *Mediterranean Fascism, 1919–1945* (New York: Harper & Row, 1971): 208–210. Introduction, editorial notes, translations by the editor, and compilation copyright 1970 by Charles F. Delzell. Reprinted by permission of HarperCollins Publishers.

MEMORANDUM

WRITTEN BY COLONEL-GENERAL JOHANNES BLASKOWITZ, COMMANDER OF THE OBER-OST MILITARY REGION, POLAND

Dated February 6, 1940

After having conquered Poland by military force during the autumn of 1939, Germany organized the land into military districts and began the process of "Germanization." Polish nationals were systematically driven from their homes, their land and livestock were confiscated, and the Poles were transported into specially designated districts or urban centers. Many of these people were assigned as slave laborers. Those who had German racial features were shipped to Germany. Huge tracts of Poland were set aside for German families moving into the area. The homes and even businesses stolen from the Polish population were given to the incoming Germans. This process became startlingly brutal with murders, tortures, and rapes occurring routinely. Jewish populations were rounded up for special treatment. Jews were sent from their homes and villages to confined urban districts in major cities including Warsaw and Lodz. There they were subject to appalling conditions with only a starvation diet provided, no work available, and no ability to leave their restricted areas. Large numbers of other Jews were rounded up in the countryside and simply gunned down and then buried in mass graves (often after being forced to dig the pits themselves). The SS was put in charge of these tasks, and a special group of police squads (which actually were death squads) handled the mass executions of Jews. These squads were known as the *Einsatzgruppen*. The soldiers of the regular army, the *Wehrmacht*, often were horrified at such policies, and significant tension developed between the *Wehrmacht* commanders and those of the notorious SS. Colonel-General Johannes Blaskowitz's memorandum below sheds light on such divisions of feeling. This document was shared with Hitler who became furious with Blaskowitz's attitude. Hitler subsequently relieved the general of his command on May 29, 1940.

. . . It is misguided to slaughter tens of thousands of Jews and Poles as is happening at present; because, in view of the huge population neither the concept
of a Polish State nor the Jews will be eliminated by doing so. On the contrary,
the way in which this slaughter is being carried out is causing great damage; . . .
[t]he consequences are:

(a) Enemy propaganda is provided with material which could nowhere have
     been more effectively devised. It is true that what the foreign radio stations
     have broadcast so far is only a tiny fraction of what has happened in real-
     ity. But we must reckon that the clamor of the outside world will con-
     tinually increase and cause great political damage, particularly since the
     atrocities have actually occurred and cannot be disproved.
(b) The acts of violence against the Jews which occur in full view of the public
     inspire among the religious Poles not only deep disgust but also great pity
     for the Jewish population, to which up to now the Poles were more or less
     hostile. In a very short time . . . our arch-enemies in the Eastern sphere—
     the Pole and the Jew. . . will, in their hatred against their tormentors,
     combine against Germany right along the line.
(c) The role of the armed forces who are compelled impotently to watch this
     crime and whose reputation . . . suffers irreparable harm, need not be re-
     ferred to again.
(d) But the worst damage which will accrue to the German nation from the
     present situation is the brutalization and moral debasement which, in a very
     short time, will spread like a plague among valuable German manpower.
        If high officials of the SS and police demand acts of violence and bru-
     tality and praise them publicly, then in a very short time we shall be faced
     with the rule of the thug. Like-minded people and those with warped
     characters will very soon come together so that, as is now the case in Po-
     land, they can give full expression to their animal and pathological in-
     stincts. It is hardly possible to keep them any longer in check, since they
     can well believe themselves officially authorized and justified in commit-
     ting any act of cruelty.
        The only way of resisting this epidemic is to subordinate those who are
     guilty and their followers to the military leadership and courts as quickly
     as possible.

. . . The attitude of the troops to the SS and police alternates between
abhorrence and hatred. Every soldier feels repelled and revolted by these crimes
which are being perpetrated in Poland by nationals of the Reich and representatives of the State authority. He does not understand how such things can
happen with impunity, particularly since they occur, so to speak, under his
protection.
     . . . The resettlement program is causing especial and growing discontent
throughout the country. It is obvious that the starving population, which is

fighting for its existence, can only observe with the greatest concern how the masses of those being resettled are left to find refuge with them completely penniless and, so to speak, naked and hungry.

It is only too understandable that these feelings reach a pitch of uncontrolled hatred at the numbers of children dying of starvation on every transport and the wagons of people frozen to death.

The idea that one can intimidate the Polish population by terrorism and rub their noses in the dirt will certainly prove to be false. This people's capacity for enduring suffering is too great for that. . . .

Source: Jeremy Noakes and Geoffrey Pridham (eds.), *Documents on Nazism, 1919–1945* (London: Jonathan Cape, 1974), 611–612.

NOTES FROM THE WANNSEE CONFERENCE

Dated January 20, 1942

On January 20, 1942, a conference was held in the Berlin suburb of Wannsee, near a picturesque lake of the same name. The conference was called by the high command of the Nazi SS to share information and coordinate the activities surrounding an enormous project. That project had been termed the "Final Solution" by Adolf Hitler and his inner circle, and its objective was the extermination of all of the Jews of Europe. What was being discussed at this conference were the actual logistical plans of the system of death camps and deportations of the Holocaust. The document below is a set of notes taken at the conference. These notes inform us who was present (representatives from the ministries of foreign affairs, the interior, justice, the eastern territories, and, of course, the SS). The notes make clear that the responsibility for this massive project was firmly in the hands of the Reichsführer SS (Heinrich Himmler), who had assigned its operational oversight to the chief of the SD, Reinhard Heydrich. Heydrich appears to have run the meeting. The notes discuss the other use of Jews in the plan as well—that of slave labor. The notes speak frankly of working Jews to death, and for those who survive such hellish conditions, having them murdered rather than released. If the heartiest Jews were released, the notes say, the Jewish race might have a chance of regenerating itself. The notes also make clear the basic logistic plan of moving Jews from the west of Europe (where they would be rounded up in deportation camps) to the east where they would be designated for extermination or hard labor. Chillingly, these notes speak of this project in a very detached way, as if it were a railroad timetable and not mass murder.

The Chief of the Security Police and the SD, SS Obrgruppenfuhrer Heydrich, began by announcing his appointment by the Reich Marshal (Goering) as the agent responsible for the preparation of the final solution of the European Jewish question, and pointed out that this meeting was being held to achieve clarity in basic questions. The Reich Marshal's wish that he should be sent a draft on the organizational, technical, and material matters regarding the final solution of the European Jewish question made it necessary that all central authorities immediately concerned with these questions should deal with them in advance so as to ensure the coordination of the lines to be taken.

The supervision of the final solution of the Jewish question was, regardless of geographical boundaries, centralized in the hands of the Reichsführer SS (Heinrich Himmler) and Chief of the German Police (Reinhard Heydrich acting for Himmler). . . .

III. The evacuation of the Jews to the east has now emerged, with the prior permission of the Führer, as a further possible solution instead of emigration. . . .

These actions, however, must be regarded only as a secondary solution. But already the practical experience is being gathered which is of great importance to the coming final solution of the Jewish question. . . .

In the process of the final solution, the Jews will be conscripted for labor in the eastern territories under appropriate administrative provisions. Large labor gangs of those fit for work will be formed, with the sexes separated, which will be sent to these areas for road construction and undoubtedly a large number of them will drop out through natural elimination. The remainder who survive— and they will certainly be those who have the greatest powers of endurance— will have to be dealt with accordingly. For, if released they would, as a natural selection of the fittest, form a germ cell from which the Jewish race could build itself up again. (This is the lesson of history).

In the process of carrying out the final solution, Europe will be combed through from west to east. . . .

Source: Jeremy Noakes and Geoffrey Pridham (eds.), *Documents on Nazism, 1919–1945* (London: Jonathan Cape, 1974), 489.

TESTIMONY OF RUDOLF HOESS AT THE NUREMBURG TRIALS

Dated April 15, 1946

After the surrender of Nazi Germany in May 1945, Allied forces rounded up and arrested all of the members of the Nazi leadership that they could find. Many of those who held top positions in the government and the military, or were involved in war crimes, eventually faced legal proceedings. The most notorious of the Nazi leadership were tried during the period from November 1945 to October 1946 at the city of Nuremburg. This proceeding was officially called the International Military Tribunal, but has since been remembered simply as the "Nuremburg Trials." Among those tried at Nuremburg was Rudolf Hoess, the commandant of the Nazi labor and death camp at Auschwitz in Poland (not to be confused with Rudolf Hess, the early secretary of the Nazi Party). Unlike most of the Nazi leadership he was extremely forthcoming and provided chilling, detailed accounts of the operations of the Holocaust. By his own admission, his operation at Auschwitz actively murdered some two and half million human beings. The testimony below describes some of the basic steps of that operation.

The "final solution" of the Jewish question meant the complete extermination of all Jews in Europe. I was ordered to establish extermination facilities at Auschwitz in June 1942. At that time, there were already . . . three other extermination camps—Belzec, Treblinka, and Wolzek. These camps were under the command of the task forces of the Security Police and SD. I visited Treblinka to find out how they carried out their extermination. The Camp Commandant at Treblinka told me that he had liquidated 80,000 in the course of six months. He was principally concerned with liquidating all the Jews from the Warsaw ghetto. He used monoxide gas and I did not think that his methods were very efficient. So when I set up the extermination building at Auschwitz, I used Cyclon B (also spelled Zyklon B), which was a crystallized prussic acid which we dropped into the death chamber from a small opening. It took from three to fifteen minutes to kill the people in the death chamber, depending upon climatic conditions. We knew when the people were dead because their screaming stopped. We usually waited about half an hour before we opened the doors and removed the bodies. After the bodies were removed our special squads took off the rings and extracted the gold from the teeth of the corpses.

Another improvement on Treblinka that we made was building our gas chambers to accommodate 2,000 people at a time, whereas at Treblinka their ten gas chambers only accommodated 200 people each. The way we selected our victims was as follows: we had two SS doctors on duty at Auschwitz to examine the incoming transports of prisoners. The prisoners would be marched past one of the doctors who would make spot decisions as they walked by. Those who were fit for work were sent into the camp. Others were sent immediately to the extermination plants. Children of tender years were invariably exterminated since by reason of their youth they were unable to work. Still another improvement made on Treblinka was that at Treblinka the victims almost always knew that they were about to be exterminated whereas at Auschwitz we endeavored to fool the victims into thinking that they were to go through a de-lousing process. Of course, they often realized our true intentions and owing to that we sometimes had riots and difficulties. Very often women would hide their children under their clothes, but of course when we found them we would send the children in to be exterminated. We were required to carry out these exterminations in secrecy but of course the foul and nauseating stench from the continuous burning of bodies permeated the entire area and all the people living in the surrounding communities knew that exterminations were going on at Auschwitz. . . .

Source: Jeremy Noakes and Geoffrey Pridham (eds.), *Documents on Nazism, 1919–1945* (London: Jonathan Cape, 1974), 490–491.

Key Questions

QUESTION 1: WAS FASCISM PRIMARILY A MODERNIZING, REVOLUTIONARY MOVEMENT, OR DID IT REPRESENT A VIOLENT REACTION AGAINST THE PROCESS OF MODERNIZATION AND REVOLUTIONARY CHANGE?

Among the most debated issues regarding the true characterization of fascism during the period from 1919 to 1945 concerns the question of whether it was primarily a modernizing and revolutionary movement or whether it was in fact a reactionary, anti-modernist movement attempting to hold back the tide of progressive change. Those analyzing fascism at the time could see this issue in diametrically opposed ways. Sir Oswald Mosley, for example, the founder of the British Union of Fascists, defined the fascist movement in his book *The Greater Britain*, in a chapter entitled, "The Modern Movement." In his analysis, he asserted that the modern world had been changed so dramatically by science, high-technology, and mass production that the new conditions had made the system of Liberal-Democracy (which he said was a product of the 19th century and designed for 19th-century challenges) quite obsolete. He believed that the essence of fascism was its ability to manage an entirely new set of modern problems with a "scientific" system of government. Others, particularly those on the political left, believed that fascism simply was the political tool of the traditional elites and Capitalists, implemented to hold back the progressive change being brought about by the forces of Marxism. Far from being modernist, they believed the real purpose of fascism was to prevent revolution and modernization—and that fascists were only too willing to employ the extreme violence necessary to do so. Such a view can be found within the title of a famous book written by American correspondent Edgar A. Mowrer in 1933, as Adolf Hitler took power; the book is called *Germany Puts the Clock Back.*

Resolving this historical question has important implications for the evaluation of the rise of fascism. A revolutionary movement—almost inherently—must be driven by mass action and the momentum of the majority of the population. Seeing fascism as essentially reactionary suggests that smaller groups of traditional elites were working together to hold back the popular will. Were Fascist regimes created by small minorities who imposed their policies on the unwilling masses? Or were fascist movements driven by large segments of the population and given mass support in power to create a new national culture? Fascism, of course, created so much chaos, death, and destruction that understanding its development is crucial today. If we hope to avoid repeating the nightmares of that age, we must be able to recognize what makes fascism possible, and hence how to combat the reappearance of such ideologies and political institutions. To avoid repeating such processes, we must be able to truly understand how those processes actually worked at the time. To gain that understanding, resolving the question posed above is vital.

Another issue that figures into the analysis of this historical question is determining the actual meaning of "modernism" or "modernity." How do we define the process of "modernization"? There has been significant scholarly reassessment within the last 25 years or so. Modernization previously had been seen as characterized by the movement from rural life to urban life, from agricultural production to industrial production, and from traditional religious influence to increasing secularism; increasing levels of individual freedoms; the transition from monarchy to increased levels of representative government; and the transition from traditional gender roles to greater levels of gender equality. Recent scholarship, however, particularly in works of scholarship studying imperialism and colonial psychology, has urged us not to accept one paradigm of "modernization," as characterized by the transitions listed above, or by the set of transitions imposed by European or "Western" powers upon the rest of the world.

The new scholarship suggests that each part of the world has taken changing circumstances and created its own paradigms of "modernity." In fact, there can be numerous or alternative "modernities," and our thinking should not be restricted to a one-dimensional conception of "modernization." This has important implications for the question discussed below and for the essayists. As we attempt to determine whether fascism represented a modernizing movement, how should we measure its modernism? Should we compare the theory and practices of fascist movements to the set of principles most often associated with "Enlightenment rationality"—such as increasing individual freedoms, representative government, and rational improvements? Or should we be open to the view that fascism represented its own particular (violent, repressive, and exclusionist) variant of high-modernism? After all, "modern" does not necessarily mean "good" or "safe" or "improved."

Dr. Rhiannon Evangelista, an expert in Italian Fascist studies, wrestles with these questions as she asserts that fascism, as a broader movement, represented a primarily revolutionary and modernizing movement. Dr. Evangelista focuses on a number of modern aspects that fascist regimes embraced, such as high-technology and industrial production. Evangelista also examines the psychological aspects of creating fascist nations in a powerful new form.

Dr. Theresa Ast, whose research has focused on Holocaust studies, takes the opposite view. Dr. Ast asserts that fascists most often embraced the irrational, and rejected the rationalist principles of the "Enlightenment." Using the memories of an idealized "glorious" past for persuasion, Ast says, Fascist regimes convinced their nations to give them extreme power to crush the advances of modernity—such as the beginnings of liberal reforms, representative government and cultural toleration.

ANSWER: DR. RHIANNON EVANGELISTA, FASCISM WAS PRIMARILY A MODERNIZING AND REVOLUTIONARY MOVEMENT

According to the fascists themselves, as well as most recent research on the fascist phenomenon, fascism primarily was a modernizing and revolutionary movement. For many years, however, scholars and the public alike have viewed fascism as a violent reaction against the process of modernization and revolutionary change. To correct this perception, we must break down some mental barriers to thinking of fascism as "modernizing" and "revolutionary," develop a proper understanding of the terms involved, and examine the progressive (though not necessarily positive) ideas and policies of Europe's fascist movements.

Why have so many understood fascism to be a reactionary movement? Part of the answer has to do with the history of the first fascist movement. In the years directly after World War I, Socialists in many European countries tried to translate the political upheaval of the war into social revolution. In Italy, Germany, Austria, and Hungary armed militias—afraid that the Russian Revolution of 1917 might spread to their own country—attacked Socialists and Socialist sympathizers. The very first movement, Italian Fascism, began this way. Most of the first observers to write astute analyses of the Fascist phenomenon were Socialists or Communists, the so-called "revolutionary" enemies of Fascism. They tended to portray the Fascists as the reactionary tool of the bourgeoisie and landowners who feared a Marxist revolution. Although this interpretation had some justification during the earliest years of Fascism, after 1922 it became increasingly clear that Fascist movements and regimes had more sophisticated goals than simply the elimination of their political enemies. According to the eminent historian of Italian Fascism Renzo De Felice, however, this view of Fascism as an anti-revolutionary reaction persisted long after the end of Fascism during World War II, particularly among scholars who worked within a Marxist framework. Therefore, despite its accuracy problems, one of the first interpretations of Fascism influenced perceptions of the phenomenon well into the postwar period.

The view of fascism as "anti-modern" has been influenced by Adolf Hitler's views on modern art and the glorification of the past by both the German and Italian regimes. It must be remembered, however, that not all fascist movements shared Hitler's view of modern art as "degenerate." Ruth Ben-Ghiat and Marla Stone, among others, for example, have demonstrated that the Italian Fascist regime promoted various types of modern art, caring little for the form of art as long as the artist was politically aligned with the regime. Therefore Fascism per se was not "against" modern artistic expression.

In the same way, be wary of misinterpreting the appeals of many fascist movements to their "glorious" pasts. Philip Morgan, a specialist in generic fascism, explains in no-nonsense British prose that

> [V]iewing fascism as essentially "anti-modern". . . just seems plain daft, I am
> afraid, even if I am caricaturing this position by pointing to the absurdity of
> the Nazis actually wanting to return Germany and Germans to the wood and
> animal skins of the pagan Germanic tribes inhabiting primeval forests, or to
> the military castes of the Medieval Teutonic knights.

Similarly, as Emilio Gentile notes, the Italian Fascists' glorification of ancient Rome was not meant to set back the clock, but instead to justify the creation of a new, Fascist empire in the Mediterranean.

Another reason why many in today's world understand fascism as reactionary and traditionalist has to do with our preconceived notions about the term "revolution" and its cognates. As both De Felice and Eugen Weber—a specialist in German history—point out, scholars and the public alike have been reluctant to describe Fascism as "revolutionary" because the word "revolution" tends to have a positive connotation. "Like the hero in a Western movie," Weber explains, "the movement that comes in riding on revolution can, as a rule, expect our sympathy." Few after World War II wished to sympathize with fascism, thus there has been a general reluctance to use the label "revolutionary" to describe it. Most definitions of the term, however, do not suggest this positive interpretation. The *Oxford English Dictionary*, for example, defines "revolution" as "a forcible overthrow of a government or social order in favor of a new system."

Fascism falls within this definition. Morgan, for example, argues that the fascists "sought the regeneration of their nations through the violent destruction of all political forms and forces which they held to be responsible for national disunity and divisiveness, and the creation of a new national order based on the moral or 'spiritual' reformation of their peoples." The aim of destroying the old order and establishing a new one is inherently modern and revolutionary. The political scientist Roger Griffin expresses a similar idea, insisting that Fascism represented "a new genus of revolutionary politics" for the 20th century.

Fascism was a revolutionary but also a modernizing movement. To discuss the relationship between fascism and modernity, the term "modern" first must be defined. As Clifton Crais notes in the *Oxford Encyclopedia of the Modern World*, this is notoriously difficult to do. Most specialists today agree, however, that the key characteristics of "modern" societies are an industrial economy, a political system based on European Enlightenment principles, and a commitment to the methods and findings of modern science. Fascist movements embraced all of these aspects of modernity. In fact, the fascists believed they were creating an "alternative" modernity—opposed to both Liberal Democracy and Communism—which would harness the advances of modern industry, politics, and science for national greatness.

Instead of calling for the abandonment of the factories and a return to an agrarian way of life, fascists embraced the advancements of industrial production and advocated the inclusion of technical experts in government. Like Franklin D. Roosevelt, both Hitler and Mussolini implemented public works projects to counteract unemployment during the Depression and to modernize their countries' infrastructures. Moreover, the fascist dictatorships implemented policies meant to modernize agriculture and increase food production, with the goal of achieving domestic self-sufficiency.

In fact, the Italian Fascists advocated (and partially implemented) Corporativism, a way of organizing labor relations in a non-antagonistic fashion, with the state acting as arbiter in labor disputes. As the Italian historian Alessio Gagliardi explains, "it was above all through the idea of Corporativism that Fascism attempted to offer itself to Italians and the whole world as a 'third way' alternative to both capitalism and socialism, as a revolutionary experiment creating a 'new State' and a different model of society." Other fascist movements—such as the Croix de Feu in France and the British Union of Fascists—also promoted Corporativism, an idea that had resonance even outside of fascist circles during the hard years of the Great Depression.

Politically, as Benito Mussolini himself explicitly stated, Fascism rejected the "modern" political philosophies of Liberal Democracy and Marxist Socialism, but it did not represent a return to pre-modern political ideas. Indeed, the fascists sought to establish a "third way" of modern politics, one that would more truly represent Enlightenment values. This was not simply rhetoric; many scholars of fascism agree. George L. Mosse, for example, argues that the "fascist style" of politics was a direct result of Enlightenment ideas.

> [T]he fascist style was in reality the climax of a "new politics" based upon the emerging eighteenth-century idea of popular sovereignty. . . . This concept . . . was given precision by the "general will," as Rousseau had expressed it, by the belief that only when all are acting together as an assembled people does man's nature as a citizen come into active existence.

The Nazis' scientific racism and eugenics policies are two of the most famous and extreme examples of fascist commitment to modern science. The Nazis (and many other fascists) believed that innate physical characteristics separated humanity into different and unequal "races" that could be studied using the tools of the biological sciences. Although the Nazis carried this idea to extremes in the Final Solution, belief in "scientific" racism was widespread in 19th- and early 20th-century Europe, as Robert W. Strayer, an expert in world history notes. Similarly, before the Nazis implemented their eugenics euthanasia program, many medical professionals and policy makers in Britain, Germany, and the United States advocated eugenicist policies, encouraging those deemed "fit" in society to breed and those "unfit" not to breed. In Europe, "eugenic thinking," insists David D. Roberts, an expert in totalitarianism, "had been widespread and seemingly progressive, even quintessentially 'modern,' and was by no means confined to fanatics in Germany."

In sum, the view that fascism was not revolutionary or modernizing has more to do with our own preconceptions about these terms and the history of the early fascist movements than with the objective realities of fascist ideas, policies, and actions during the interwar period. Fascism's commitment to a comprehensive industrial economy, the advancements of modern science, and the manifestation of a new politics based on popular sovereignty marked it as particularly modernizing and revolutionary.

ANSWER: THERESA AST, FASCISM WAS PRIMARILY A REACTIONARY AND ANTI-MODERNIST MOVEMENT

This essay asserts that fascism—as a broad political movement—primarily was reactionary or "anti-modernist." Although there have been many contemporary fascists who claimed that fascism represented a cutting-edge, modernizing movement, there were certainly other contemporaries who saw it as just the opposite. In fact, contemporary analysis of fascism, even that conducted by fascists themselves, often was inconsistent, confused, and even contradictory. This makes determining the true nature of fascism, according to fascists' own discourse, quite problematic. Because of this fact, this essay concentrates on the analysis of more recent historians and political scientists as they assess the period. Using this approach, it becomes clear that the various fascist movements (so often different from one another), shared an almost unanimous rejection of the driving set of principles behind modernity—what can collectively be termed "Enlightenment rationality."

Fascist leaders inveighed against the principles of the Enlightenment, which had emerged in 18th-century Europe, and which was expanding its influence throughout the 19th century. The principles of the Enlightenment stood for ever-increasing individual liberties, the rule of law, and increased representative government, along with cultural relativism and tolerance of different religious and cultural groups. Fascist discourse from 1919 to 1945, and the actions taken by fascist dictatorial regimes, made the elimination of these principles part of their core values: representative government was entirely eliminated in favor of single-party dictatorships; individual liberties were repressed as subordinate to the collective needs of the "national" community; and, of course, any cultural or ethnic groups not seen as part of that national community were denounced, purged, and persecuted. Can such a collection of theories and practices be seen as "modernizing"?

Richard Thurlow, in *Fascism: Perspectives in History,* writes that it is important to consider many factors when examining the nature of fascism. The serious student of history and politics will consider the intellectual revolt against the Enlightenment; the liberalism of the late 19th century; and the economic and cultural discontents and frustrations occasioned by industrialization, modernization, and the First World War. The social and economic unrest associated with the failure of imperialism in Africa, the radicalization of World War I, and reaction to the Bolshevik Revolution—an extreme fear of rising Communism—also were contributing elements in the rise of fascism. After the First World War, fascism appealed to many European citizens who were frustrated, disillusioned, or disaffected for a variety of reasons. Italy and

Germany, having achieved nationhood comparatively late in the 19th century, had a much smaller window for developing Liberal and Democratic ideals or parliamentary procedures.

Between 1890 and 1914 proto-fascist ideas and concepts emerged within the context of a conservative cult of the irrational and recently developed scientific traditions. Some scholars focus instead on radical social movements of the revolutionary left. In his book *Fascism: Its Origins and Development*, Alexander De Grand observed that Mussolini and the Italian Fascist Party were a mass of contradictions making it difficult to determine exactly where the party was situated politically. The same would be true of German National Socialism.

Italian Fascism's Syndicalism or Corporatism, a form of Socialism under which political representation is based upon trade and industry, leads De Grand to describe Fascism as a possible "third way" between Capitalism and Communism. Under Mussolini, however, the power of Corporatism declined and its dominance or influence in Italian politics proved to be illusory. At the same time, the influence of traditional conservative parties and business interests remained almost unchanged. Until he instituted the war economy in the mid-1930s, Mussolini permitted industrialists to manage their companies with minimal government interference. Despite his "anti-Capitalist rhetoric," Mussolini reduced business taxes, permitted powerful business cartels, mandated wage reductions for workers, and rescinded the law guaranteeing an eight-hour work day.

Some scholars find it difficult to characterize fascist governments as Conservative or Liberal, to situate fascism within a reactionary or revolutionary framework. Roger Eatwell, for example, described fascism as possessing "a reactionary right-wing, mythical side . . . but also [having] rational left-wing influences which focused on modern state . . . planning." Historians could focus on the seeming incompatibility between conservative ideology and fascism's embrace of highly industrial society, including modern science and technology. As Jeffrey Herf points out in his book *Reactionary Modernism*, there is a striking contradiction between fascist ideology and practice. Herf's conclusion that the Nazis were pragmatists who utilized modern technology and methods to achieve anti-modernist and anti-Liberal political goals also can be applied to Italian Fascism.

Prior to World War I, Italy and Germany—as politically Conservative nations—embraced rather limited Liberal concepts and Democratic processes. The landed gentry, politicians, upper-class industrialists, and middle-class business owners were concerned about the rise of Socialism and the growth of labor unions. They focused on protecting national elites and industries, and embraced militant opportunism and imperialism to oppose "the leveling aspirations of liberal democracy and socialism." Fascist elites welcomed a conservative, reactionary approach to preserving the socioeconomic status quo. They did not favor a Liberal or modern revolution.

In *The Italian Dictatorship*, R. J. B. Bosworth asserts that Italian Fascists vigorously oppressed Socialists, siding with "landowners, industry, and all those elements of wealth, power, and status" within the Conservative nation. Mussolini first made his reputation sending squads of Blackshirts to brutally beat striking workers and peasants in 1920–1921. In spite of the theoretical principles of Italian syndicalism, which mandated the establishment of independent worker's associations, in practice, Fascist Corporatism was used to destroy labor movements and suppress political dissent.

The Nazis moved aggressively against independent labor unions, abolishing them as early as May 1933 (just four months after the Nazis came to power), replacing them with the Nazi Labor Front, and against Socialist movements and parties by making them illegal. If "revolutionary or Socialist" anti-capitalism existed under Hitler, it was very narrowly defined, applying only to "Jewish" industrialists, business owners, and shop keepers. National Socialists permitted all non-Jewish German Capitalists to continue managing their companies.

Hitler was a pragmatist about most issues, and was willing to wait for suitable conditions to implement his ideological goals. To further his grand vision, he was careful not to alienate traditional political or social institutions on the right. When Hitler needed new leaders and institutions to implement his goals, he authorized parallel organizations and associations (*Gleichschaltung*), which in time absorbed any organization unwilling to cooperate with National Socialist principals.

Italian Fascists regularly emphasized their "glorious and illustrious past." Mussolini admired the martial values of the Roman generals; they served as a pattern for Italian Fascists. The Roman Imperial ethos stressed the primacy and glory of empire, unquestioning obedience to the supreme leader, and submission of individual personality and will to the needs of the empire. This created an ideology that attracted followers, controlled the masses, and alleviated the need for class-based politics. National Socialist culture drew from Imperial Rome, Norse mythology, sun mysticism, and various occult beliefs and practices.

To generate "unity of the nation," Italian Fascists supported conservative political, economic, and cultural forces within society. In other words, they zealously protected the status quo; their goals were primarily reactionary, rather than revolutionary. Although the leadership often talked about "revolution," the symbols they used, according to Bosworth, "were drawn from the history of Classical Rome, the corporate life of the Middle Ages, and the virile creativity of the Renaissance." In metaphor and symbol Italian and German Fascists always were referring back to an idealized, virtuous, and mythical past. As the supposed inheritors of Caesar's mantle, both regimes remained staunchly conservative and authoritarian—reactionary rather than revolutionary.

National Socialists were vehemently opposed to modern bourgeois culture and confiscated and publicly burned modernist literature. They promoted German literature and art that described rural life, the Volk—the peasant farmers—and expressed longing for a simpler, pre-industrial society. National Socialists were appalled by Modern Art, staging a public showing of "Degenerate Art, Produced by Liberals, Democrats, Jazz-Playing American Negroes, and Jews." They rejected modernism in theater and films. German Fascists, according to Jeffrey Herf, selectively borrowed from earlier cultural traditions, in particular Romanticism, using motifs, metaphors, and symbols affirming Nazi ideology.

Italian Fascism was not as critical of Modernist culture. Mabel Berezin found that Italian Fascists respected theater as a cultural vehicle, and intervened very little in the film and theater industries. Based on her research, however, Isabella Sanchez, contends that the "Italian government heavily censored films that contradicted Fascist ideology to avoid revolts," and artists were forced to join a Professional and Artists Syndicate, but "were not required to subscribe to an official view of art, which meant that Fascist Italy did not face a loss in major artists" as did Nazi Germany.

So, in what way were the mid-20th-century Fascists modern? How did German and, to a lesser extent, Italian Fascists embrace modernity? Both regimes focused on pragmatic achievements that resulted in successful conquest, annexation of territory, and governance. They invested in improved weapons, tanks, planes, and ships; technological processes and industrial efficiency were highly valued. Fascists were able to develop pragmatic and rational approaches to production, and reject the political and social values usually associated with modernity—Liberalism, parliamentary politics, expanded individual rights, and balanced and reasonably benevolent government. "Technology had exerted a fascination for fascist intellectuals" throughout Europe; they were interested in power and understood the role that technology could play. It is not difficult to understand how fascists—committed to Romanticism, the illiberal, the irrational, and geographic expansion—could apprehend the immense utilitarian potential of modern science, technology, and methods of production. The Germans were better at this than the Italians, but the "reactionary modernists," as Herf refers to them, were able to separate technology from modern Liberalism and reframed technology in language that emphasized technology's tremendous benefits for

the modern nation-state. The German and Italian dictatorships were fundamentally reactionary and anti-revolutionary regimes, which made limited
and strategic use of selected narrow aspects of modernity.

CLOSING

Did fascism—as expressed in a few powerful regimes and in a number of
smaller movements—represent a primarily modernizing movement or was it
primarily reactionary and anti-modernist? Dr. Evangelista's analysis points
out some of the older notions that obstruct the view of fascism as a modernizing movement. Evangelista points to Hitler's famous rejection of modern
art and the view that Marxists were the progressives being held back from
modernizing changes by obscurantist fascist repression. Dr. Evangelista goes
on to assert, however—citing fascists of the period and recent scholarship—
that fascists embraced high technology, science, and mass production, and
any other modernist technique that could further their ultra-nationalist objectives. They were, in fact, creating their own "alternative" modernity.

Dr. Ast's analysis insists that fascist violence and repression was anti-
modern in nature. Ast uses primarily recent scholarship, suggesting that contemporary discourse on that subject is contradictory and problematic. The
fascist regimes' repudiation of representative government, suppression of individual liberties, and intolerance of difference, however, simply cannot be
seen as modernizing. Dr. Ast acknowledges the fascist embracing of science
and engineering, but reminds us that it was mostly applied as the means to
bring about irrational, obscurantist, and aggressive ends. Ast concludes by
asserting that fascists were willing to use "selected narrow aspects of modernity" to accomplish their chiefly anti-modern agendas.

DOING MORE

Ben-Ghiat, Ruth, *Fascist Modernities: Italy, 1922–1945* (Berkeley: University of Cali-
fornia Press, 2001).
Bosworth, R. J. B., *The Italian Dictatorship: Problems and Perspectives in the Interpre-
tation of Mussolini and Fascism* (London: Arnold, 1998).
Griffin, Roger, *Modernism and Fascism: The Sense of a Beginning Under Mussolini and
Hitler* (Basingstoke: Palgrave, 2007).
Herf, Jeffrey, *Reactionary Modernism: Technology, Culture, and Politics in Weimar and
the Third Reich* (New York: Cambridge University Press, 1984).
Mowrer, Edgar A., *Germany Puts the Clock Back* (New York: William Morrow Co.
1933).
Paxton, Robert O., *The Anatomy of Fascism* (New York: Knopf, 2004).
Renton, Dave, *Fascism: Theory and Practice* (London: Pluto, 1999).

QUESTION 2: WERE RACISM AND ANTI-SEMITISM AN ESSENTIAL PART OF FASCIST IDEOLOGY OR WERE SUCH PRIORITIES RESTRICTED TO A FEW PARTICULAR CASES?

On the nights of November 9–10, 1938, there erupted in Nazi Germany mass rioting, looting, smashing of property, and physical assaults on ordinary people. This violence and chaos raged throughout the German nation and the Austrian territories just acquired by Germany. The violence was sponsored by—and mostly carried out by—agents of the Nazi State and the target was clear—Germany's Jewish community. The nightmare of *Kristallnacht*, as it came to be known, marked a significant threshold in terms of world opinion, so outraging other nations that several cut off diplomatic relations with Germany or removed their ambassadors. It became impossible—even for foreign supporters of Nazi Germany—to ignore or downplay the intensity of the Nazi State's anti-Semitism. Anti-Semitism and racial prejudice in general, however, had been a core Nazi principle from the beginning. Karl Marx had pioneered the idea that it was the struggle between classes that drove human historical events. Adolf Hitler asserted, however, in works such as *Mein Kampf*, that it was the struggle between races. Hitler and his Nazis capitalized on an existing anti-Semitism within Germany that dated back to the Middle Ages. Nazi ideology, however, was fanatic in its accusations about the Jews' role in creating the economic, social, and moral problems in Germany. Nazism from its earliest days preached the need to eliminate the Jews and their influence from the national community—which they were supposedly corroding from the inside. By 1941, when the Germans were consolidating their conquered territories in Eastern Europe, Jews and other non-Aryan ethnic groups were identified, forcibly ejected from their homes, and moved into segregated areas to make way for German colonists. Although many other groups were sent into forced labor, the Jews were rounded up and either installed in restricted ghettos in the cities (such as Warsaw and Lodz), or taken *en masse* to be gunned down in executions and thrown into mass graves—most often after having been forced to dig the pits themselves. The Holocaust had begun.

By the following year, 1942, the network of death camps was beginning to operate and the Jews from all over occupied Europe were fed into an industrialized system of killing camps and slave-labor programs. When Allied armies finally liberated these camps, their horrors shocked the world; and the estimates of the dead climbed to between 11 and 14 million victims. More than six million of these victims were Jews. The Holocaust seemed like the culminating nightmare in human history—the logical final destination of fascist ideology when translated into action and with unlimited power.

The horrors of the Holocaust, understandably, were so great that they deeply influenced the scholarship on the subject for decades after 1945. Gradually, however, scholars are re-assessing the place of anti-Semitism and outright racism within the ideology of fascism in general. The Nazi regime was always the most radical of any of the movements when it came to the question of racial theory and anti-Semitism. From the beginning the Nazi Party had based its vision of the future German state on concepts that equated "race" with "nation" and "state." Aryans made up the German nation, and racial non-Aryans simply were not part of the nation, based on their genetics. In power, the Nazis were able to convert this concept into legal reality, removing citizenship from non-Aryans, particularly those identified as Jews. Were other fascist regimes and movements motivated and driven by the same conceptions? Was the concept of the "racial nation" a foundational precept in all fascist thinking? Was each major fascist movement inclined to persecute, purge, and violate those identified as specifically "racial others," and particularly Jews? This remains an ongoing debate amongst scholars of the fascist era. It has vitally important implications, because the answer to that question contributes to a quick determination as to the credibility of fascism and for those who, today, borrow from the fascist political formula. If fascism is inherently racist, and any fascist regime that becomes established eventually will have the need to persecute and murder racial others, then any political state that even resembles the fascism of 1919–1945 is discredited as adopting and endorsing beliefs that enabled the Holocaust.

Conversely, if it is found that Nazi Germany only represents one strange aberration of the period, and that other fascist ideologies were not necessarily bound up with race, then it is plausible to assert that those who followed fascism at the time simply were trying to make a better world in a terribly difficult time and had no inherently malicious or evil intent. It suggests that if parts of fascist practices are adopted (such as the Corporative economic model or military-style regimentation of political ceremonies) in a modern regime, it will not necessarily lead to another round of the persecution and murder of innocent people simply because of their ethnicity.

Arriving at a simple answer is quite difficult. There is no question at all about the racial attitudes of the Nazi regime; however, Mussolini's Italy presents a more complicated question. In general, the Italians did not write about, speak publicly about, or pass laws about racial issues during their formative period or during the majority of the Mussolini dictatorship. It was even famously remembered that Mussolini had a Jewish mistress, and that there were Jewish members of his Blackshirts. After the conquest of Abyssinia in 1936, however, Mussolini's relationship with the democracies became quite tenuous. For support and security he increasingly turned to friendship with Hitler's Germany. By 1937, Galeazzo Ciano wrote in his diary that

Mussolini was ranting about Jews and the need for a Jewish policy. By 1938, the Italian government had issued a formal proclamation on the importance of race (*Il Manifesto della Razza*) and had passed laws diminishing the rights of Africans and Jews. Does this mean that the Fascists in Italy finally reached the inevitable stage of racial antipathy that was always potentially part of their belief system? Or does it indicate that racism had never been part of Italian Fascism at all, until Mussolini so forcibly was influenced by Hitler and the Nazi Party's unique brand of fascism only after 1936?

Other Fascist cases provide similar challenges. The British Union of Fascists (BUF), led by Sir Oswald Mosley, launched its program in 1932, announcing that its program completely rejected the racial views of the Nazis. Mosley emphasized that with a vast empire full of different races, racism was totally impractical for the British variant of fascism. He held no grudge against Jews at all, he said, and there were even said to be Jewish members of the BUF. After 1934, however, with the popularity of his movement waning fast, Mosley and the BUF turned to vigorous anti-Semitism. Their newspaper, *Action*, became something of a stridently racist scandal sheet. Was this simple political opportunism? Which policy indicates the true, essential nature of British fascism?

The essays provided below tackle this tangled and difficult issue. First, Barbara Stamey, whose research has focused on the victims of the Holocaust, takes the position that racism and anti-Semitism were and are essential to fascist ideology. Although there might not be specific mention of Jews in contemporary fascist writing, in many cases it lurks beneath the surface. Stamey takes the position that the bedrock principle of fascism is intense nationalism, and such fanatic nationalism inherently degrades or diminishes any group considered not part of the national community. This position aligns with that of scholar Mark Neocleous, whose 1997 article "Racism, Fascism, and Nationalism" asserted that "nationalism is necessarily xenophobic—that is, xenophobia is part of the logic of nationalism—and thus always remains an invitation to anti-Semitism and racism."

The second essay is written by Dr. Eugene Berger, a specialist in the politics of the Spanish-speaking world. In it he examines a number of fascist regimes that are not always considered in the attempts to define fascism. For Dr. Berger, the Nazi model was unique in its radical racism and other regimes—such as those in Spain, Portugal, Austria, and even some South American examples—simply did not engage with the racial issue. Different races having not formed a significant part of their nation's experience, racial explanations for the nation's problems simply didn't work. Although most shared the tendency to create "internal enemies," those enemies were not necessarily racial or ethnic in nature.

ANSWER: BARBARA STAMEY, RACISM AND ANTI-SEMITISM WERE AN ESSENTIAL PART OF FASCIST IDEOLOGY AND PRACTICE

The term "racism" or "anti-Semitism" is not found in the scholarly definition of fascism; however, almost all definitions of Fascism include nationalism. Nationalism is racist in theory and in practice. Anti-Semitism is a millennia-old form of racism. Enemies and "others" are required by fascists in their various quests for national superiority, both internal and external, and this essential element was provided by general racism and, where applicable, anti-Semitism. Ideas of inherent subservience are built into nationalist thinking (if members of the national community are believed to be superior relative to others, then the others must, of course, be inferior) and an understanding of the evolution or racist ideology and the roles it has played in nationalism show how this factor was and is a vital ingredient of fascist ideology.

Racism and anti-Semitism were essential in the minds of fascists as a means to achieving the goals of the nation. Racism, in the form of anti-Semitism, was central to Hitler's ideology of Nazism, as set out in *Mein Kampf*. The place of anti-Semitism in Mussolini's Italian Fascism, however, is far less clear. Even in Italy, however, in the early days of the Fascist takeover, according to scholar R. J. B. Bosworth there were populist attacks on non-Italian ethnic groups in areas like Trento. Eventually, of course, after Mussolini's conquest of Abyssinia, he issued a declaration on the importance of race and passed racist and anti-Semitic legislation curtailing the rights of these peoples. Fascists and fascist-inspired authoritarians used racism and anti-Semitism as a means to unite their citizens against an "other," providing a tool to be used in building support for the mobilization of the masses. This forced the assimilation of different ethnic groups within their boundaries, or justified persecuting and purging them. The culture and history of the nation involved, the personality of the dictator, and the degree to which the leader chose to retain the traditional trappings of hierarchy helped determined which ideas fascist-like regimes would use.

In the formative age of fascism, race was used interchangeably with ethnicity and racism and anti-Semitism were accepted as parts of nationalist traditions. This was certainly the opinion of numerous writers of the period, for instance Carleton Stevens Coon in his book *The Races of Europe* or R. W. Seton-Watson in his article, "The Problem of Revision and the Slav World," both published in the 1930s. Even though it is not spelled out in the many definitions of fascism, the prevailing central European tradition of a race-oriented nationalism of the time was essential to fascist ideology.

Historians have identified two types of racism during the fascist era, "cultural racism," and what is known as "biological racism." Scholar of fascism Kevin Passmore writes, " 'Cultural racism' is less extreme and allows for assimilation—always resting on racist assumptions—especially discriminatory where it involves oppressive measures such as closure of minority language schools." Mussolini practiced this type of racism when he persecuted and forced the assimilation of Slovenes in the territory of South Tyrol which had been assigned to Italy after World War I. "Biological racism," however, is the conception that a racial, ethnic, or even religious group is biologically distinct and that both its physical and cultural differences are a product of this biological difference. According to this thinking, this leaves no possibility of assimilation of that group into the national community. Therefore, if a national community hopes to eliminate the "foreign" influences of this different and distinct group, the only methods available are voluntary removal, forceful ejection, or extermination. This path of logic, tied to the conception of "biological" racial difference, is what author Daniel Jonah Goldhagen termed "eliminationist anti-Semitism" in Germany, in his highly controversial book, *Hitler's Willing Executioners* (1996).

Although the extreme racialism of Nazi Germany is beyond question, perhaps the thorniest issue in trying to resolve the question about the place of racism and anti-Semitism in fascist ideology revolves around Italian Fascism under Mussolini. The Italian Fascist movement—and then the regime—largely ignored racism early on. By 1938, however, it was implementing dramatic racial policies. As Italy is the location where Fascism was born and where it was first translated into political power, it is crucial to resolve where such attitudes were positioned in the Italian case. Many of the fascist beliefs, symbols, practices, and movements were developed in direct imitation of the Italian model.

There is a conspicuous lack of racist discourse in the earlier written material from Fascist Italy. Racism and anti-Semitism were as deeply ingrained in the integral fabric of the period and in Fascism as an ideology that it was not necessary to include it in the written definition which Mussolini was eventually forced to formulate, "Fascism: Doctrines and Institutions," found in the 1932 edition of the *Enciclopedia Italiana*.

In his biography of Mussolini, Denis Mack Smith writes, "There is for example no reference in this article to the racialism that soon after became a fundamental fascist doctrine." Many important current scholars, however, do include race as a characteristic of fascism. In the preface to his book, *The Nature of Fascism*, noted fascist scholar Roger Griffin states, "Its [Fascism's] raw materials were such forces as militarism, racism, charismatic leadership, populist nationalism. . . ." Kevin Passmore explains, "Fascism won't tolerate diversity of identities, or the notion that a person can simultaneously fulfil her or his duties as a citizen and espouse other identities." Even more explicitly, Passmore says that,

> As an ultranationalist ideology, fascism is unabashedly racist. . . . Citizenship and its benefits are accorded or denied on the basis of conformity to, or possession of, characteristics alleged to be "national," be they biological, cultural, religious, or political. Nationalism and racism pervade all aspects of fascist practice, from welfare provisions and family policy to diplomacy. Those deemed to be outside the nation face an uncertain future—extermination in the worst case.

Mussolini is touted by some scholars as the best example that racism is not an essential ideology of fascism. In speaking of Mussolini's regime, scholar George L. Mosse takes this position writing that, "Racism and anti-Semitism were not a necessary component of fascism, and certainly not of those parts of the movement that looked for their model to Italy, where until 1936, racism was not part of official doctrine." "Official" is a key designation here and certainly Mussolini used the tool of racism differently and more selectively. Though his use of racism was not as severe as that of Hitler, he felt free to use racism to suit his needs—as was seen in South Tyrol, Libya, Ethiopia, and finally against Italian Jewish citizens. He did not accept Hitler's biological racism mainly because it placed the Italian race somewhat beneath that of the German Aryan race. The anti-Semitic policies finally implemented in 1938 always had been available to Mussolini, though he had never thought or moved in that direction until he became increasingly tied to Hitler's Germany for reasons of Italy's national security. Nonetheless, as Meir Michaelis points out in his book, *Mussolini and the Jews*, "The Fascist drive for monolithic unity ('everything within the State, nothing outside the State, nothing against the State') was a potential threat to the Jews from the very beginning (a fact which was well understood by the Jewish leaders.)"

Modern students of Italian Fascism are frustrated with Mussolini's inconsistencies of policy, and certainly people of the period were equally confused. Mussolini ignored and rejected racism or anti-Semitism until the mid-1930s, after his Ethiopian conquest, when race became a present issue. After that period, however, Mussolini implemented dramatic racial laws that denied racial "others" of basic rights and sought to keep the Italian "race" pure. Which policy reflects the true nature of Mussolini himself and of his variant of Fascism? Giovanni Gentile, minister of public instruction in Mussolini's first cabinet, points out a key characteristic of Mussolini's policy making in an article for *Foreign Affairs Magazine*, published in January 1928. "The real 'views' of the Duce," Gentile said, "are those which he formulates and exe-cutes at one and the same time." In other words, it is Mussolini's deeds which must be judged, not words or posturing. In the end, Mussolini made the Ital-ian movement as racist as any of the Fascist movements.

Mussolini appears to have turned to vigorous racialism partly as a tactic to defend against any reduction of enthusiasm for his regime amongst the younger generations of Italy. Ultra-Nationalists, almost by definition, would be drawn to ideas of their own racial superiority, and be reinvigorated by this new emphasis. Additionally, the younger generation needed distraction from the declining social and economic conditions within Italy. Despite all the bombast, the economic resources of the country were being drained away by the commitment to the civil war in Spain and the settlement of Ethiopia. By depriving the Jews (and women) of their holdings, jobs, and positions in companies and at the universities, Mussolini could placate these men by having them fill the vacant positions. Furthermore, at the time of the implementation of racial laws, Mussolini was facing several other challenges that could be solved with anti-Semitic directives. In an article titled "Racism in Italy," in the January 1939 issue of *Foreign Affairs*, Martin Agronsky wrote that Mussolini blamed Jews for his inability to obtain loans in Europe and America and sought revenge on Italian Jews, despite their small numbers in Italy.

During the early years of Fascism, Mussolini often used anti-Semitic and racist rhetoric. Michaelis wrote,

> Throughout his career he both attacked and defended the Jews. As early as 1917 he identified the Bolshevik Revolution with the "synagogue"; but as late as 1944 he insisted that he was "not anti-Semite." As early as 1919 he accused the Jews of plotting against the "Aryan race"; but as late as 1944 he denied the existence of a Jewish problem in Italy. As early as 1921 he referred to the Italian people as "this our Aryan and Mediterranean stock (stirpe)"; but as late as 1944 he deplored Hitler's racialist aberrations, with special reference to the "final solution."

Despite this double-talk, however, if taking the advice of Giovanni Gentile and focusing on Mussolini's deeds, the fact remains that at the end of the Second World War 7,680 out of 44,500 Italian Jews had perished. The Jew-ish-Italian community had been ripped apart and scattered, and lives were destroyed. Most Jewish Italians never would recover their previous vigor and prosperity. The number dead is small as compared to the millions who per-ished under Hitler's adaptation of fascism but, even so, it represents nearly 20% of the Italian Jewish community.

Racism and anti-Semitism were essential ideologies in the fascist toolbox to be used to achieve the goals of the fascist leaders and the nations. Racism in the form of anti-Semitism was more central to Hitler's ideology, and the racism and anti-Semitism in Mussolini's Italian Fascism were far more subtle and haphazard befitting the conflicted and contradictory personality of Il Duce. It is clear that, as Passmore writes, "While racism took different forms in different countries, it was 'available' to fascists everywhere."

ANSWER: EUGENE BERGER, RACISM AND ANTI-SEMITISM WERE NOT ESSENTIAL INGREDIENTS OF FASCIST IDEOLOGY OR PRACTICE

The Holocaust undoubtedly was the most sinister outgrowth of European fascism. Some scholars, such as Aristotle Kallis, have argued that the Nuremburg tribunals "revealed the extent to which fascist regimes . . . had contributed to an unprecedented campaign of violence and annihilation, mostly against the continent's Jewish populations but also involving other ethnic, racial, religious, and social non-conformist groups." Many fascist movements including, but not limited to, Nazi Germany, used racism and anti-Semitism to help develop the essential fascist element of the "internal enemy." Fascism, however, *did* have many more targets for their suspicion and violence—apart from Jews and ethnic minorities. As described below, racism and anti-Semitism were not essential to fascist ideology.

Hitler's atrocities make it difficult to argue that anti-Semitism played *no* part in fascism, but was it fundamental or formative? All true fascist states go through an early phase that Robert Paxton calls "marking the internal enemies." By marginalizing other groups the Nationalists try to establish a "collective superiority" that could take many forms, including racism and anti-Semitism. In Nazi Germany this was initiated with a one-day boycott of Jewish businesses in April 1933, and the Nuremburg Laws of September 1935. European Nationalists in Romania, Hungary, and a handful of other states also targeted Jews, but none turned the rise of fascism into genocide. (Romania was quite complicit in the Holocaust and committed its own massacre of Jews in the early 1940s, but as Fascists there were not the dominant power, it can't be claimed that Romanian fascists had any sort of fully developed "fascist ideology," anti-Semitic, racist, or otherwise.) In short, German racism was unique.

Germany's "mystical racism" had origins at least as far back as the 18th century and, according to scholar Stanley Payne, painted Jews as the "most bitter racial foe." Hitler's "doctrine of demonic racial anti-Semitism was not new, having been advanced in varying degrees by diverse French, Russian,

German and Austrian ideologues in the late nineteenth century, but (his had a) new virulence and a special centrality." However, Hitler's hatreds were "re-markable" and he divided problems into "simple dualities."

So if "demonic anti-Semitism" was present in neighboring countries, did fascist regimes in those countries use it to come to power? The answer, some-what surprisingly, is "no." Perhaps the second-most infamous fascist in world history was Benito Mussolini in Italy. His rise to power involved a combina-tion of nationalist regeneration, the myth of ancient Rome, Corporatism, violence, party formation, electoral victories, and institutional reform. How-ever, none of those formative elements seem to be anti-Semitism or racism. According to Payne, Mussolini's internal enemies were mostly Liberals, "bol-shevists" and Masons.

In Spain, Francisco Franco came to power through civil war, and as a result had a much more readily identifiable internal enemy. The objects of Spanish Nationalist repression were "leftist leaders and activists in general and anyone suspected of opposing the Nationalist movement in particular." With the es-tablishment of the *estado nuevo* beginning in 1939, another source of internal enemies was the Basque and Catalonian regionalists. Franco denounced their separatist agendas as harmful to "True Spain," and national integrity. But they were not at all denounced as ethnic "others" or as racial inferiors. In fact, Franco was demanding that those elements be forced to remain within the nation and to assimilate.

In neighboring Portugal, the origins of popular fascist mobilization were largely in the *Integralismo Lusitanio* (IL). Integralism was based on traditional anti-Liberalism, "historical" nationalism and ruralism opposed to industriali-zation. The internal enemies of the Integralists, according to the leading scholar of the Portuguese extreme-right Antonio Cost Pinto, were "Jacobin and anti-clerical republicanism, along with Masonry." When Portuguese fas-cism came of age under Rolão Preto, he emerged as the leader of IL. Later, under the Salazar dictatorship, there continued to be a sense that "the real internal enemy . . . was "the Liberal Republic."

Some scholars are hesitant to extend a discussion of fascism outside of Europe, but Latin America had the closest thing to "genuine fascist regime(s)" in Brazil and Argentina. These cases can also help in examining the rise of nationalism further outside of the shadow of the Holocaust. In Brazil, the *Ação Integralista Brasileira* (AIB), according to Robert O. Paxton, "was the closest to an indigenous mass fascist party." Its founder Plinio Salgado met Mussolini and went on to "merge indigenous Brazilian historical imagery . . . with the more overtly fascist aspects of his program." Argentina also had a figure in Juan Domingo Perón who, more than Vargas, matched the image of a "fascist *jefe*." Perón came to power through mass demonstration and the organization of labor unions, not through the traditionally oppressive steps of European contemporaries. Oppression instead came during his dictatorship (1946–55), which shared several elements with Nazi Germany and Fascist Italy (parades, control of the press, repressive police, violence against the Left) but, conspicuously, not racism or anti-Semitism.

If fascist ideology is not inherently racist or anti-Semitic, we must examine how Jews and ethnic minorities were treated in the aforementioned fascist regimes. If fascism wasn't endemically anti-Semitic or racist, perhaps Hitler's influence meant that fascism in Austria and Hungary was forced to become so. In fact, the opposite seems to be the case. The Austrian Fatherland Front was able to use its closeness with Italian Fascism to ward off widespread anti-Semitism. In fact, until the *Anschluss*, much of the character of Austrian fascism was based on its asserting its independence and separate identity from Germany. The Fatherland Front emphasized Austria's Catholicism over Germany's Protestantism, for example, and for the most part rejected the racism and anti-Semitism so prominent in Nazism. In 1930s Nationalist Hungary, there were two anti-Jewish laws in the 1930s that followed an increasing cooperation with Germany. This anti-Semitism, however, also could be partly attributed to the Magyarization of the newly contracted Hungarian state and its marginalization of *all* ethnic minorities, including but not limited to Jews.

What of Spain then; a nation that expelled all Jews in 1492? There were several attempts by Germany to expand Spain's support of the Nazi regime, especially after Nazi occupation of France in 1940. Spain largely stood firm however. It did not sign the Tripartite Pact and did not support Hitler's treatment of the Jews. Stanley Payne points out that "during the first part of the war some 30,000 Jews had received safe passage through Spain, and there is no indication of any Jew who reached Spanish soil being turned back to German authorities."

Neighboring Portugal's nationalists also had a Germanophilic element, although it still remained neutral during World War II itself. Lusitanian Nationalism mentioned the threat of syndicalists, Communists, foreign aggression, and Bolshevism as well, but not Jews or ethnic minorities. In fact, according to Cost Pinto, Rolão Preto actually thought that racism could be counterproductive to Portuguese Nationalism. Preto wanted to "destroy the useless laments before the Race's Wailing Wall."

In Italy, anti-Semitism and racism appeared in Mussolini's regime, but only long after his rise to power. In 1936, Italy passed racial regulations in reaction to its invasion of Ethiopia and then in 1938 published the "Manifesto of Italian Racism." That same year, Italy banned Jewish teachers from public schools and eventually purged Jews from "major institutions." This turn against Jews was somewhat surprising. Jews in Italy were a small and well-integrated minority in Italy by the 20th century, and did not seem to be the target of widespread discrimination in WWI or in the 1920s. In fact, Stanley Payne reminds us, 230 Jewish Fascists participated in the March on Rome and by 1938 the party had more than 10,000 "adult Jewish members."

Across the Atlantic, Brazilian fascism did include "overtly fascist aspects" such as anti-Semitism, but had also a laundry list of almost all the aspects noted above. Plinio Salgado's broad vision was important in building Integralism to more than 180,000 members, but the party lacked the focus necessary to take the presidency. In neighboring Argentina, Juan Domingo Perón turned the police on the press and certain leftists but, says Paxton, "(his dictatorship) lacked the diabolized internal/external enemy—Jews or others—that seems an essential ingredient of fascism."

Neither racism nor anti-Semitism was essential to fascist ideology. The more examples examined, the more apparent it is that no internal enemy fit every nationalist leader's purposes perfectly. Plinio Salgado tried to attach the Tupi Indian culture, "dictatorship, nationalism, protectionalism, corporatism, anti-Semitism, goose steps, a proposed Secretariat for Moral and Physical Education, green shirts and black armbands with the Greek letter sigma" to *Ação Integralista Brasileira* ideology. Ultimately however, the more indigenous program of President Getulio Vargas won out, as it was not "typically" fascist but addressed Brazil's unique realities. Benito Mussolini tried to "latinize" international fascism and reach out to Spain, Portugal, and Brazil with his *"Braco Largo."* Adolf Hitler tried to export Nazi anti-Semitism to Austria. These efforts aside, the fact is that the most effective fascism was homegrown. More often than not, these homegrown movements chose not to use racism or anti-Semitism to build critical initial support.

CLOSING

Were racism and anti-Semitism essential components of fascist ideology and practice? Barbara Stamey's essay asserts that they were. To make her argument, she focuses on one regime in particular. Although there is some argument as to whether the Franco regime in Spain, the Salazar regime in Portugal, or the Fatherland Front in Austria were truly fascist, there is no argument about Italian Fascism being "the original." Establishing whether that regime was essentially racist, then, is crucial to the argument. Stamey acknowledges that Mussolini did not specifically list racism as one of his defining issues in his own written definition. But, Stamey also cites Giovanni Gentile's assertion that to truly know Mussolini's convictions, one had to observe his actions. In the end, says Stamey, Fascist Italy limited the rights of Africans and Jews, and sent thousands of Jews to their deaths, exterminating approximately 20% of Italy's Jewish community. Whatever the content of Italian Fascist discourse, these were the concrete results.

Dr. Berger, however, challenges this by examining the Italian case and several others. Berger concentrates on the "formative" period of fascist movements and looks at fascism in Austria, Spain, Portugal, Brazil, and Argentina. He makes the point that in the formation of Austrian fascism, for instance, rejection of German identity was a crucial element, and rejecting the Nazi racial attitudes was part of this. In Portugal, Brazil, and Argentina, these regimes marked "internal enemies," but did not identify them by race or ethnicity. Berger also points out the very interesting contradiction, that during the Franco regime in Spain, ethnic others such as the Basques and Catalans were not urged to leave, or to be identified as different in any way. Just the opposite, they were forced to assimilate into "True Spain," putting away their thoughts of separatism, and cultural differences.

DOING MORE

Burleigh, Michael, and Wolfgang Wippermann, "The 'Uniqueness' of Nazi Racialism," *The Racial State: Germany 1933–1945* (Cambridge: Cambridge University Press, 1991): 44–51.

Goldhagen, Daniel Jonah, *Hitler's Willing Executioners: Ordinary Germans and the Holocaust* (New York: Vintage, 1997).

Kallis, Aristotle, "Fascism and the Jews: From the Internationalization to a Fascist Anti-Semitism," *Holocaust Studies: A Journal of Culture and History* (Summer/Autumn, 2009): 15–34.

Neocleous, Mark, "Racism, Fascism, and Nationalism," *The Fascism Reader* ed. Aristotle Kallis (London: Routledge, 2003).

Paxton, Robert O., *The Anatomy of Fascism* (New York: Alfred A. Knopf, 2004).

Payne, Stanley G., *The Franco Regime: 1936–1975* (Madison: The University of Wisconsin Press, 1987).

Sarfatti, Michele, *The Jews in Mussolini's Italy: From Equality to Persecution* (Madison: University of Wisconsin Press, 2006).

QUESTION 3: WAS FASCIST IDEOLOGY BASED UPON MILITARY CONQUEST AND EXPANSION, OR DID FASCISTS EQUALLY ADVOCATE WITHDRAWAL AND NATIONAL INSULATION?

The way that fascist dictatorship most deeply impacted world history is in its bringing about (and fighting in) the Second World War. The Second World War arguably stands as the largest-scale single event in all of history; it affected the most human beings, involved the most geographical territory, and created the greatest amount of death and destruction of any of the monumental events in modern recorded history. No single natural disaster or human development so radically changed the period of time that immediately followed it. World War II directly caused the death of approximately 60 million people, which far exceeds even the large-scale disasters of the European colonization of the New World and the Atlantic slave trade. Not surprisingly then, the role of the fascist dictatorships in escalating the tensions that eventually brought about that terrible war, and the role of these dictatorships in fighting it, tend to be the central focus of the study of fascism.

The period during which the two dictatorships of Fascist Italy and Nazi Germany escalated world tensions was dominated by concerns about their military aggression and territorial expansion. Japan launched a campaign of conquest during 1931 by invading and conquering Manchuria. Later the Japanese extended these conquests to areas of China, the Philippines, Singapore, Burma, and multiple island territories in the Pacific. There are people who do not see the Japanese government as necessarily "fascist" until the period under the dictatorship of Hideki Tojo (1941–1944). For those who do consider the government of Imperial Japan to be at least "fascist-inspired," however, there is no doubt as to its intense ambitions of territorial expansion. In Europe, Mussolini's Italy had secured some small—and negotiated— territorial expansion during the 1920s. In 1935, however, Italy embarked on a provocative war of conquest that threw the diplomatic world into crisis. This was the invasion of Abyssinia—the last truly independent African state, led by its emperor, Haile Selassie. Abyssinia was a member of the League of Nations, and so the prospect of one prominent member attacking and conquering another had frightening implications. The acknowledged role of the League of Nations was to serve as a diplomatic organ of world government, and to preserve the world order created by the Paris Peace Conference. If Mussolini was simply allowed to attack and conquer another member nation, then the League's authority would be instantly discredited. Because of such chilling prospects, diplomats from the democracies worked furiously to prepare a solution that would prevent war and at least leave the appearance of the League's authority and its members' cooperation intact. Eventually, however, the most that the League and its most prominent members could manage were weak economic sanctions, and Italy proceeded with its brutal conquest of Abyssinia.

Soon after, in 1936, Hitler moved into the Rhineland—blatantly violating the Versailles Treaty—and both Hitler and Mussolini sent significant aid to the Spanish "Nationalists" under Franco. In 1938 Hitler annexed Austria, and then brought the world to acute crisis again in September of that year with his plans to annex parts of Czechoslovakia. Eventually an agreement was loosely put in place between Britain, France, Italy, and Germany that gave Hitler the German-speaking lands of Czechoslovakia (the Sudetenland), but also confirmed that this would be Hitler's last territorial expansion. Hitler violated this agreement almost immediately, moving into the rest of Czechoslovakia during early 1939. His massive invasion of Poland in September 1939 launched the Second World War, as the democracies agreed that the constant aggression of the fascist dictatorships no longer could be tolerated without permanently undermining world stability.

The policies of the democracies in these years spoke to the tendency of fascist dictatorships to need to expand. Britain's government—under the Conservatives Stanley Baldwin and then Neville Chamberlain—pursued a policy of "Appeasement." This policy attempted to allow the dictators reasonable territorial expansions, enough to correct the most problematic punishments from the postwar settlement. If they were allowed these acquisitions, the thinking went, the problems of the Paris Peace Conference could be repaired and the dictatorships would be satisfied—and the world could return to peace and cooperation. The policy failed. As many people insisted at the time, such fascist dictatorships *never* could be satisfied, because militarism, aggression, and conquest were at the essence of their national systems. The fascist belief system achieved its aggrandizing of the national community by means of overpowering other national communities—and then exploiting the resources acquired in the process. The behavior of Italy and Germany during the Second World War would seem to support this assertion; after war was declared, they did not fight a limited war with Poland, Britain, and France. Instead, Germany attacked and conquered Poland, Denmark, Norway, Holland, Belgium, Luxemburg, France, Hungary, and other countries. It also attacked Britain and the Soviet Union, though it never conquered them. Italy attacked—with the intention to conquer—Southern France, British Somaliland, Greece, and Egypt. Surely this long list of behaviors makes it beyond argument that fascism was positively based on military conquest and territorial expansion.

In the cases of Italy and Germany this seems quite plausible. Viewing the Japanese state of the period as being fascist only strengthens the argument. There were other fascist regimes and movements, however, which did not necessarily emphasize conquest or expansion in their rhetoric, political programs, or actions. There were some regimes that entirely ignored such issues. There were others that dreamt of conquest but lacked the means. Still others actually emphasized a different approach altogether, advocating withdrawal from the chaotic conditions of the world, emphasizing the need for economic autarky, and urging the building of armaments for defense rather than aggression. Is it possible, then, that aggressive territorial expansion and conquest is not necessarily an essential component of the fascist belief system?

The two essays provided below examine this contradiction. The first was written by Dr. Nathan Orgill, an expert on modern German history and the World Wars. His essay makes the case that expansion at the expense of others was built into the fascist belief system. Dr. Orgill focuses on the Italian and German cases, but also mentions Spanish and British Fascism as well. The second essay is by Dr. Patrick Zander, the editor of this book. Dr. Zander's research has focused on British Fascism of the period. Zander makes the case that systems other than that of Italy and Germany—particularly the Austrian, Spanish, and British—demonstrate that a program of expansion was not a central feature of these movements. In fact, there was an opposite emphasis on withdrawal and isolation.

ANSWER: NATHAN ORGILL, FASCIST IDEOLOGY WAS FOUNDED UPON THE PURSUIT OF MILITARY CONQUEST AND TERRITORIAL EXPANSION

The various fascist movements of interwar Europe have long seemed subjects ripe for comparative analysis. Perhaps the least obvious way of comparing 20th-century fascism, however, has been in the realm foreign policy and military conquest. Indeed, the historiographical consensus—at least in the two most salient examples of Italy and Germany—has seemed to point in the opposite direction. Whereas the historiography of German foreign policy has most often seen Adolf Hitler's pre-war diplomacy as the result of a specific program developed before he came into power and put to work after 1933, the historiography of Italian foreign policy has interpreted Benito Mussolini's international maneuvers as largely incoherent, the work of an opportunist whose main concerns lay elsewhere. The water seems even more muddied when examining Europe's lesser interwar "fascisms"—such as Francisco Franco's Spain or Vichy France, where the very record of the regimes involved seems to preclude any notion that an expansionist agenda could somehow be an integral component of a generic definition of fascism.

As Robert Paxton has recently asserted in his *Anatomy of Fascism*, however, perhaps the way to think about these differences is to draw a distinction between varying stages of development—distinguishing nascent types of fascism in some national settings that never developed far beyond the early stages of the genesis and consolidation, from the more mature varieties that succeeded in seizing and exercising power before either radicalizing or facing "entropy." Although almost all fascist movements emphasized the integration and the strengthening of a national community, venerated violence and will in achieving those ends, and proclaimed a Social Darwinist ideal and "the right of the chosen people to dominate others without restraint from any kind of human or divine law," only two really succeeded in seizing and consolidating power to an extent that allowed them to pursue an expansionist foreign policy.

Almost all major fascist movements in early 20th-century Europe viewed struggle between the races of the world, war, and territorial expansion as a normal part of international politics. The Nationalist program of the *Falangists* in Spain, for instance, called for a revival of Spanish imperialism and the wiping out of foreign elements. Although much of the prewar period saw *Falangism* focused on securing and solidifying power at home, the occupation of Tangier in mid-June 1940 can be seen as having been at least partially motivated by an expansionist agenda, as Stanley Payne has hinted in *The Franco Regime*.

Even Oswald Mosley's British Union of Fascists, which proclaimed a "Britain First!" policy of economic protectionism and stridently pressed appeasement as a response to the reckless diplomacy of the Axis, saw empire as the direct and natural outgrowth of the inequality of the races of the world. In the June 7, 1935 issue of his party organ, *The Blackshirt*, Mosley deplored that "British statesmanship" was "busy giving away its own Empire in India and elsewhere" making it "the first Empire in history that has been given away." If the fascists of Britain seemed more focused on national consolidation and less interested in foreign war and expansion than their comrades in other countries, it was to some extent explained by the fact that their empire was an old and apparently decadent one, rather than a vibrant, growing one.

For many years, the historiography of Italian foreign policy up to the Second World War tended to portray Mussolini as a statesman who lacked any coherent, ideologically driven policy. The best example of this tradition was the work of a former Italian dissident, Gaetano Salvemini, whose *Prelude to World War II* viewed Fascist foreign policy as simply a hollow attempt to appease the organs of the press and public opinion in Italy—and Mussolini himself as merely a master propagandist without any tangible long-term policy goals. Nevertheless, that the Fascist movement in Italy at least had an expansionist façade seems beyond doubt.

The 1921 platform of the Italian Fascist Party, for example, excoriated the League of Nations, announced Italy's natural role as the dominant and influential power in the Mediterranean, and pressed for the strengthening of Italy's colonial empire and of the army and navy. Likewise, in the edition of the *Enciclopedia Italiana* published in 1932, an entry on "*La Dottrina del*

Fascismo" (ordinarily interpreted as written by Mussolini himself), valorized war as an instrument of international politics. Denying pacifism and the "utility of perpetual peace," it declared that "war alone brings up to their highest tension all human energies and puts the stamp of nobility upon the peoples who have the courage to meet it." Moreover, the concrete expressions of an expansionist impulse—the Abyssinian campaign of 1935–36, Italy's intervention in the Spanish Civil War in the summer of 1936, the formation of the Rome-Berlin Axis the following October, the belated and ill-conceived attack on France in mid-June 1940, and the subsequent invasions of British Somaliland, Egypt, and Greece between August and October 1940—point as much to an ideological bent in Mussolini's foreign policy as they do to cheap attempts to score points with the Italian public.

Beginning in the 1970s, some English-speaking scholars of Fascist Italy began to ask just this question. It seemed possible that a line of continuity existed between the bellicose Mussolini of the second half of the 1930s and his early diplomatic ventures in the 1920s. In *Mussolini's Early Diplomacy* by Alan Cassels, for instance, the Duce was portrayed as the architect of an energetic foreign policy as early as 1923. Mussolini had made various moves in the direction of Asia Minor but was restrained abruptly by the murder of Giacomo Matteotti in June 1924—an event that brought about a domestic crisis severe enough to make restraint abroad seem necessary. According to Cassels, Mussolini felt secure by 1925, however, and was able to establish a virtual protectorate over Albania and subsequently identified France as Italy's main competitor. By 1927, Mussolini's indecisive years were all but ended; he could embark on a more ambitious foreign policy. The Duce was, in Cassels's view, "an ideologue and trafficker in revisionism, and [a] spokesman for discontented, aggressive nationalism."

A compelling argument can be made that the unmistakable dissimilarity in success and degree of intensity that seems to distinguish Fascist Italy from Nazi Germany might really be the result of differences of military capability and tradition in the two countries, rather than an expression of major differences of ideology. In an analysis of Mussolini's policy on the eve of Italian participation in the Second World War, *Mussolini Unleashed*, Macgregor Knox found an even greater degree of homegrown aggressiveness in Fascist diplomacy than had been recognized by previous historians. The main difference he identified between Hitler and Mussolini was that Germany's army was stronger militarily. As a result, Germany's success in war led contemporaries and historians alike to take Hitler's ideological aims more seriously, while simultaneously seeing Mussolini and his regime as somehow less serious in their devotion to conquest, war, and empire. Knox uncovered a consistent program in Mussolini's devotion to the acquisition of "*spazio vitale*," the Italian variety of "living space," in the Mediterranean and North Africa. Although King Victor Emmanuel III and leaders in the military were hesitant to support any decision for war, when Mussolini did finally get his war in 1940, the Duce "was triumphant. He had 'realized his true dream,' . . . to become '*condottiere* of the nation at war.'" These sentiments were echoed in Knox's broader comparative history of the expansionist policies of Italy and Germany in the era of the World Wars, *Common Destiny*, as well as in the more deliberate comparative account of Aristotle Kallis, *Fascist Ideology*, both published in 2000.

It is in the German context, however, that an intentionalist approach linking ideology and policy formulation seems to carry the most weight. In the 1960s, A. J. P. Taylor sparked a major controversy with his provocative book, *Origins of the Second World War,* by asserting that Nazi foreign policy was not dictated by ideological underpinnings or marked by forethought and will. Instead, Taylor saw Hitler as a traditional European statesman who opportunistically pursued objectives that, taken together, resembled the power politics of earlier centuries.

The most important historiographical contributions since then largely have argued the opposite case, however, pointing to ideology as the most important explanatory factor in German foreign policy after 1933. In *Mein Kampf,* clearly and publicly, Hitler articulated broader expansionist aims based upon a rejection of the changes made during the Paris peace settlement following World War I. He viewed the question of German foreign policy as pointing directly to the foremost duty of a "völkisch state . . . to secure the existence of the race"—both in relation to agricultural production and raw materials, as well as to military and geopolitical security. The borders of 1914 seemed such a "political absurdity" as to approach the level of a crime; Germany had to end the policy of advancing in the south and west, "turning our eyes toward the land in the east." Indeed, the search for "new land" in Eastern Europe meant *Lebensraum* conquered specifically from "Russia and the border states that are subject to her." Many of these ideas were reiterated and elaborated in Hitler's so-called "second book" written in 1928, which remained unpublished until long after the fall of Nazi Germany.

When examined alongside other documents central to the debate—such as the famous Hossbach memorandum of 1937, which Hugh Trevor Roper saw as the key "blueprint" that refuted Taylor—the available evidence seems to point to a more or less fixed plan that led directly from the rejection of Versailles to a war of expansion ultimately aimed at Russia. As delineated most clearly by Andreas Hilgruber, Hitler's foreign policy can be interpreted as a stage-by-stage program (*Stufenplan*) for expansion in Europe. Hilgruber posited a basically three-step plan which he argued Hitler developed and put into action. In the dictator's lifetime the first step was to achieve German ascendency in Europe by peacefully revising the Versailles settlement, waging of a series of short localized wars against individual powers, and culminating in a major war against the Soviet Union to ensure dominance on the Continent and destroy Germany's most dangerous enemies—the Bolsheviks and the Jews. After this, Germany would challenge Britain and force it into the position of junior partner. Finally, Germany would build up its power and the generation of leaders following Hitler would take the struggle to the world level in an ultimate showdown with the United States.

The concept of Hitler's foreign policy being dictated by a step-by-step plan sometimes is seen as having been even more explicitly articulated as a five-point foreign-policy program. As Jeremy Noakes and Geoffrey Pridham described it in their book, *Nazism 1919–1945*, this path to war led directly from Hitler's "Saturday surprises"—the shaking off, in March 1935, of the arms limits imposed in 1919, and the remilitarization of the Rhineland in March 1936—to the breaking up of France's alliance network in Eastern Europe; the transformation of Austria, Czechoslovakia, and Poland into satellites of Germany; the crushing of France and the securing of Germany's western border; and finally to the destruction Russia and acquisition of "living space" as the final step allowing Germany to make a bid for global domination. As recorded in the October 1937 Hossbach memorandum, Hitler seems to have made allowance for contingencies—that Germany might not have a favorable opportunity to act before 1943, or alternatively that France might become embroiled in a domestic crisis or a foreign war that would enable him to strike sooner—but he was nevertheless guided by a notion of a basic path to follow and ultimate aims and goals.

Gerhard Weinberg argued in his magisterial treatment of Nazi foreign policy from 1933 to 1939—*Hitler's Foreign Policy*—that the so-called Führer "had some very definite, fixed ideas on foreign policy before he came into power," and two key concepts ultimately provided the ideological foundation for his foreign policy: race and space. The first was the notion of a pure, Germanic race at the apex of a hierarchy of races, having a natural right and obligation to take the second, "living space," as a necessity to provide the nation a viable future. Hitler walked a fine line between an opportunistic policy and a coherent and consistent one. Before 1933 he had been very open about these ideas, but after coming to power he was not as frank about his long-term plans in public, even though the two concepts ultimately continued to underpin all his decisions, internationally as well as domestically.

Altogether, then, it seems hard to deny that an expansionist ideology and glorification of war not only informed but were central to Europe's fascist movements in the era of the World Wars. An emphasis on the central role played by ideology helps to restore an important factor in the original context of international politics in the 1930s, especially for those nations most capable of fulfilling the foreign-policy programs of the fascist movements that dominated their societies. Indeed, in the nations where fascism had gained control of government and was able to maintain the military capability to impose the nations' will on foreign peoples and nations, there was an increasing tendency to pursue ideologically motivated goals and objectives leading up to World War II. It can hardly be maintained that Hitler's Germany and Mussolini's Italy were not driven by at least a general preconceived program that gave direction to their diplomacy. Ultimately, these ideas help to account for the increasingly belligerent policies of both powers after 1935.

ANSWER: PATRICK G. ZANDER, MILITARY CONQUEST AND TERRITORIAL EXPANSION WERE NOT ESSENTIAL COMPONENTS OF FASCIST IDEOLOGY

During the interwar period the dictatorships of Fascist Italy and Nazi Germany embarked upon an aggressive program of expansionist conquest and annexations of neighboring nations. This string of aggressive invasions began in October 1935 with Italy's attack and eventual conquest of Abyssinia (modern Ethiopia). Abyssinia was a member of the League of Nations, thus there ensued a diplomatic crisis as the democracies of Britain and France attempted to peacefully satiate Italy's appetite for new territory in East Africa without completely undermining the credibility of the League's authority. Italy would have no part of any mitigating solutions, however, and drove on to complete victory in Abyssinia, using poison gas and bombing Red Cross medical stations along the way. Mussolini reacted to the mild economic sanctions imposed upon Italy by the League with defiance and belligerence, and soon after moved closer to the Hitler regime. Mussolini was absolutely bent on imperial conquest and would not be denied. During 1936, Adolf Hitler reoccupied the Rhineland, and in 1938 bullied and threatened the Austrian government to the point that Germany was able to annex that nation and absorb it into the boundaries of the German Reich. Czechoslovakia would follow in 1938, as is well known, and then in 1939 Hitler and Mussolini both moved again. Mussolini moved into Albania and Hitler launched a massive invasion into Poland, commencing the Second World War.

In the Second World War, Hitler's Germany came to occupy and dominate nearly the entire European continent through invasions, outright conquest, and the installation of friendly puppet governments. Italy followed Germany into the war and launched its own invasions of Southern France, British

Somaliland, Egypt, and Greece. Italy and Germany joined forces with Imperial Japan which was involved in its own massive project of imperial expansion in the Pacific Rim. In 1941, Hitler launched his largest invasion into the Soviet Union, despite being alliance partners with that nation. That invasion fulfilled one of the central tenets of the Nazi Party program, as explained in Hitler's book *Mein Kampf*. In that book, Hitler had made clear that Germany had a "historic destiny" to conquer the East of Europe (and especially the Soviet Union) for the expansion of the Aryan race and its culture. Eventually, of course, the coalition of Britain, the United States, and the Soviet Union, among others, worked together to crush the Axis Powers by 1945. The Allied Powers agreed that any negotiated peace was unacceptable, as continued aggressive expansion and the disruption of world stability that the fascist dictatorships threatened was unacceptable for the future peace of the world. It would seem then, that part of the very definition of fascism was the need to attack and conquer others in the constant pursuit of territorial expansion. In other words, the aggrandizement sought by fascist ultra-nationalists for their own nation had to be obtained at the expense of other nations and peoples.

The magnitude of the disaster of the Second World War naturally focuses attention on the attacks, conquests, and expansion by Fascist Italy and Nazi Germany. It is important, however, to be careful not to examine these two cases exclusively when seeking to understand the nature of fascism as a wider political phenomenon. That Germany and Italy were obsessed with war and territorial expansion is beyond question. An examination of other fascist regimes and movements of the period, however, shows that Italy and Germany actually were exceptional in the intensity of their expansionist rhetoric and aggressive behaviors. Other movements around Europe emphasized the need for national withdrawal and insulation from the economic and political chaos.

One such case was the fascist movement in Britain. The movement's largest organization was the British Union of Fascists (BUF), led by Sir Oswald Mosley. In his book *The Greater Britain* and in numerous other BUF publications, Mosley made it clear that BUF policy included no intention of threatening or invading other territories. Britain had all it needed, he continually stressed, both at home and within its existing empire to create a self-sufficient and self-contained imperial economy. A fascist Britain, Mosley said, would arm itself with the most modern weaponry to protect itself against any aggressor, but sought no territorial expansion for itself. Mosley and the BUF emphasized the need for redeveloping agriculture to guarantee that Britain had an assured food supply in case of world emergency, and the BUF endorsed a program of self-sufficiency including producing petroleum from coal to eliminate the need for oil imports. Far from a policy of expansion or conquest, the BUF chiefly was concerned with withdrawal and isolation. As Mosley wrote in *10 Points of Fascism,* "Great nations can be self-contained once they are organized and scientifically protected from the shocks and dislocations of world chaos. . . . A self-contained Empire will be *withdrawn* from that struggle, and the risks of war will be diminished."

The British Union of Fascists produced a great deal of written discourse and a quite thorough political program, but that organization never put a single member in parliament. So, their words can be analyzed, but historians cannot determine what would have happened if the BUF had taken power. Were there fascist regimes that held power, but did not pursue a program of militarized expansion? The answer is most assuredly yes.

The Fatherland Front, formed in Austria during 1934, proclaimed no territorial ambitions, and its leaders did not pursue any. That government, however, only lasted a matter of months before its dictator, Engelbert Dollfuss, was murdered by Austrian Nazis in a failed coup attempt. In Spain, however, there was a fascist movement in operation by 1933 in the form of the *Falange Espanola* and then a Fascist dictatorship was created by Francisco Franco and lasted from 1939 to 1975. In the *Falange's* list of principles, the Twenty-Seven Points (retained by the Franco regime as the Twenty-Six Points), Jose Antonio Primo de Rivera insisted that Spain should once more seek an empire. He wrote, "We have the determination to build an Empire. We affirm that Spain's historic fulfillment lies in Empire. We claim for Spain a preeminent position in Europe." Neither of these ambitions, however, was realistic for Spain's national situation. The Franco regime did not seek territorial expansion. Instead, Franco imposed a policy of serious economic and cultural isolation on the Spanish nation. In his book, *A Time of Silence: Civil War and the Culture of Repression in Franco's Spain 1936–1945,* published in 1998, scholar Michael Richards demonstrates that Franco imposed this restrictive combination of economic autarky and cultural isolation as a sort of punishment for the Spanish people's embrace of liberal, progressive ideas during the years of the Republic.

Spanish fascists might have dreamt of a renewed Empire, but national realities made this an unrealistic policy for its dictator to follow. Austria's leaders of the Fatherland Front, likewise, had no realistic ability to expand and thus focused their emphasis on internal repressions and maintaining an independent identity from Germany. Britain already had a vast and thriving empire and thus had no need for imperial expansion. Italy and Germany, however, had very different national circumstances. Germany had had its overseas colonies taken away as part of the multiple humiliations of the Versailles Treaty. Italy, like Germany, had been late to the imperial game and had assembled a small and weak empire. Then at the Paris Peace Conference Italy was denied the territories it felt were its due after being on the winning side in the First World War.

For both Germany and Italy, territorial expansion provided the national prestige each dictator craved and matched their highest nationalist priorities. Fulfilling the perceived highest priorities of the "national community" was the essence of fascism. In some cases this was served by territorial expansion and aggressive conquest, but for other nations this was not the case, and instead other priorities were followed. In Austria, Spain, and Britain, those movements, in their words or in their deeds, advocated policies in an almost opposite direction—that of creating a self-contained, autarkic economy and a political withdrawal from the center of world affairs.

CLOSING

In the two essays provided above, the contributors examine a challenging dilemma. Was expansion and conquest part of the essence of the Fascist system? Although the aggressive expansion of Italy and Germany leading to and during the Second World War makes this seem almost obvious, examining the rhetoric and actions of other regimes makes this less certain. Dr. Orgill uses some classic historiography in making his case, and addresses the important argument made by A. J. P. Taylor that Hitler's aggression was merely opportunistic and simply in the same mold as the European conquests of the previous century. In the end, though, Orgill uses documentary evidence (e.g., the Hossbach Memorandum) and the work of historians such as Gerhard Weinberg to assert that Nazi conquests, like the Italian, were part of an ideological impulse and not mere opportunism. It is interesting that Orgill uses examples from Spanish and British Fascism to make his point.

Looking at those same cases (Britain and Spain), Dr. Zander draws a different conclusion. Although he acknowledges the pro-imperial rhetoric of the *Falange Espanola*, he asserts that this did not match national realities. Thus, under Franco, Spain did not pursue any meaningful attempts at conquest. Instead, Dr. Zander uses Michael Richards' scholarship to remind us that Franco, in fact, imposed a repressive policy of economic autarky and cultural isolation for Spain that would last into the 1950s. Zander also uses the examples of Austria, and particularly the British Union of Fascists, to demonstrate that where different national situations existed (Austria fighting to remain independent and too small for external conquests, and Britain already holding a vast empire), there might not be any national priority for aggressive expansion. According to Zander, it was such national situations that determined whether a fascist movement was bent on external conquests, rather than being a fundamental impulse that was present in every fascist movement.

DOING MORE

Carr, William, *Arms, Autarky, and Aggression: A Study in German Foreign Policy, 1933–1945* (New York: Norton, 1973).

Kallis, Aristotle, *Fascist Ideology: Territory and Expansionism in Italy and Germany, 1922–1945* (London: Routledge, 2000).

Mosley, Sir Oswald, *The Greater Britain* (London: BUF, 1932).

Payne, Stanley G., *The Franco Regime, 1936–1975* (Madison: University of Wisconsin Press, 1987).

Richards, Michael, *A Time of Silence: Civil War and the Culture of Repression in Franco's Spain 1936–1945* (New York: Cambridge University Press, 1998).

Skidelsky, Robert, *Oswald Mosley* (New York: Holt, Rinehart & Winston, 1975).

Thurlow, Richard C., *Fascism in Britain: A History, 1918–1985* (New York: Blackwell, 1987).

Weinberg, Gerhard L., *The Foreign Policy of Hitler's Germany: The Road to World War II 1933–1939* (New York: Enigma Books, 2005).

Selected Annotated Bibliography

ONLINE SOURCES

History Learning Site, www.historylearningsite.co.uk
The History Learning Site is maintained as a public service but including advertisements. It contains a large catalog of in-depth entries on dozens of subjects related to early 20th-century history, including life in Fascist Italy and an entire section on Nazi Germany.

Oswald Mosley.com, www.oswaldmosley.com
This website is maintained by "The Friends of Sir Oswald Mosley." There is a good deal of material on the site dedicated to the history of the British fascist movement of the 1930s. Although the site provides a public service in furnishing historical material, it also advocates Mosley's political message, which is extremely controversial and unpopular.

"Oxford Bibliographies," http://www.oxfordbibliographies.com
A fine public service and educational website, "Oxford Bibliographies" is an excellent place to begin learning about nearly any subject. An extensive subject list includes a significant list of sources. The source lists provided include surveys, academic-level works, and collections of primary sources. For the present subject, the heading "The Challenge of Fascism" and the materials include an introductory reading list compiled by scholar David E. Roberts.

"Spartacus Educational," www.Spartacus-educational.com/index.html
Spartacus Educational is a historical website maintained by the historical author John Simkin in the United Kingdom. It includes a remarkable collection of in-depth

biographies of individuals from many historical epochs, and it has a particularly extensive catalog of profiles from the interwar and World War II period. The profiles often contain controversial material, but it is generally well-sourced.

PRINT SOURCES

General Surveys of Fascism

Passmore, Kevin. 2014. *Fascism: A Very Short Introduction.* New York: Oxford University Press.
Clearly written and clearly organized, Passmore's book is a concise introduction to the subject of the rise of fascism. It reviews the basic chain of events leading to the creation of fascist regimes in Italy and Germany, along with a review of the essence of the ideology of the various fascist movements.

Paxton, Robert O. 2004. *The Anatomy of Fascism.* New York: Knopf.
In this book, Paxton wrestles with the difficulty of interpreting fascism and suggests a new approach to its study. Paxton makes the point that there are stages to the development of a fascist movement: early development, fighting for power, taking power, and maintaining power. During each one of these stages, Paxton suggests, the relationships and policies of fascist movements can change and thus any comparative work should take this into consideration.

Payne, Stanley G. 1996. *A History of Fascism 1914–1945.* Madison: University of Wisconsin Press.
Payne's book is one of the finest overall surveys of fascism as a general political phenomenon. Taking a comparative approach, he includes a chapter on all the major regimes and movements. At the end of the book is a particularly useful section that reviews all of the many major scholarly interpretations of fascism.

Surveys of the Italian Fascist State

Bosworth, R. J. B. 2005. *Mussolini's Italy: Life Under the Dictatorship 1915–1945.* New York: Allen Lane.
Bosworth provides a very thorough examination of the influence of Mussolini's regime into all the many areas of Italian life. His overall thesis suggests that there were clear limits to the level at which Mussolini's fascist state could penetrate; as such, Italy's fascist revolution did not meaningfully change many of the traditional institutions of Italian society.

Bosworth, R. J. B. 2002. *Mussolini.* New York: Oxford University Press.
This is the most recent thorough biography of Benito Mussolini by the scholar who is perhaps the leading authority on Fascist Italy working in the English language.

Bosworth has written extensively on all aspects of Italy in the fascist era and his biography is considered to be among the most definitive.

DeGrand, Alexander. 2000. *Italian Fascism: Its Origins and Development.* Lincoln: University of Nebraska Press.
DeGrand provides a clearly written and structured study of the development, ideology, and institutional structures of Italian fascism. The book is designed as a study tool for high school and undergraduate-level students.

Finaldi, Giuseppe. 2008. *Mussolini and Italian Fascism.* New York: Pearson/ Longman.
Concise and manageable, Finaldi's book provides an outstanding study tool for the high school or undergraduate-level student. It provides an accessible narrative, and highlights the most important people, places, events, and concepts together with clear definitions. The book also includes a documents section and a useful glossary.

Surveys of Nazism

Evans, Richard J. 2003. *The Coming of the Third Reich.* London: Allen Lane.
Evans, Richard J. 2005. *The Third Reich in Power 1933–1939.* London: Allen Lane.

Evans, Richard J. 2008. *The Third Reich at War 1939–1945.* London: Allen Lane.
Evans' three-volume set offers the most complete overview of the Nazi phenomenon that exists. It includes analysis and insight into virtually any feature of Nazism that a reader might seek. It also has one of the most complete lists of sources on Nazism available.

Gellately, Robert. 2001. *Backing Hitler: Consent and Coercion in Nazi Germany.* Oxford: Oxford University Press.
Gellately examines the development of the Nazi regime with a particular focus. He helps explain how the Nazi regime was able to take power and how it was able to retain power through the mass support of ordinary Germans.

Kershaw, Sir Ian. 1999. *Hitler, 1889–1936: Hubris.* New York: W.W. Norton.
Kershaw, Sir Ian. 2000. *Hitler 1936–1945: Nemesis.* New York: W.W. Norton.
Sir Ian Kershaw's two-volume biography of Adolf Hitler is considered the definitive work on the subject. It is an extremely thorough work and dense with detail, but is clearly written and has a very exhaustive bibliography and index.

Mitchell, Allan. 1997. *The Nazi Revolution: Hitler's Dictatorship and the German Nation.* Boston: Houghton Mifflin.
Mitchell's book is a compact and concise analysis of Nazism with a structured approach that emphasizes the revolutionary changes brought about by the Nazi regime. It is quite useful for students.

Shirer, William L. 1960. *The Rise and Fall of the Third Reich: A History of Nazi Germany* New York: Simon and Schuster.
William L. Shirer uses his experience of being a newspaper reporter living in Nazi Germany during the Nazi regime to compile the most complete one-volume survey of Nazism available. The book covers the development of Nazism from the birth of Hitler until Germany's surrender at the end of the Second World War.

Spanish Fascism, the Spanish Civil War, and the Franco Regime

Beevor, Antony. 2006. *The Battle for Spain: The Spanish Civil War 1936–39.* London: Wiedenfield and Nicolson.
This work is the most recent and thorough account of the breakdown of the Spanish Republic and the Civil War that followed. It explains the complex series of political events and provides a thorough narrative of the events of the war.

Payne, Stanley G. 1999. *Fascism in Spain, 1923–1977.* Madison: University of Wisconsin Press.
Payne's book examines the explicitly fascist movement in Spain. The analysis emphasizes the role of the *Falange Espanola* and does not see the Franco regime as a truly fascist dictatorship. Payne ends his analysis by explaining why fascism failed to take hold in Spain (though other scholars would maintain that fascism did come to power in that country under Franco).

Preston, Paul. 1990. *The Politics of Revenge: Fascism and the Military in 20th-Century Spain.* Boston: Unwin Hyman.
Preston's book reviews the continuous role of Spain's military and its interventions in Spain's political system. By dissecting the Franco regime and reviewing its actions and relationships, Preston makes a convincing argument for the fascist nature of the Franco dictatorship.

Surveys of the British Fascist Movement

Linehan, Thomas, P. 2000. *British Fascism, 1918–39: Parties, Ideology and Culture.* Manchester: Manchester University Press.
Linehan's book examines all the major British fascist organizations active during the interwar period and thoroughly reviews their political programs and activities. It also reviews the extreme right views on greater cultural issues such as attitudes toward women, industry and technology, and urbanization.

Thurlow, Richard C. 1998. *Fascism in Britain: From Oswald Mosley's Blackshirts to the National Front.* London: I.B. Tauris.
Thurlow's book is a fine review of the most important British fascist organizations active during the interwar period. What distinguishes his book is his examination of the extreme right-wing groups that developed after 1945 (including the Union

Movement and the National Front) and the links he identifies with the pre-war generation of fascist groups.

Surveys of the French Fascist Movement

Davies, Peter. 2002. *The Extreme Right in France, 1789 to the Present: From De Maistre to Le Pen.* New York: Routledge.
Davies' concise book traces the progression of the ideas and traditions of the far right through the 19th century and into the 20th. It traces the high-Nationalist intellectual movement in France from 1871 to 1914 that some call "proto-fascism," and examines the French fascist organizations such as the *Action Francaise* and the *Croix de Feu.* The book also looks at the continuation of the far-right tendency through groups such as the OAS in the 1960s and the Le Pen movement in the present day. It is an excellent study tool for students.

Soucy, Robert. 1986. *French Fascism: The First Wave, 1924–1933.* New Haven: Yale University Press.
Soucy, Robert. 1995. *French Fascism: The Second Wave, 1933–1939.* New Haven: Yale University Press.
Soucy's two-part series examines the ideologies and political programs of the major French fascist organizations through the interwar period. He engages with the difficult historical question as to whether France actually developed a true fascist movement before the Vichy era. His assertion is that France did develop a widespread fascist movement, although it was fragmented and variegated.

Sweets, John F. 1986. *Choices in Vichy France: The French Under Nazi Occupation* New York: Oxford University Press.
This book examines the political aspects of the Vichy French regime as well as the aspects of daily life under the dictatorship. It also deals with the difficult question of whether French citizens had a choice when compelled to follow or aid the Nazi regime.

Williams, Charles. 2005. *Petain: How the Hero of France Became a Convicted Traitor and Changed the Course of History.* New York: Palgrave.
A manageable biography for high school and undergraduate students that concentrates particularly on Petain's involvement in the coming of the Vichy regime, his government, and the subsequent question of his treason—Williams' analysis is more sympathetic than many previous analyses.

Primary Sources—Personal Accounts and Documentary Readers

Ciano, Count Galeazzo. 1953. *Ciano's Hidden Diaries, 1937–39.* Translated by Andreas Mayor. New York: Dutton.
Ciano, Count Galeazzo. 1946. *The Ciano Diaries, 1939–43.* Edited by Hugh Gibson. New York: Doubleday.

These volumes of the diaries of Count Ciano cover his time as Italy's foreign minister. Ciano reveals much about true attitudes of Benito Mussolini and the machinations within the fascist government behind the scenes.

Delzell, Charles (ed.). 1970. *Mediterranean Fascism, 1919–1945.* New York: Harper & Row.
This is a compilation of the important documents from the Italian fascist era as well as the Spanish fascist movement and the time of the Spanish Civil War. It is extremely thorough and includes primary documents on the origins of fascism, the inner workings of the fascist regime, Italy at war, the ideology of the *Falange Espanola,* and the Franco regime.

Goebbels, Joseph. 1983 *The Goebbels Diaries.* Translated and edited by Fred Taylor. New York: Putnam.
This is the set of diaries spanning 1939 to 1945 and written by Hitler's propaganda minister. The book provides important insights into the belief system of Nazism, the cult of the Führer, and the thought processes behind the manipulation of public opinion in the Nazi regime.

Hitler, Adolf. 1971 [1925–1926]. *Mein Kampf.* Translated by Ralph Manheim. Boston: Houghton Mifflin.
Mein Kampf is Adolf Hitler's autobiography and the manifesto of the Nazi Party. It is perhaps the most essential document recording the ideology and objectives of Hitler and the Nazi Party. Included in the book are Hitler's explanations of his belief in racial struggle, his intense anti-Semitism, and his determination to attack and conquer the nations of Eastern Europe.

Noakes, Jeremy, and Geoffrey Pridham (eds.). 1974. *Documents on Nazism, 1919–1945.* London: Jonathan Cape.
This is an extremely complete and well-organized collection of primary documents from the Nazi movement and the Nazi regime. From the early formation of the Nazi Party, this collection includes documents from the days of the Holocaust to end of the Second World War. Each document is accompanied by a helpful explanation and analysis, making it accessible and useful for students.

Index

Page numbers in **bold** indicate main entries.

About the Editor and Contributors

EDITOR

PATRICK G. ZANDER, PhD, earned his MA in history from Georgia State University, and his MS and PhD from the Georgia Institute of Technology. Zander is the author of numerous articles and reference works, including sections on fascism in ABC-CLIO's *World History Encyclopedia*. In 2009, he received the Duncan C. Tanner Prize from the Oxford University Press journal, *Twentieth Century British History*, for his article about the interwar British fascist movement. His current project is a book about the various European resistance movements of the Second World War. He is assistant professor of history at Georgia Gwinnett College, Atlanta, Georgia, where he teaches modern British and European history as well as courses on comparative fascism.

CONTRIBUTORS

THERESA AST, PhD, earned her graduate degree at Emory University. She is professor of history at Reinhardt University, teaching courses on European history and the Holocaust. Dr. Ast has published two books, *Confronting the Holocaust: American Soldiers Enter Concentration Camps* and *Dressing the Bones* (poetry). She currently is working on a book about her grandparents, both of whom were Polish immigrants who survived the Nazi and Soviet invasions.

EUGENE BERGER, PhD, is an associate professor of history at Georgia Gwinnett College in Lawrenceville, Georgia. Dr. Berger received his MA and

PhD in Latin American history from Vanderbilt University. He completed his dissertation research in Seville at the Archive of the Indies and has made separate research trips to Chile and, most recently, to Peru as part of a National Science Foundation grant. He has published articles in *Encyclopedia of Latin America* and *The Latin Americanist*.

RHIANNON EVANGELISTA, PhD, received her degree from Emory University. Dr. Evangelista is a limited-term assistant professor at Kennesaw State University. Evangelista specializes in 20th-century Italian history and the history of regime change. Her publications include "The Particular Kindness of Friends: Ex-Fascists, Clientage, and the Transition to Democracy in Italy, 1945–1960" (forthcoming in *Modern Italy*). Evangelista currently is writing a book about former fascists in Italy's post–World War II regime change.

BARBARA LINGERFELT STAMEY is a graduate of Reinhardt University and holds a BA in history and a BA in religion. Stamey earned a Master's of Theological Studies from Candler School of Theology at Emory University, where her studies concentrated on Jewish history. Her master's thesis focused on Jewish experiences of the Holocaust.

NATHAN N. ORGILL, PhD, completed his undergraduate degree at Fresno State and received his doctorate in European history from Duke University. Dr. Orgill's research focuses on modern European international and military history, the history of journalism, and modern Germany. He has published book chapters on European diplomatic history and several entries on German military history. Orgill presently is completing a study examining the press and politics of the July Crisis of 1914. He serves as book review editor for H-German and currently is an associate professor of history at Georgia Gwinnett College in Atlanta, Georgia.

www.ingramcontent.com/pod-product-compliance
Lightning Source LLC
Chambersburg PA
CBHW070358270326
41926CB00014B/2606